# INFORMATION AND COMMUNICATION TECHNOLOGY AND THE TEACHER OF THE FUTURE

## IFIP – The International Federation for Information Processing

IFIP was founded in 1960 under the auspices of UNESCO, following the First World Computer Congress held in Paris the previous year. An umbrella organization for societies working in information processing, IFIP's aim is two-fold: to support information processing within its member countries and to encourage technology transfer to developing nations. As its mission statement clearly states,

> *IFIP's mission is to be the leading, truly international, apolitical organization which encourages and assists in the development, exploitation and application of information technology for the benefit of all people.*

IFIP is a non-profitmaking organization, run almost solely by 2500 volunteers. It operates through a number of technical committees, which organize events and publications. IFIP's events range from an international congress to local seminars, but the most important are:

- The IFIP World Computer Congress, held every second year;
- Open conferences;
- Working conferences.

The flagship event is the IFIP World Computer Congress, at which both invited and contributed papers are presented. Contributed papers are rigorously refereed and the rejection rate is high.

As with the Congress, participation in the open conferences is open to all and papers may be invited or submitted. Again, submitted papers are stringently refereed.

The working conferences are structured differently. They are usually run by a working group and attendance is small and by invitation only. Their purpose is to create an atmosphere conducive to innovation and development. Refereeing is less rigorous and papers are subjected to extensive group discussion.

Publications arising from IFIP events vary. The papers presented at the IFIP World Computer Congress and at open conferences are published as conference proceedings, while the results of the working conferences are often published as collections of selected and edited papers.

Any national society whose primary activity is in information may apply to become a full member of IFIP, although full membership is restricted to one society per country. Full members are entitled to vote at the annual General Assembly, National societies preferring a less committed involvement may apply for associate or corresponding membership. Associate members enjoy the same benefits as full members, but without voting rights. Corresponding members are not represented in IFIP bodies. Affiliated membership is open to non-national societies, and individual and honorary membership schemes are also offered.

# INFORMATION AND COMMUNICATION TECHNOLOGY AND THE TEACHER OF THE FUTURE

***IFIP TC3 / WG3.1 & WG3.3 Working Conference on ICT and the Teacher of the Future***
***January 27–31, 2003, Melbourne, Australia***

*Edited by*

**Carolyn Dowling**
*Australian Catholic University*
*Australia*

**Kwok-Wing Lai**
*University of Otago*
*New Zealand*

KLUWER ACADEMIC PUBLISHERS
BOSTON / DORDRECHT / LONDON

**Distributors for North, Central and South America:**
Kluwer Academic Publishers
101 Philip Drive
Assinippi Park
Norwell, Massachusetts 02061 USA
Telephone (781) 871-6600
Fax (781) 681-9045
E-Mail <kluwer@wkap.com>

**Distributors for all other countries:**
Kluwer Academic Publishers Group
Post Office Box 322
3300 AH Dordrecht, THE NETHERLANDS
Telephone 31 78 6576 000
Fax 31 78 6576 254
E-Mail <services@wkap.nl>

Electronic Services <http://www.wkap.nl>

**Library of Congress Cataloging-in-Publication Data**

A C.I.P. Catalogue record for this book is available from the Library of Congress.

Information and Communication Technology and the Teacher of the Future
Edited by Carolyn Dowling and Kwok-Wing Lai
ISBN 1-4020-7604-5



*Printed on acid-free paper.*
Printed in United Kingdom by Biddles / IBT Global.

# Contents

Melbourne 2003 Committees ix

Melbourne 2003 Sponsors x

Preface
CAROLYN DOWLING AND KWOK-WING LAI xi

**Section 1: Setting the Scene – The Keynote Addresses**

The Teaching Profession: A Networked Profession in New Networked Environments
BERNARD CORNU 3

Designing Learning Experiences: Supporting Teachers in the Process of Technology Change
BARRY HARPER 15

The Teacher – A Forgotten Stakeholder?
DERYN WATSON 29

**Section 2: The Teacher of the Future as a Professional**

ICT, National Policies, and their Impact on Schools and Teachers' Development
ROSA MARIA BOTTINO 41

Using an Educational Consensus to Reach Educational Technology Tipping Point
ROGER CARLSEN 49

Path to the Future: Generative Evaluation for Simultaneous Renewal of ICT in Teacher Education and K-12 Schools
NIKI DAVIS, MARI KEMIS AND NATALIE JOHNSON 53

ICT and Future Teachers: Are We Preparing for E-learning?
ANTHONY JONES 65

Developing a European Pioneer Teacher Community for School Innovation
VITTORIO MIDORO, STEFANIA BOCCONI, ALLAN MARTIN, FRANCESCA POZZI AND LUIGI SARTI 71

A New Qualification and Certification for Specialist ICT Teachers
SIGRID SCHUBERT 85

In Service Teacher Development Using ICT: First Step in Lifelong Learning
JOSÉ ARMANDO VALENTE 97

Raising the Standards: ICT and the Teacher of the Future
IAN WEBB AND TONI DOWNES 109

Professional Development Needs of Teachers Managing Self-Guided Learning
WOLFGANG WEBER 115

Reports of Focus Group Discussions:
Group A – The Teacher as a Professional: Fostering Professionalism
Chair: RAYMOND MOREL, Rapporteur: PAUL NICHOLSON 125
Group B – The Professional Teacher: Contexts, Capabilities and Competencies
Chair: SIGRID SCHUBERT, Rapporteur: TONI DOWNES 129

**Section 3: Classroom Roles of the Teacher of the Future**

Developing ICT Leadership Skills for Teachers of the Future
DIANNE CHAMBERS 137

The Effects of Attitudes, Pedagogical Practices and Teachers' Roles on the Incorporation of ICT into the School Curriculum
MARGARET COX 145

From Facilitator to Knowledge-Builder: A New Role for the Teacher of the Future
ELIZABETH HARTNELL-YOUNG 159

Teacher Empowerment and Minimalist Design
WING-WAH KI, ALBERT LING-SUNG CHUNG AND HO-CHEONG LAM 165

Innovative Classroom Practices and the Teacher of the Future
NANCY LAW 171

From Teacher Education to Professional Development for E-learning in an E-society
RAYMOND MOREL, JEAN-CLAUDE DOMENJOZ, CHARLES LACHAT AND CHRISTINE ROSSI 183

Technology Matters But Good Teachers Matter More
GEOFF ROMEO 191

Reports of Focus Group Discussions:
Group C – The Role of the Teacher
Chair: MARGARET COX, Rapporteur: STEVE KENNEWELL 203
Group D – The Role of Teachers: Lifelong Learners in a Community of Practice
Chair: WOLFGANG WEBER, Rapporteur: TREES HAAKSMA 209

**Section 4: Teaching and Learning Environments of the Future**

Mathematical Teaching and Learning Environment Mediated by ICT
GIAMPAOLO CHIAPPINI, BETTINA PEDEMONTE AND ELISABETTA ROBOTTI 217

Distant Actors on a Digital Campus, or Sharing and Crumbling Pedagogical Responsibility
HÉLÈNE GODINET 229

ICT and the Quality of Teaching: Some Hungarian Results of the OECD ICT Project
ANDREA KÁRPÁTI 235

Developing Research Models for ICT-Based Pedagogy
STEVE KENNEWELL 247

Technology Access: Resources Wasted in Computer Laboratories
KRISTIAN KIILI 251

Teacher in the Mobile World
JARI MULTISILTA, HARRI KEIHO AND HARRI KETAMO 257

Using Portable Computer Technologies to Support Learning Environments
PAUL NEWHOUSE 267

E-Learning, ICT, and Learning Portals for Schools
FERRAN RUIZ TARRAGÓ 279

Slash 21: A New School and a New Way of Learning
HENK VAN DIETEN 291

Reports of Focus Group Discussions:
Group E – Teaching Environments: Key Influences and Considerations
Chair: MIKE KENDALL, Rapporteur: JAN WIBE 295
Group F – Knowledge Building Communities: Creating New Learning and Teaching Environments
Chair: JARI MULTISILTA, Rapporteur: BERNARD CORNU 301

Index of Contributors 307

## Melbourne 2003 Committees

### Programme Committee

**Chair:** Pieter Hogenbirk, The Netherlands

**Members:**

| | |
|---|---|
| Herminia Azinian | Argentina |
| Rosa Maria Bottino | Italy |
| Carolyn Dowling | Australia |
| Kwok-Wing Lai | New Zealand |
| Harriet Taylor | USA |
| Anne McDougall | Australia |
| Wolfgang Weber | Germany |

**Editors:**

| | |
|---|---|
| Carolyn Dowling | Australia |
| Kwok-Wing Lai | New Zealand |

### Organising Committee

Anne McDougall
Carolyn Dowling
Paul Nicholson
Jill Vincent
Ros McDougall
Dianne Chambers
John Murnane
Geoff Romeo
John Vincent

## Melbourne 2003 Sponsors

The University of Melbourne

Australian Computer Society

ICT in Education Victoria

Australian Council for Computers in Education

Apple (Australia)

# Preface

Carolyn Dowling
*Australian Catholic University*

Kwok-Wing Lai
*University of Otago*

This book is one of the outcomes of a Working Conference on the topic of 'ICT and the Teacher of the Future', which took place in Melbourne, Australia, in January 2003. The conference was held under the auspices of the International Federation for Information Processing (IFIP). Technical Committee 3 (TC3) of IFIP, through the activities of its seven Working Groups, focuses on different aspects of the impact of Information and Communication Technologies on Education. The conference that was the impetus for this publication was organised jointly by Working Group 3.1 (Secondary Education) and Working Group 3.3 (Research).

In addition to the text of the papers delivered by the three keynote speakers, the book comprises a selection of the papers presented by delegates at the conference, along with reports of the discussions of Focus Groups working in each topic area.

All of the papers presented at the conference were reviewed by members of the International Programme Committee and the National Organising Committee. Those selected for publication as chapters in this book have subsequently undergone an additional process of collaborative editing before qualifying for inclusion. It is our belief that these papers collectively present a very comprehensive overview of the concerns and developments in the use of Information and Communication Technologies that are currently of relevance to educators and educational policy makers across the globe. While the papers in one sense incorporate wide-ranging perspectives deriving from varying national contexts, their grouping within topic areas reveals more commonalities of concern than differences.

The first topic area, *The Teacher of the Future as a Professional*, focuses on the changing requirements for both the initial preparation and the continuing professional education of teachers. These concerns are often expressed, particularly by educators in the field, in terms of the constant and seemingly increasing pressure to simply keep up with new technological developments of relevance to education. The deeper issues, however, as reflected in the selected papers, relate not merely to the acquisition of technological competencies, but rather to gaining and maintaining an understanding of the relationship between the capabilities of the technology and pedagogical theory and practice. It is this very complex requirement that can be seen as mounting the greatest challenge to the professionalism of the teacher of the future.

The second area, *Classroom Roles of the Teacher of the Future* is concerned more specifically with the way in which developments in Information and Communication Technologies are changing the way in which teachers interact with students. Even within the more traditionally organised, basically face-to-face classroom, both the capabilities of the technology and the expectations raised by it are creating subtle but important shifts in the perceived role of the teacher. Within electronic environments, these effects are far more obvious. The papers that make up this section of the book explore different aspects of this issue.

Finally, the section *Teaching and Learning Environments of the Future* examines a range of pedagogical scenarios in differing stages of development and implementation, each of which provides a special insight into how the 'classroom of the future' might function. It is worth noting that, while this topic area was designated at the conference itself as 'teaching environments of the future', the emphases and terminology of the papers themselves appeared to favour a clearer emphasis on 'learning', as reflected in the wording used in this book.

The Focus Group Reports that complete each section of the book represent an important component of the professional interactions that are part of an IFIP Working Conference. The opportunity for delegates to meet together in a structured context for significant amounts of time to discuss and debate the material presented in the papers related to each topic area is invaluable in terms of synthesising the key issues and of identifying themes for further research and development.

As editors of this book we have enjoyed and have benefited significantly from the privilege of interacting closely, both face-to-face and through the medium of ICT, with innovative educational theoreticians and practitioners from many different countries. One of the key attributes of Information and

Communication Technologies is the ability to dissolve a number of the practical barriers to interaction between people, including teachers and students, of different nationalities and different degrees of geographical separation. We are pleased that this book reflects, albeit in microcosm, the types of benefit that derive from such global interaction.

# Section 1

# Setting the Scene - The Keynote Addresses

# The Teaching Profession: A Networked Profession in New Networked Environments

Bernard Cornu
*La Villa Media, Grenoble, France*
*bernard.cornu@la-metro.org*

**Abstract:** The information and communication society is a networked society. We reflect on the concept of a network and identify some profound changes in society.

In such a society, knowledge is changing, new knowledge appears, and the structuring of knowledge is evolving. Access to knowledge is changing. The networked form of knowledge makes an evolution of educational systems and structures towards a networked organisation necessary. Complexity, which is a key characteristic of new knowledge in the new society, is reinforced and structured by networks.

The teacher's role is becoming more and more complex. We analyse some of the ways it is evolving, see how new technologies force us to confront the core roles of the teacher and reinforce some specific aspects of his/her profession, particularly the role as a mediator, and the role in the development of the collective intelligence.

The teacher is now dealing differently with time and space; he/she uses new learning environments, which are more global and link pedagogy and school life within its whole. The growing complexity and the changes in education lead not only to an evolving teaching profession, but also to new teaching professions.

Starting from different possible scenarios for the school of the future, we suggest possible scenarios for the teacher of the future, and see the teacher's place in national policies.

ICT makes teaching more and more a profession, not only a vocation. The question now is not only to improve education with the help of ICT, but also to transform education and learning, as society is transformed.

Information and Communication Technology (ICT) has a profound impact on Society and on Education. ICT not only provides new and supplementary tools able to help improve teaching or learning; it profoundly transforms Society, Education and Knowledge. The teaching profession is at the core of such changes, and is itself transformed by ICT. The role of the teacher is changing, the way the teacher works is changing. We have to distinguish the essential components of the teaching profession, the ones that are stable, and the ones that are changing. And we have to try to anticipate the main changes, in order not to be merely subjected to them, but to master and direct them.

## 1. A NETWORKED SOCIETY

A major change brought by ICT is networking. Most of our organisations, which were before of a hierarchical type ('tree-type' or 'pyramid-type'), are now moving to networks.

A network is a set of nodes and edges, the edges linking the nodes. It is a complex organisation, and a continuously evolving set. ICT has hugely increased the possibility of linking people, and linking objects. A complex network is progressively being elaborated, making our society a networked society. The Internet is one of the visible parts of the networked society; it links mainly computers, and, behind these computers, sites and people.

A network has important properties. The main one is that there are always several paths for going from one node to another (in a pyramidal structure, there is only one path from one point to another).

Let us look at some examples:

- Accessing an item of information in a book. In a traditional organisation, one had to use a 'hierarchical' path, going through bibliographies, library directories, name of the author, title of the book, table of contents, chapter number, page number, etc. In a networked system (like the Internet and with the use of search engines), one can access directly one word, one concept, one sentence in a book, without even going through the title of the book or the author's name.
- Communicating with people in a hierarchical system requires knowledge of the structure, the hierarchy and the rules. You can communicate with some people through other people, you often communicate with a 'function', not necessarily a person. In a networked system with tools like e-mail, one can communicate directly with a person, without knowing his/her position, his/her location, etc.
- Our educational systems are organized on a 'pyramidal type' basis: at the top, the Minister of Education, then Directors, Inspectors, principals,

head teachers, teachers, pupils.... The pupils are organised in classrooms. One can think that in the networked society, such an organisation cannot be satisfying, and that new types of organisations will appear in educational systems, based on network principles.

Networks are permanently enriching and are becoming increasingly complex. Let us consider the Internet: Each web site is usually built according to a 'tree' structure. But one can create many new links, enriching the circulation in the 'tree', and each web site progressively becomes a kind of network between pages, resources, information ... and the set of all web sites makes a huge network, whose complexity is permanently growing, and with new nodes and new edges appearing at each moment.

A network can be considered in different ways. One can network people, and thus constitute a group of people who are connected in a network system. One can network information, and obtain a huge Information Network. In reality, we often think in a mixed way, linking people with people, people with information, information with other information.

There is not only one network, but there are many of them: local networks, particular networks ... they can themselves be networked, in order to create bigger networks, up to the 'global network', the network of networks...

For technologists, the links are important. For users, it is the nodes that are important: the people to connect, the information to connect. Merckelbach and Dupas (2002) suggest the metaphor of the spider and the giraffe. In a spider's web, what is important is the threads, and in between there is only emptiness. But if we look at a giraffe's skin, we see stains with lines in between, and it forms a network in which the important element is the stains. A network aims at connecting people, connecting information, and what is connected is more important than the edges connecting them. But the way they are connected is important as well: it creates proximities, it creates sub-networks, it creates new relationships.

In all domains, the network structure of society has consequences for the economy, social life, leisure, politics, etc. In education, it has major consequences, for knowledge itself, for the way one can access knowledge, for educational systems, for teaching and learning, and particularly for the teaching profession.

## 2. NEW KNOWLEDGE, NEW ACCESS TO KNOWLEDGE

ICT changes knowledge itself. This is clear within each discipline, and one can easily describe such changes. Concepts, processes, methods, and resources available are evolving under the effect of ICT.

One must be careful not to confuse information and knowledge. Information is a raw object, most of the time independent of people. Knowledge is more elaborated: at the society level, it is a constituted set of information, with its own coherence, linked with main issues or questions, and linked with possible uses.

The Internet is at first a network of information. Education needs networks of knowledge, and it is the role of educators to elaborate such networks. In such a network, the edges are not only links between information; the edges contribute to the meaning of the knowledge, and each edge or link brings an 'added value' to the network of knowledge. Each item of knowledge is enriched by the links it has with other pieces of knowledge.

Conversely, knowledge, which was up to now stored in books and in libraries, is now networked; the networked dimension of knowledge is made possible because knowledge is in a digital form. Because knowledge is now networked, it is more rich and complex.

Complexity and networking are linked concepts. In a more and more complex world, networking as a tool enables us to address complexity and complex objects. Networking helps us to understand better the growing complexity of the world. Therefore, networking is profoundly linked to the evolution of Society: more complex implies more networked, and more networked makes it more complex.

As an example of complexity in the field of education, the French sociologist Morin (2001) suggests that the traditional disciplines can no longer be enough to address the complex problems of Society and Humanity. He proposes seven necessary kinds of knowledge for the education of the future:

- Detecting error and illusion. Teach the weaknesses of knowledge: what is human knowledge? Teach its errors, its illusions. Teach how to know what to know is!

- Principles of pertinent knowledge. One must be able to take into account global and fundamental problems, in which partial and local knowledge will then be used. Knowledge cannot be split into disciplines. One must be able to consider the objects of knowledge in their context, in their complexity, in their whole.

- Teaching the human condition. Teach the unity and the complexity of human nature. This needs input from biology, from human sciences, from literature, from philosophy. Teach the relationship between the unity and the diversity of what is human.

- Global identity. Teach knowledge at a world-wide level. Teach the history of the planetary era, teach the solidarity between all the parts of the world.

- Confronting uncertainties. Sciences have established a lot of certainties, but they also have revealed many uncertainties. Teach the uncertainties in physics, in biology, in history.

- Understanding each other. Teach understanding; understanding in all its meanings, mutual understanding between human beings. And teach what misunderstanding is. It is a crucial basis for peace education.

- Ethics for the human genre. Teach the world. Teach the ethics of humanity preparing citizens of the world. Teach how democracy relates to the mutual control between society and individuals.

Such a new 'curriculum', in which traditional disciplines do not disappear but are included in a different way, illustrates how knowledge is interlaced, and needs a networked approach.

Not only knowledge is profoundly changed by ICT, but also the way one can access knowledge. Knowledge is no longer only in books, in libraries, in the Teacher's head; it is available in many places, at any time, and it is distributed in a networked form. Being able to access knowledge means being able to find appropriate paths in complex networks. But the wide and easy availability of knowledge brings new difficulties: knowledge, as it is, is not necessarily validated, its accuracy is not visible, and the user needs to be able to sort and validate the knowledge he/she finds; knowledge is not clearly different from information in the resources available, and the user has to be able to find appropriate knowledge among the huge amount of information. Here is clearly a major role for the Teacher, not only to deliver knowledge to the pupils, but to help them find accurate knowledge, to help them circulate in the network of knowledge.

## 3. COLLECTIVE INTELLIGENCE

In the networked society, intelligence is no longer only an individual matter. Traditionally, education aims at developing the individual intelligence of the students. But now, society needs a new kind of intelligence, a collective intelligence. This is necessary in many professions, this is necessary for citizenship. Collective intelligence is not only the addition of individual intelligences; there is a specific collective dimension in this new intelligence.

Collective intelligence can be approached through a network of individual intelligences, individual intelligences, with relationships which make them complementary, which enrich each of them and make them more efficient, and which help solve problems which need not only individual intelligence but a collective one.

Lévy (1994) has shown how the Internet is linked with the development of a collective intelligence. He has described on many occasions how the Internet is mainly a tool, the more recent we found for perfecting our intelligence through cooperation and exchange ... The true revolution of Internet is not at all a revolution of machines, but of communication between human beings ... the Internet enhances our capacity for collective learning and intelligence ... Each community realises that it is one of the dimensions of the production of human sense ... the Internet forces us to experiment new ways of being together ... The ethic of collective intelligence, consisting in interlacing different points of view ...

The collective intelligence is made possible because communication is possible, because people are networked, because everybody can be connected to everybody. Connectivity makes collective intelligence exist; this is why De Kerckhove (2001) speaks about 'connective intelligence'.

The classroom is the first place were collective intelligence can be built and used. This is also a major role for the teacher.

## 4. NEW PROFESSION, NEW PROFESSIONS

A lot of new competencies are needed for teachers: competencies linked with technology (they must be able to use the new tools, to make them work), competencies linked with the new pedagogical possibilities (they have to be 'pedagogical engineers'), competencies linked with the new knowledge and the new networked form of knowledge, competencies linked with the new expectations Society has towards teachers. Adding together all these competencies, it could seem impossible to provide any teacher with all of them. Clearly, the teacher's competency can no longer be described only with a list of definite abilities. The teacher's competency needs to evolve and adapt all his/her career long. It is a collective competency: we need teams having a set of competencies, not necessarily each teacher having all of them.

ICT has certainly increased the competencies teachers need; but there are core expectations from Society towards teachers. The French National Commission for Unesco (Cornu, 2001) has studied the changes in the teaching profession. The teaching profession is based on the 'four pillars of Education': Learning to know, Learning to do, Learning to live together and learning to live with others, Learning to be. The teaching profession takes place in a world marked by increasing tensions, such as the tension between local and global, the tension between tradition and modernity, the tension between short term and long term, the tension between spiritual and material values. Education, in most countries, is facing new dimensions, with the increasement of democratisation, complexification and globalisation. In such a context, teachers have two major roles:

- Forming citizens in a world marked by change and dominated by the ephemeral; transmitting the basic values of society and the universal values of humanity.
- Instilling knowledge, when knowledge has changed and accessing knowledge has changed.

Clearly the teachers' competencies and activities have been increased, and the profession is getting more and more complex. But, rather than adding and adding new expectations, one could say that ICT and the variety of possibilities it permits confirm the essential and core role of the teacher. Since Socrates, the teacher has been the mediator between knowledge and the student; since Socrates, the face-to-face relationship between the teacher and the pupil has been the core role of the teacher. Balle (1999) says that ICT does not profoundly affect the status of the teacher, nor the fundamental vocation of school, but enables them to do better the best things that they do and that only they can do.

The human dimension of the teaching profession appears to be essential, and this dimension cannot be replaced by technology. But the human dimension can be supported and enhanced by technology, since ICT reinforces the possibilities of communicating and individualizing teaching.

Thus, even if ICT provokes profound perturbations in the profession of the teacher and his/her daily activity, the core characteristics are stable. If there is a 'new teaching profession', it is not in the fundamental mission, but in the way the profession is practised every day, in the tools and resources available, in the diversity of possible pedagogical methods.

But besides the teaching profession, new professions are appearing in Education: engineers and technicians, technological assistants, pedagogical assistants, educators of different types ... It is too early to describe precisely these new professions, which we can see around us in schools and universities. The teacher will not remain the only educative actor; recentered on his/her core role, he/she will be surrounded and assisted by other kinds of professionals.

## 5. NEW VIRTUAL LEARNING ENVIRONMENTS

Being a teacher in the networked society needs specific tools and environments.

First of all, teachers need to be networked, at different levels: at the local level (teachers in a given school), at other kinds of levels (for example national level, or teachers in a given discipline, or teachers in international networks...) and more generally in the 'global network'. Networking enriches the resources available for the teacher, networking enhances collaborative working among teachers, and networking enriches the possibilities for teachers to interact with their pupils. One can see how many groups are formed for teachers to cooperate: discussion forums, interest groups, etc.

Among the new tools available for teachers, virtual learning environments are essential. One can see them appear under different names: digital schoolbag, digital campus, virtual schools, digital working environments ... They aim at globalizing all the activities of schools' actors: teachers, students, but also parents, administrators, etc. They provide different types of facilities:

- Resources: accessing resources, organizing and storing resources, creating and producing resources, etc.
- Communication tools: e-mail, Intranet, access to the Internet...
- Collaborative working tools.

Most such environments are conceived on a modular basis, so that they can be enriched continuously, and can interoperate with other systems. They take into account 'nomadism', making possible complementarity between activities at school and activities out of the school. They have two major interests:

- providing school actors with new tools, adapted to the new needs of a 'networked' education, and anticipating the future evolutions of education;
- making concrete the 'unity' of education: traditionally, pedagogy is separated from administration, and school is separated from home. Such environments consider the pupil's life as a whole, school's life as a whole, and this enriches the complementarity of different situations.

Virtual learning environments are based on a plurality of actors and on a plurality of activities. They illustrate some of the evolutions in the teaching profession.

# 6. SCENARIOS FOR THE FUTURE

In a recent study, the OECD (2001) has developed six scenarios for the school of the future up to 2020. The scenarios are clustered into three categories: 'Attempting to Maintain the Status Quo', 'Re-schooling' and 'De-schooling'. Two aspects are important:

- None of these scenarios will happen in its pure form, the reality will be more complex and mixed; but the six scenarios give trends, which we must take into account;
- There is no inevitability in the future: actors must decide where they want to go, and such scenarios may help in decision-making.

It is useful to consider, for each of the scenarios, what happens for teachers and the teaching profession. In this paragraph, we borrow some sentences from the OECD document.

The 'status quo' scenarios consider that the basic features of existing systems are maintained into the future.

- In the first scenario, 'Bureaucratic School Systems Continue', school systems continue to be strong, with a pressure towards uniformity, and resistance to radical change. Individual classroom and teacher models remain dominant. The use of ICT continues to grow without changing schools' main organisational structures. In such a scenario, teachers form a strong corps, generally with the status of civil service. The evolution of the role and status of teachers in such a scenario is just the continuation of the present situation. Teaching is considered as an 'individual art'.
- In the second scenario, teacher shortage leads to a crisis: 'Teacher exodus - The 'meltdown scenario''. The teaching profession is rapidly ageing, and gets less and less attractive. ICT may appear as a possible response to teacher shortage. Salaries increase in order to attract more teachers, but this has detrimental consequences for investments in areas such as ICT and physical infrastructure. In this scenario, there is a major difficulty in recruiting enough teachers, and the market of 'school at home' is developing, with new types of professionals.

The 're-schooling' scenarios are based on major investments and widespread recognition for schools and the professionals, with a high priority accorded to both quality and equity.

- In the scenario 'Schools as Core Social Centres', the focus is on socialisation goals and schools in communities. School is recognized as the most effective bulwark against social, family and community fragmentation. It is now heavily defined by collective and community tasks. This leads to extensive shared responsibilities between schools and other community bodies. The focus of learning broadens with more explicit attention given to non-cognitive outcomes, values and citizenship. Significant investments would be made to update the quality of premises and equipment in general and to open school facilities to the community. ICT is used extensively, especially its communication capabilities. In this scenario, teachers have a high-level status and various types of contracts. Around them would be many other professionals, community players, parents, etc.

- The other scenario: 'Schools as Focused Learning Organisations', has a stronger knowledge orientation. New forms of evaluation and competence assessment flourish. ICT are used extensively alongside other learning media. Schools look like 'learning organisations'. Flourishing research on pedagogy and the science of learning is systematically applied. Schools management uses teams, networks and diverse sources of expertise. Teachers enjoy favourable conditions and are highly motivated, with strong emphasis on R&D, continuous professional development, group activities, networking (including internationally). Contractual arrangements might well be diverse, with mobility in and out of teaching. We meet the concept of 'networked teachers in a networked society'.

The two 'de-schooling' scenarios see the dismantling of school systems.

- In the scenario 'Learning Networks and the Network Society', new forms of co-operative networks come to predominate. Dissatisfaction leads to the abandonment of schools in favour of a multitude of learning networks, quickened by the extensive possibilities of powerful, inexpensive ICT. The emerging 'network society' leads to the dismantling of school systems. Greater expression is given to learning for different cultures and values through networks of community interests. Small group, home schooling and individualised arrangements become widespread. There would be a substantial reduction in public facilities and institutionalised premises for schools, but major investments in ICT could be expected. In such a scenario, there is no longer reliance on particular professionals called 'teachers': the demarcations between teacher and student, parent and teacher, education and community, blur and sometimes break down. New learning professionals emerge, whether employed locally to teach or as consultants (home teaching, educational 'hot lines', office consultancy...).

- The scenario 'Extending the Market Model' is the result of competitive mechanisms. Existing market features in education are significantly extended as governments encourage diversification in a broader environment of market-led change. Many new providers are stimulated to come into the learning market. The most valued learning is importantly determined by choices and demands. There is a substantially reduced role for public education authorities, and entrepreneurial management modes are more prominent. In such a situation, new learning and educational professions are created in the market.

Such scenarios show different trends for possible evolutions of the teaching profession. Will teaching be mainly an art, a vocation, or a profession? How will the shortage of teachers affect the nature of the profession? Will the school be reinforced, or will it disintegrate? Will education focus mainly on knowledge and disciplines, or on values and citizenship? How will the status of teachers evolve? How will the market affect the teaching profession? Asking such questions may help us master the evolution.

## 7. TEACHERS AND NATIONAL POLICIES

It is clear that teachers play a major role in national educational policies.

The expectations that society has of teachers are changing and growing in complexity. National policies have to take this into account and to express these expectations. They also have to enable teachers to complete their tasks and roles in relation to these expectations.

The social status of teachers is a key element of a national policy; not only teachers' salaries, but also the way they are considered in society, the role they have as public service agents.

Will teachers mostly remain in the public service, or shall we see more and more private educational actors? A national policy must address this type of question.

And national policy must also accompany the teaching profession in the changes due to ICT. For example, ICT creates new tasks for teachers; they do not only have to be in the classroom with their pupils, then at home for preparing their lessons, but they have a wide diversity of different activities: team work with colleagues, being available for pupils, physically or at a distance through e-mail or other means of communication, working in small groups with pupils, spending time to design digital resources, etc. The official duties of a teacher usually do not take these new tasks into account, and as a consequence only the most motivated teachers spend time on such innovative tasks. In the future, precise descriptions of teachers' tasks and precise description of their obligations will be needed. There will not be only one way to be a teacher, but a diversity in the possible activities for a teacher. Making explicit this diversity, showing the different ways of being a teacher, showing how a teacher can take part in innovation, increasing the social status of the teachers, are necessary items for reducing the shortage of teachers in the future.

It is interesting to note that most of these points were addressed in the 'Recommendation Concerning the Status of Teachers' (Unesco, 1966), adopted by the Unesco Special Intergovernmental Conference on the Status of Teachers in ... October 1966!

The political dimension of the teacher's mission must not be considered only at the national level. Globalisation and internationalisation also occur in the Education field, and lead to major questions, both political and ethical. International concerns about education (such as the one expressed by the Dakar Forum – 'Education for All') should also influence the teaching profession, and help teachers to take into account the questions that are posed at the global level.

## 8. CONCLUSION...

The changes in Society, and particularly those due to ICT, provoke major changes in the teaching profession. Being a teacher cannot now be considered only as an art, as a vocation; it is more and more a profession, with all the dimensions linked with such a concept: working conditions, status, preparation and pre-service training, professional development and in-service training, innovation, etc.

Teachers have gone through a progression (Unesco/IFIP, 2000): ICT has first emerged as new concepts, new tools, new resources, with no evidence that it could be used in education; then they started applying ICT to their professional activity, looking at how teaching could be changed by the use of new tools. In a third phase, teachers went to the integration of ICT into education. But now we are entering the phase of transformation. ICT can no longer be simply considered as a collection of tools for improving teaching and learning; a profound transformation has started, and teachers are the main agents of this transformation.

## REFERENCES

Balle, F. (1999). Les NTIC: Outils au service de la formation à l'enseignement. *Les Technologies de l'Information et de la Communication et Leur Avenir en Éducation, XXVII*(2).

Cornu, B. (2001). *Winds of Change in the Teaching Profession*. Paris: French National Commission for Unesco.

De Kerckhove, D. (2001). *Principles of Cyberarchitecture*. Boston: Birkhäuser.

Lévy, P. (1994). *L'Intelligence Collective*. Paris: La Découverte.

Merckelbach, S. & Dupas, P. (2002). *L'Araignée, la Girafe et les Réseaux de Proximité*. Freiberg: Ordinata.

Morin, E. (2001). *Seven Complex Lessons in Education for the Future*. Paris: Unesco Publishing.

OECD/CERI (2001). *What schools for the future?* Paris: OECD.

Unesco (1966). *Recommendation Concerning the Status of Teachers*. Paris: Unesco.

Unesco/IFIP (2000). *Information and Communication Technology in Secondary Education: a curriculum for schools*. Paris: Unesco.

# Designing Learning Experiences: Supporting Teachers in the Process of Technology Change

Barry Harper
*Faculty of Education, University of Wollongong*
*barry_harper@uow.edu.au*

**Abstract:** As teachers adopt technology in their classrooms and develop the pedagogical models that will allow them to make use of the affordances of the technology, we are seeing improved learning outcomes and high-quality learning demonstrated. The pedagogical models that are showing the most promise come from ideas about how designers can implement the class of theories referred to as constructivism. Designers of technology-based learning environments can draw on the work of the many writers who have sought to develop guidelines and heuristics to support new modes of learning (see for example, Grabinger, 1996; Hannafin & Land, 1997; Squires, 1996). Constructivist frameworks are based upon the argument for learners being placed in authentic environments that incorporate sophisticated representations of context through such constructs as virtual "worlds". Learning experiences, which adopt these approaches, designed around bounded resources, such as CD-ROM technologies, are now well documented and many teachers have been making extensive use of these environments for some time. One such project, Exploring the Nardoo, which has been developed within constructivist frameworks as a virtual world has been acclaimed for its illustration of these concepts. The product displays varying degrees of fidelity of representation, learner immersion and active participation and has been shown to offer learning advantages for users.

However, teachers need to continue to address the constantly changing nature of the capability of the technology, and potential learning opportunities offered by these changes. Unbounded environments, such as the World Wide Web, have offered a new set of affordances and now the concept of learning objects is set to again require teachers to re-conceptualise learning experiences for their students. The concept of a 'learning object' has developed from the movement to create reusable learning resources. Significant investment in content, described in terms of standards, which can be reused and re-purposed in education settings, is becoming a priority nationally (The Le@rning Federation, http://socci.edna.edu.au/newcms/view_page.asp) and internationally (Ariadne: http://ariadne.unil.ch/, Merlot: http://taste.merlot.org/, LRX: http://www.lrx.com.au/). Teachers are now seeking tools to make effective use of the myriad of learning objects that are now being developed, in such entities as digital libraries, to construct meaningful learning environments.

This paper will review the changes in pedagogy which ICT based learning environments have been able to facilitate, report on research findings on learning outcomes for a series of innovative bounded CD-ROM learning environments, and review the potential of learning object technologies to again challenge teachers striving for high quality learning from their students.

# 1. INTRODUCTION

As teachers adopt technology in their classrooms, safe in the understanding that the weight of argument and evidence supports pedagogy, not the technology (Clarke, 1985, 1999), as the key to successful learning design, we are seeing the development of pedagogical models which will allow teachers to make use of the affordances of the technology. The pedagogical models which are showing the most promise in demonstrating improved learning outcomes and high quality learning come from ideas about how designers can implement contemporary theories of learning which support knowledge construction through learner-centred settings (e.g. Bostock, 1998; Duffy & Cunningham, 1996) via activity-based tasks and collaborative learning which are scaffolded and supported by teachers or tools (e.g. Vygotsky, 1978). Designers of technology-based learning environments can draw on the work of the many writers who have sought to develop guidelines and heuristics to support new modes of learning (see for example, Grabinger, 1996; Hannafin and Land, 1997; Squires, 1996). These frameworks are based upon the argument for learners being placed in authentic environments that incorporate sophisticated representations of context through such constructs as virtual worlds. Learning experiences that adopt these approaches, designed around bounded resources, such as CD-ROM technologies, are now well documented, and many teachers have been making extensive use of these environments for some time.

However, teachers need to continue to address the constantly changing nature of the capability of the technology, and potential learning opportunities offered by these changes. Unbounded environments, such as the World Wide Web, have offered a new set of affordances. With this development broader concepts about learner-learner interactions have been illustrated and are being implemented through a broad range of curriculum initiatives. This access to rich resources from world-wide sources has resulted in significantly wider use of technology, but has also helped to drive the broader view of reusability.

The current significant investment in content, described in terms of standards, which can be reused and re-purposed in education settings, is becoming a priority nationally and internationally. The resulting construct of 'learning objects' is set to again require teachers to re-conceptualise learning experiences for their students. Teachers are now seeking tools and exemplars to construct meaningful learning environments through making effective use of the myriad of learning objects that are now being developed, in such entities as digital libraries.

This paper will review the changes in pedagogy which ICT based learning environments have been able to facilitate, report on research findings on learning outcomes for a series of innovative bounded CD-ROM learning environments, and review the potential of learning object technologies to again challenge teachers striving for high quality learning from their students.

## 2. BOUNDED LEARNING ENVIRONMENTS

*Exploring the Nardoo* (1996) is an innovative project that illustrates the development of learning environments based on contemporary theoretical constructs. This project was developed as a virtual world and has been acclaimed for its illustration of these concepts. The product displays varying degrees of fidelity of representation, learner immersion and active participation and has been shown to offer learning advantages for users. *Exploring the Nardoo* (Harper et al., 2000a, 2000b; Hedberg et al., 1998a, 1998b) has been well described and has been the focus of a number of specific studies in classrooms which have investigated learner response, the use of genre embedded templates and simulations and problem solving. The learning environment is characterised by a research centre (Figure 1) within the context of an inland river environment. A set of cognitive tools (Harper et al., 2000) supports learners in their investigation of authentic problems, with a rich set of resources as reference sources.

In an initial investigation of a broad view of learner response to the package, a structured and an ill-structured problem were set for two groups of year nine students and the construction of ideas by collaborative pairs of students was logged. Details of the study have been reported in Harper et al. (2000). Students perceived the rich tasks as being in context, motivating and worth spending a significant amount of time to develop possible solutions to the investigations. Students needed minimal instruction in the use of the cognitive tools and they developed extended arguments with multiple solutions to the investigations undertaken. In general, the ill-structured problem group did produce more complex and complete solutions to the task. As they did not have a defined task to solve but rather had to generate a series of hypotheses, they sought to be comprehensive and complete. More often, the structured problem group, sought to answer only the questions asked of them, and did not seek to find alternative explanations or to find other issues embedded in the investigation.

*Figure 1.* The Water Research Centre of *Exploring the Nardoo*

Gordon (1998) showed in her study that students who used the genre template cognitive tool, scored higher on learning outcome measures than students who did not. While the results endorsed the value of the templates in supporting student reporting, the static nature of the templates only improved the structure of the reports and not the quality of the arguments chosen. Further work on the development of more context sensitive assistance to improve reflection and assessment of the quality of the responses generated is underway and is showing promising results.

A study focused on probing learner problem solving to support design of more appropriate learner assistance for this package (Brickell, 2002) has reported on the use of a variety of support frameworks to assist learners in arguing their solutions, with the support frameworks resulting in greater learner achievement when using the package.

Corderoy (2002) in investigating the use of the algal bloom simulator by students has found an improvement in the process and success of formation of new knowledge links (knowledge acquisition) for students who study an ecological process (blue-green algal bloom development), using the interactive multimedia-based simulation of these processes as opposed to those who study them using rich resources without access to the simulator. He has also reported an improvement in the level of understanding of relationships (cause/effect) for students who study the ecological process using the simulators.

The range of studies reported has probed specific aspects of an individual package. However, they do illustrate improved learning outcomes when learners are engaged with learning environment designs based on contemporary views of learning, where the designs make use of the affordances of the technology, but are focused on theoretical constructs which lead to effective pedagogy.

## 3. UNBOUNDED LEARNING ENVIRONMENTS

Unbounded environments, such as the World Wide Web, are now offering a new set of pedagogical opportunities, especially in information access and collaborative processes. This technology shows particular promise for supporting meaningful learning through flexible delivery modes and a capacity to link and connect those involved in the learning process (e.g. Duschatel & Spahn, 1996; Levin, 1999). However, pedagogical issues have often been overshadowed by developments in the technology and unfounded claims of outstanding success attributed to use of the technology seem to be just as prevalent during the development of this technology as with previous new technologies. Salomon (1998) supported this concern and has noted that for the first time in history, technologies are outpacing pedagogical and psychological rationale for design of high quality learning.

Despite the possibilities existing for rich electronic learning based on this technology, for the most part, pedagogically sound and exciting Web courseware tools have yet to be developed to take advantage of such opportunities. Nevertheless, broader concepts about learner-learner interactions have been illustrated and are being implemented through a broad range of curriculum initiatives not only at the school level, but also at the higher education level where there is a different focus. Additionally, a body of literature is starting to report on innovative tools, with strong pedagogical underpinning. Bonk (1998) has reported on interactive tools for on-line portfolio feedback, profile commenting, and Web link rating, while Oliver and McLoughlin (1999) are building tools for on-line debate, reflection, concept mapping and student surveying and discussion.

A number of international initiatives have been developed to help illustrate good pedagogy and to support instructors in incorporating these exemplars into higher education courses, including teacher preparation. Significant projects that are informing the process currently include:

- Merlot, a database of small and large-scale interactive learning elements (http://taste.merlot.org/),
- the Ariadne project, which created tools and methodologies for producing, managing and reusing computer-based pedagogical elements and telematics supported training curricula (http://ariadne.unil.ch/), and
- the SoURCE project which identifies existing technology-based learning materials that have been shown to be successful and to replicate the successful environments as generic tools for teachers in other settings (http://www.source.ac.uk/).

An Australian University Teaching Committee (AUTC) project making some impact in this area, *ICT-Based Learning Designs* (www.learningdesigns.uow.edu.au) has recently been launched. The aim of this project is to assist university teachers in creating high quality flexible learning experiences for students by providing a range of generic resources/tools/templates that draw upon successful flexible learning projects that utilise ICT and which may be generalised beyond the scope of the individual project. Successful ICT-based learning projects are those that demonstrate improved learning outcomes.

The study conducted by Alexander and McKenzie (1998) highlighted that one contributing factor towards a successful learning outcome for an ICT-based learning project was the learning design employed. Thus, this project strove to accomplish its aim through the following process:

- the identification of a range of learning designs that have been demonstrated to contribute to high quality learning experiences and which can be applied generically;
- the design and subsequent development of a series of re-useable software, templates and/or exemplars for the learning designs previously identified; and
- the development of a series of guidelines for good practice in the use of or implementation of the software, templates and/or exemplars in new contexts.

Crucial to the success of this project was the development of an evaluation instrument, the *Evaluation and Redevelopment Framework* (ERF), with a twofold purpose:

- to facilitate the identification of learning designs that foster high quality learning experiences; and
- to provide a mechanism to determine whether such learning activity designs have the potential for re-development in a more generic form.

One of the initial activities of the project, to facilitate the development of the ERF, involved determining what constitutes "high quality learning". Two key researchers in the field of learning in higher education, David Boud and Mike Prosser, were commissioned to develop a paper on high quality learning. Their ideas together with feedback from the project team led to the development of a set of "Key Principles for High Quality Student Learning in Higher Education – From a Learning Perspective" (Boud & Prosser, 2001). The four principles, which are holistic in that they incorporate both learning outcomes and learning processes, describe key characteristics that underpin high quality learning in the higher education context. The principles are based upon an experience-based learner-centred view of learning and consist of learner engagement, acknowledgement of context, challenging learners and practice. The principles can be more fully described as: -

1. **Engage learners through:**
   - building on their learning intents generally and their particular expectations of the activity in question;
   - acknowledging and taking account of their prior experience, both their knowledge and experience of situations which might impinge on the present ones;
   - mobilising their will and desire and developing some kind of emotional engagement with the task in hand;
   - providing them with a sense of agency with respect to the activity or significant parts of it; and
   - recognising that learning is a social act and involves other learners for at least part of the activity.
2. **Acknowledge context through:**
   - involvement with problems in context;
   - recognising the context of the learner (who may see themselves as decontexualised);
   - maintaining an awareness of the cultural assumptions and stereotyping which may be incorporated in the context;
   - situating learning tasks within disciplinary or professional or practical knowledge as appropriate;
   - taking account of the site of application of what is to be learned (this poses different challenges when the learner is currently engaged in the site of application and when they are not);
   - appreciating the knowledge demands on students and equipping them to deal with them; and
   - ensuring that there is a clear alignment between the activities in which students will be engaged and the ways in which they will be assessed.

3. **Challenge learners through:**
   - prompting them to seek and discern variation in the knowledge and experiences in which they are involved;
   - questioning the assumptions they bring to the activity and the assumptions they develop through it;
   - encouraging them to see what is provided as a means to wider ends and go beyond what is provided; and
   - creating situations in which they are required to take responsibility for their own learning and to shape the activity to their own ends.
4. **Involve practice through:**
   - demonstrating what has been learned for themselves and for others;
   - gaining feedback at strategic points in learning, but also recognising that finding ways of gaining feedback for one self other than that provided is also important;
   - reflecting on and making sense of their experiences. Continuous exposure to new activities without integration and consolidation within the learner's framework is not conducive to good learning; and
   - developing confidence in performance from practice.

The ERF tool has been applied to a significant number of learning designs submitted to the project and the analysis has been used to select a range of projects considered to have the potential to support the key principles and be redeveloped as generic designs. The project has been published through a web environment with mechanisms for instructors to access the learning design exemplars, re-usable software, templates, tools etc, and guidelines for good practice in the use of or implementation of the software, templates and/or exemplars in new contexts. Additionally, the designs will be represented through a visual representation which draws from the work of Oliver (1999) and Herrington (2001), to illustrate the learning design in a temporal format (Figure 2).

The rationale for this construct is to provide a common form of communication to explain and illustrate each different kind of learning design and highlight its key features. Figure 3 illustrates this concept where the resources, learner activity or task and the learner support are all considered as separate, but essential components of a learning design. This representation of the designs has been developed to help link the resources to the issue of reusability, both of the learning design, and the learning resources described as resources or supports.

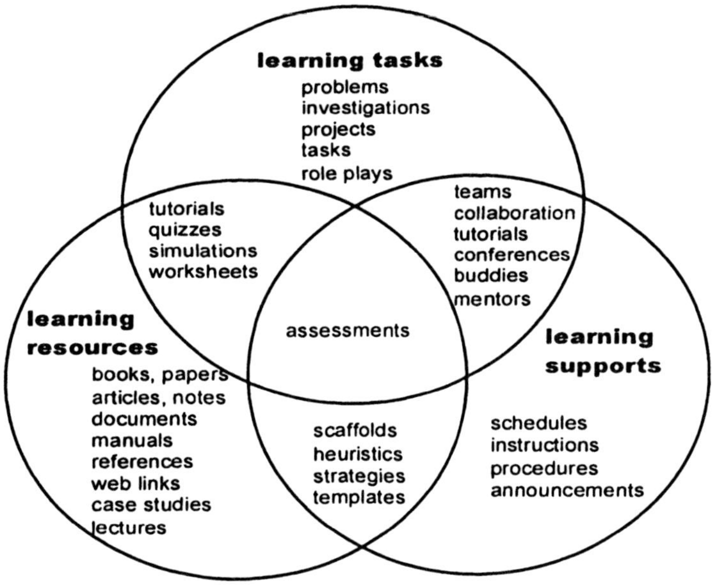


*Figure 2.* Elements of a learning design (based on Oliver, 1999 and Oliver & Herrington, 2001)

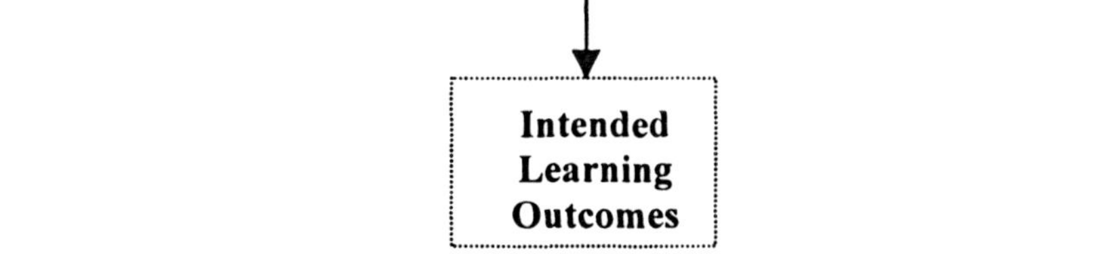


*Figure 3.* Representation of a learning sequence as resources, activities and supports

## 4. REUSABILITY DRIVING LEARNING ENVIRONMENT DESIGN

The access to rich resources world-wide has resulted in significantly wider use, but has also helped to drive the broader view of reusability. The issue of reusability of learning environments and their associated components has now developed as a major agenda for learning with both reusability at the small content chunk level and the learning design level being investigated, but not necessarily in conjunction with one another. The current significant investment in content, described in terms of standards, which can be reused and re-purposed in education settings, is becoming a priority nationally and internationally. A myriad of learning objects are now being developed, through such projects as the Learning Federation initiative for development of a significant K-12 repository of curriculum specific learning objects (http://socci.edna.edu.au/ newcms/view_page.asp), CLOE, the Cooperative Learning Object Exchange of Ontario (http://cloe.on.ca), Merlot and a raft of digital libraries (Marlino & Sumner, 2002).

Unfortunately, there is still a significant chasm between those researchers working on standards and describing and designing learning object metadata, and those interested in the learning settings in which these objects will need to be recombined as learning designs. Currently there seems to be two approaches to use of multimedia content in learning. The first is to develop learning designs based on our knowledge of best practice. This is a time consuming process and requires access to quality exemplars. Significant advances are being made through projects such as the SoURCE project: http://www.source.ac.uk/ which is developing instances of learning designs and theAUTC project described above on use of ICT in learning (Harper et al., 2000) which is developing mechanisms to streamline this process through generic learning designs and symbolic languages. However, these, and similar projects have not addressed reuse or management of resources in any specific way.

The second approach has evolved from information systems and is characterised by the current research in learning objects through learning technology standards. Standardization is a means to ensure interoperability between systems and this has been approached both through learning management systems and learning environments standardization initiatives. These initiatives, such as IEEE Learning Technology Standards Committee (LTSC), Instructional Management Systems (IMS) Project, or the Advanced Distributed Learning Network (ADLNET) have developed a broad range of standards, from high-level specifications for architectures to bindings for certain components. However, most of these approaches focus on the reuse of content. These specifications do not provide adequate concepts for modelling pedagogy. What is missing is a way of taking the advantages from both of these approaches and developing a new way forward which would revolutionise the eLearning space i.e. a way of bringing together the power of quality learning designs and the concepts of reusability of learning resources as learning objects or digital learning items.

## 5. PEDAGOGICAL MODELS

Koper (2001) and Pawlowski (2001) argue that the current representation of metadata does not provide an adequate representation of pedagogical concepts for the linking of learning objects described via standards and learning designs.. Additionally, there is no adequate mapping of content-oriented representation to a pedagogy-oriented representation. A variety of models are being developed to close the gap including a *Tutorial Markup Language (TML)* (Netquest, 2000) for development of tutorial systems. A more promising approach for the representation of pedagogical concepts is the Educational Modelling Language (EML) (Koper, 2001) which is based on a meta-model for pedagogical modelling. However, Pawlowski has argued that currently, there is no mapping to other standards such as SCORM and that in order to use both standards, a common framework needs to be specified such as the Essen Learning Model (ELM) (Pawlowski, 2000). The designers claim that this model serves as a base for a high-quality design of learning environments from a pedagogical and content perspective.

The difficulty with many of these models is that they do not differentiate the learner task, set in a particular context, from the learning supports and the learning resources which facilitate the learning experience, thus allowing use of digital libraries of digital items such as those described by Marlino and Sumner (2002). What is needed is a model that describes the central learner experience and provides an effective and real connection to digital learning objects in a framework that will be easy for trainers, instructors and teachers to use to construct rich learning experiences. Additionally, before teachers can have access to these resources, quality tools will need to be developed for their use.

## 6. CONCLUSION

Technology has the potential and demonstrated facility to support good pedagogy with a key outcome of this alliance high quality learning in rich educational settings. There is ample evidence to support this claim, but we often overlook the relationship between technology and pedagogy when new technologies become available. Learning objects have been the major focus of the current reusability debate, but much of the good work being done on learning designs as reusable objects is currently not being effectively addressed as part of the debate. For example, the tools for linking learning objects with quality learning designs are only now being conceptualised and there are very few examples available. The construct of learning objects is set to again require teachers to re-conceptualise learning experiences for their students, and require teacher preparation programs to support their students in developing the skills in design and well as tool use. We can all hope that Gavriel Salomon's call for new pedagogical models for the new affordances offered by this new technology will be taken up in higher education, particularly in teacher preparation, and in classrooms, with the reusability debate resulting in more efficient development of quality learning settings for learners.

## ACKNOWLEGEMENT

The author would like to acknowledge that the section of this paper to do with the AUTC project, was made possible through participation in the 2000-2002 Australian Universities Teaching Committee project titled: "Information and Communication Technologies and Their Role in Flexible Learning" funded through the Higher Education Innovation Programme (HEIP) via the Commonwealth Department of Education, Science and Training. Consortium: Project Team - Professor Barry Harper (University of Wollongong), Professor Ron Oliver (Edith Cowan University), Professor John Hedberg (University of Wollongong), Professor Sandra Wills (University of Wollongong); Research Team – Dr Jan Herrington (Edith Cowan University), Dr Garry Hoban (University of Wollongong), Dr Lori Lockyer (University of Wollongong), Associate Professor Catherine McLoughlin (Australian Catholic University). For information about this project visit the project web site: http: //www.learningdesigns.uow.edu.au or contact: Project Manager, Dr Shirley Agostinho (University of Wollongong).

## REFERENCES

Alexander, S. & McKenzie, J. (1998). *An Evaluation of Information Technology Projects for University Learning*. Canberra: CAUT, AGPS.

Bonk, C. (1998). *Pedagogical Activities on the "Smartweb": Mentoring Undergraduate Educational Psychology Students*. Paper presented at the American Educational Research Annual Meeting, April 14, San Diego, CA. Retrieved September 11, 1998 from http://php.indiana.edu/~cjbonk/smart_paper.html

Boud, D. & Prosser, M. (2001). *Key Principles for High Quality Student Learning in Higher Education – From a Learning Perspective*. Paper presented at a workshop held on April 27, 2001 for the AUTC funded project: Information and Communication Technologies and Their Role in Flexible Learning, Sydney, Australia.

Bostock, S. (1998). Constructivism in mass education: A case study. *British Journal of Educational Technology*, 29(3), 225-240.

Brickell, G., (2002). *Problem Solving in Technology Supported Learning Environments*. Unpublished doctoral thesis, University of Wollongong.

Clarke, R. E. (1985). Evidence for confounding in computer-based instruction studies: Analyzing the meta-analyses. *Educational Communications and Technology Journal, 33*(4), 249-262.

Clarke, R. E. (1999). The cognitive science and human performance technology. In H. D. Stolovitsch & E. J. Keeps, *Handbook of Human Performance Technology* (pp. 82-95). San Francisco: Jossey-Bass-Pfeiffer.

Corderoy, R., (2002). *Designing Simulations to Improve Learning Outcomes in Ecological Education*. Unpublished doctoral thesis, University of Wollongong.

Duffy, T. M. & Cunningham, D. J. (1996). Constructivism: Implications for the design and delivery of instruction. In D. H. Jonassen (Ed.), *Handbook of Research for Educational Communications and Technology* (pp. 170-198). New York: Macmillan Library Reference USA.

Duschatel, P. & Spahn, S. (1996). *Design for Web-based Learning*. Paper presented at the WebNet'96, World Conference of The Web Society, San Francisco, USA.

*Exploring the Nardoo* (1996). Canberra: Interactive Multimedia, Project Manager Barry Harper, Instructional Design Barry Harper, John Hedberg, Rob Wright, Grant Farr and Christine Brown (a CD ROM-based interactive multimedia package produced in collaboration with NSW Dept of Land and Water Conservation).

Gordon, J. (1998). *Learning with Technology Tools*. Unpublished doctoral thesis, University of Wollongong.

Grabinger, R. S. (1996). Rich environments for active learning. In D. H. Jonassen (Ed.), *Handbook of Research for Educational Communications and Technology* (pp. 665-692) New York: Macmillan Library Reference USA.

Hannafin, M. J. & Land, S. M. (1997). The foundations and assumptions of technology-enhanced student centred learning environments. *Instructional Science*, 25, 167-202.

Harper, B., Hedberg, G. & Wright, R. (2000a). Who benefits from virtuality? *Computers and Education, 34*, 163-176.

Harper, B., Squires, D. & McDougall, A. (2000b). Constructivist simulations in the multimedia age. *Journal of Educational Multimedia and Hypermedia, 9*(2), 115-130.

Harper, B., Hedberg, J., Corderoy, R..& Wright, R. (2000). Employing cognitive tools within interactive multimedia applications. In S. P. Lajoie (Ed.), *Computers as Cognitive Tools: The Next Generation* (pp. 227-245). Mahwah, NJ: Lawrence Erlbaum Publishers.

Hedberg, J., Harper, B., Lockyer, L., Ferry, B., Brown, C. & Wright, R. (1998a). Supporting ill-structured problem solving in interactive multimedia learning environments. In T. Ottmann & I. Tomek (Eds.), *Proceedings of ED-MEDIA/ED-TELECOM 98 World Conference on Educational Multimedia and Hypermedia & World Conference on Educational Telecommunications* (Vol. 1, pp. 496-501). Charlottesville, VA: Association for the Advancement of Computing in Education.

Hedberg, J., Harper, B., Lockyer, L., Ferry, B., Brown, C. & Wright, R. (1998b). Supporting learners to solve ill-structured problems. In R. M. Corderoy (Ed.), *Proceedings of the 15th Annual Conference of the Australasian Society for Computers in Learning in Tertiary Education* (pp. 317-327). Wollongong, NSW: University of Wollongong.

IEEE Learning Technology Standards Committee (2000). *Draft Standard for Computer-Managed Instruction (CMI), Version 3.4*. Retrieved May 5, 2001 from http://ltsc.ieee.org/doc/wg11/CMI-Sem34.doc

IEEE Learning Technology Standards Committee (2001). *Draft Standard for Learning Object Metadata, Version 6.1.* Retrieved May 30, 2001 from http://ltsc.ieee.org/doc/wg12/LOMv6.1.html

Koper, R. (2001). *Modeling units of study from a pedagogical perspective – the pedagogical meta-model behind EML.* Retrieved July 1, 2001 from http://eml.ou.nl/introduction/articles.htm

Levin, J. (1999). Dimensions of network-based learning. *International Journal of Educational Technology*, 2(1).

Marlino, M. & Sumner,T. (2002). Educational digital libraries; building community; building libraries. *Proceedings of ED-MEDIA 2002, World Conference on Educational Multimedia, Hypermedia & Telecommunications* (pp.1223-1225). Denver Colorado, USA: Association for the Advancement of Computing in Education.

Netquest (2000). *Tutorial Markup Language (TML).* Retrieved September 25, 2000 from http://www.ilrt.bris.ac.uk/netquest/liveserver/TML_INSTALL/doc/tml.html

Oliver, R. (1999). Exploring strategies for on-line teaching and learning. *Distance Education, 20*(2), 240-254.

Oliver, R. & McLoughlin, C. (1999). Curriculum and learning-resource issues arising from the use of Web-based course support systems. *International Journal of Educational Telecommunication, 5*(4), 419-438.

Pawlowski, J. M. (2000). The Essen Learning Model – A Multi-Level Development Model. *Staff and Education Development International, 4.*

Pawlowski, J. M. (2001). *Das Essener-Lern-Modell (ELM): Ein Vorgehensmodell zur Entwicklung Computerunterstützter Lernumgebungen* [The Essen-Learning Model (ELM): A Development Model for the Development of Computer-Supported Learning Environments]. Unpublished dissertation. University of Essen, Germany.

Squires, D. (1996). Can multimedia support constructivist learning? *Teaching Review, 4*(2), 10-17.

Salomon, G. (1998). Novel constructivist learning environments and novel technologies: Some issues to be concerned with. *Research Dialogue in Learning and Instruction, 1*, 3-12.

Vygotsky, L. (1978). *Mind in society.* Cambridge, Massachusetts: Harvard University Press.

# The Teacher – A Forgotten Stakeholder?

Deryn Watson
*Department of Education and Professional Studies, King's College London, Waterloo Road, London SE1 9NN, UK, deryn.watson@kcl.ac.uk*

**Abstract:** There are a number of tensions and debates embedded in any consideration of the teacher, ICT and the future. In this complex climate, it is possible to argue that too little attention has been paid to the act of teaching. With widely available and different forms of information and knowledge, learners still need to learn how to learn and to think. Teachers are the essential part of ensuring this process of transformation. Their professional judgement and voice are essential in this process.

## 1. INTRODUCTION

The perspective from which I will discuss the role of the teacher in an ICT world is informed by literature on innovation and change, professional development, and ICT and teaching and learning, which I present at the end as a bibliography. An exploration of ICT as an innovation and its relationship to, and influence upon, change in education is not only current and at the heart of our interests, but is particularly complex as the nature of the technology itself is dynamic. Thus we are attempting to analyse and understand a fast moving innovation with attributes that shift in both complexity and ranking of significance. Understanding such a mobile innovation and its relationship to education, which itself is neither static nor fixed, needs models of change. For me, the linear models, often developed to understand the management of change, provide too simplistic a representation of such reality. This is in part because a further layer of complexity lies in the substantial societal changes within which this educational and technological relationship is developing. And these societal changes, part triggered by information and communication technologies, add to the shifting contexts in which we are operating.

My analysis of this literature and the papers and discussions published in this volume, is built around what I see as a cluster of debates and tensions embedded in the themes of this conference. A useful way of perceiving such tensions, often used in analysis in applied social sciences, is to explore their characteristics as if located at opposite ends of a pole. Such analysis, by focussing on the characterisation of difference, may subsequently sharpen our understanding of such debates and tensions, but also clarify the continuities that underlie them. I am convinced we should recognise some residual tensions in our field, and indeed take responsibility for some of the discourse that suggests enormous benefits for the use of ICT in education when research often reflects patchy and inconclusive effects. In this paper I will set out to use this device of identifying differences around each of the four themes of the conference: the roles of the teacher, the teaching environment, the teacher and society, and the teacher as professional.

I intend to explore each theme as if the four represent a series of nested boxes, or stacked Russian painted dolls. The inner box is the teacher as professional, the next their roles, then the environment and the final outer box, or the largest of the Russian dolls, is the teacher and society. These boxes provide a simple form of scaffolding for the basis of my analysis. But while they represent the overall structure of my intent, in order to build, or scaffold the stack, I am choosing to start with the second box.

## 2. THE ROLES OF THE TEACHER

In this climate of educational and societal change surrounding the introduction of ICT, the teacher often falls between two classifications – that of a conservative resister of change, and that of a pioneer and interpreter of change. Those who focus on teachers as a block to innovation will produce and impose prescriptions for change to include the externally devised new curriculum and in-service courses to promote an innovation. This approach is, in effect, designed to redress a deficit model of teachers. This can be illustrated by the number of times teachers are referred to as the object of the imperative – 'teachers must', 'teachers should'. The problem with this model is that it can too easily ignore existing perceptions and experiences of teachers. At the opposite end of the pole is the belief that lasting innovations work if they are introduced or emerge 'bottom up', that is from within the corpus of practising teachers. They adopt and adapt the innovation to suit the needs of their learners and classrooms. The problem here is the innovation often remains trapped within individual or small group's interpretations and use, and rarely develops into a consensus to influence the majority.

Educational innovation and change does occur, but Fullan (1991) has repeatedly reminded us of two factors – that teachers lie at the heart of change, and that planned major innovations are often less successful than those which succeed through what I am choosing to call a form of 'consensus of practice'. That is, teachers and related groups, such as professional associations and advisers, find enough potential common ground and value in an innovation for it to be adapted, adopted and become a regular part of their pedagogy. Sarason (1990) suggests that the problem is not what to do, but what to think. He reminds us that no-one warmly seeks, let alone embraces, significant intellectual and personal change. Change is difficult – we must address the issue of power, and power relationships, to ensure the desired change is to be achieved. The value of many of the papers and discussions in this volume is that this is what they are addressing.

Much of the work on the role of teachers and the use of ICT appears to be caught in a pincer movement between a substantial and important discussion on theories of learning, and an equally important consideration of models of teachers' knowledge. Our understanding of the psychology of learning includes our shifting understanding of how students construct and situate knowledge. There has been an interesting partnership between educational psychology and educational ICT – and this has spawned experimental research and many applications have been devised around models of learning. This work has been valuable, and not simply in association with the use of ICT, as all educationalists are continually trying to model and understand the processes of learning. Valuable though this is, there appears to me a relative absence of corresponding discussions about how teachers can or do assimilate research about learning and translate such approaches into their teaching.

Writing about teachers and ICT is increasingly focused on the nature of teachers' knowledge, and thus how and where ICT 'should' be incorporated into it. There are useful models of the various component parts of teachers' knowledge. These are now commonly agreed to have as a basis three interlocking sets, to include subject knowledge, the knowledge of schooling, and the translation of both these in combination to arrive at pedagogic knowledge. The latter refers to knowledge to suit curriculum and learning at different levels of complexity. Thus for example a geography teacher knows and understands geography and the nature of geographical thinking, understands schools and learning, and translates that into curriculum and teaching, that is their pedagogy, of for instance the significance of plate tectonics to seven and seventeen years olds. The addition of knowledge about ICT within a pedagogic frame is a welcome recognition that this is an integral and not separate part of the complex knowledge base of teachers. Because it is here that the enormous asset that ICT can be to pedagogy, and the changes in perception about knowledge that it can herald, are best achieved.

And yet we do have evidence that teachers are not necessarily enamoured of this ICT 'knowledge' or of its incorporation into their pedagogic armoury. We know teachers often face a dichotomy with respect to ICT use. Is ICT a skill to be learned and used as part of their pedagogy, or is ICT a means to support their pedagogy? There is still an ambiguity of what we construe as ICT use in education. Not all ICT knowledge and use has been good; there has often been too much emphasis on the fact that it is being used, without enough attention being paid to the validity of its use. Good is often very good – and in such a way that it is difficult to evaluate its impact; but often ICT use is not good, at a low level, with the emphasis on the technology and skills not clearly enough related to teachers' other three knowledges. And we know that part of the problem lies in the fact that good pedagogic ICT use involves complexity. It takes time to come to grips with both the technology and its potential service to the subject/knowledge base for which a teacher is responsible. Teachers will spend this time if they believe that ICT will support their pedagogic philosophy; they will not make a sustained effort if it does not.

So it seems clear that our current construct of the role of the teacher is fraught with contradictions. On the one hand we recognise the teacher as the basic constructor of the pedagogic environment, of the subject and content base of schooling; on the other hand we have the apparent lessening of the significance of the teacher relative to the emphasis on the learners, and their construction of knowledge. But both these emphases are but background to the foremost role of the teacher, which is to teach. Where in the debate is a discussion on what Shulman (1987) refers to as 'the act of teaching'? This is where their comprehension and reasoning, transformation and reflection form the basis of actual teaching. It would seem to me that the attention given to the new environment provided by ICT is in danger of eclipsing the act of teaching.

## 3. TEACHING ENVIRONMENTS

ICT has been responsible for a substantial shift in the environment for learning; teachers can be distributed in time and space – face to face, hybrid, distributed, teams. Distributed networks, fora and access to information rightly force us to ask questions about the location of learning. Here we see another dichotomy – learning within defined frames of time and space, compared with learning at any time and anywhere. There are substantial advantages of the web, for access to information from a range of sources and distance learning. These are often characterised as a new learning environment, a replacement for the traditional setting of a classroom – in which the tables of desks may be set out in rows or clusters. And the characterisation of a classroom as 'traditional' by the ICT community often implies this is bad. It seems to me that this polar painting of the new as automatically good and the traditional as bad misrepresents the complex relationship between learners, teachers and the actuality of the learning environment.

I would argue that the prime context for learning is how and where maximum interaction between teachers, learners and knowledge can be achieved. With the emphasis on independent learning, few address the reality of location as a ground base for the new wider reach that the technology provides. Yet this base provides the development of situated learning communities. I note that many on-line environments emulate the notion of a room, a place to which learners feel they belong and where activities 'occur', whether more formal sessions, seminars, discussions or general chat. Learning is an individual activity, but not exclusively. We know that the social dimension of groups, both formal and informal, enhances the learning for a number of reasons, which include interaction between learners, the vocal exploration of ideas, the development of social skills, a counter to isolation, the broadening of social networks. The web opens up the classroom, not simply to access information, but to contacts with other communities; thus it should be seen as an additional asset to the classroom, rather than its rival or replacement.

But for my purposes in this paper, the value of the classroom, however it is constructed or perceived, is that it is the home base where the act of teaching occurs. Much is written about the teacher in this new ICT environment as causing a shift from teaching to guiding, a facilitator – as if current constructs of the act of teaching were dominated only by the 'transmitter of knowledge' model. This is a simplistic characterisation; I feel equally uncomfortable with the phrases such as 'from sage on the stage to guide on the side'. The roles of tutor – coach, guide, companion, supporter – are important in this environment, but not, I would contend, at the expense of teaching itself.

The focus on the supportive, tutoring role suggests learners in school do not need more than agenda setting. But teachers are in charge – they are empowered by society to be responsible for learners to learn how to learn and to think. Authority is located in a physical institution – and here authority is not primarily associated with power, but with responsibility. Who is in charge? Who assumes the pedagogic responsibility? This voice is not an authority on knowledge, but the voice of someone in charge of a process. Many may consider a class outmoded, but it is where groups of learners share a common experience, a particular voice, and an interpretation – the teacher's voice.

Access to data, to information, to knowledge is not the same as learning. Some of the literature, both about the teachers' knowledge, and the wider avenues to knowledge available to students, seems to suggest that knowledge is a box of something, bounded and wrapped as a gift to be available or given to learners. A box of knowledge is an odd thing – knowledge is organic, it shifts, grows, and changes in these fluid times. Our geographical knowledge, for example, as with so many other subjects, has broadened and changed over the years, and most recently through the advent of satellite imagery and geographical information systems. It is the use of the noun, knowledge, which obscures the heart of the matter. The act of teaching is about verbs - to enable learners to know, to think, to understand. It is through the continual interaction with the elucidation and reasoning of teachers that learners become more proficient in thinking and understanding. Thence they can increasingly assume more responsibility for their learning. Teaching, even with the advent of the technology and widening access to information and knowledge, seems to me to be an essential part of learning. It is teachers who are responsible for ensuring the transformation from ignorance or confusion to knowing, thinking and understanding.

## 4. THE TEACHER IN SOCIETY

There are relatively few published contributions from within the ICT community on the theme of the teacher and society. But the reality is that debate about education and the use of ICT is not happening in isolation. Teachers, learners, managers, parents, communities are all but part of the world in which we live. Indeed education has a strong compact with society as part of the way with which society progresses and copes with change. Developing countries place a high premium on the role and function of schools and teachers that we in the developed world sometimes forget, and often take for granted. And the social, political and economic structures in the world have changed dramatically in part because of the growth of the technology and increased globalisation.

There has been a close association for some time between the perceived benefits of ICT and economic growth in a competitive world. Governments have promoted the use of ICT in education as part of an agenda to prepare an economically successful society by ensuring that its citizens have employable skills. Curriculum has been defined in association with the development of essential ICT skills, thus leading to the dichotomy of purpose already mentioned. As Wood (2002) has stated, there is an axis of tension between teachers as technicians – that is, as deliverers of a skills based agenda – and teachers as professionals, who know pedagogy and pupils.

There is a further tension for professionals between what society expects of teachers – from the specific association with skills of pedagogic knowledge to much broader issues in society. The role of teachers lies well beyond the development of cognitive skills. They are expected, and wish, to address issues such as inequity, personal and group rights, safety and values. The current high profile worries about security and risk and the threat to human rights and liberties in association with ICT – all these fall on the shoulders of teachers. The teachers in many communities are under pressure, from governments and parents and society in general – to welcome and embrace the technology, grapple with the measurable outcomes of skills, use it proficiently in subject teaching, and address the tensions ICT brings to society.

So how do teachers respond to this pressure and to being stretched between competing goals? They leave – they are leaving education, and new graduates are not entering the profession. There is substantial attrition after 2 and 10 years of service in the UK. The discourse in society about teachers in certain contexts is negative and damaging.

## 5. THE TEACHER AS PROFESSIONAL

The reason I have left the teacher as professional until last is because I believe the tension between the teacher as a technician or professional lies beneath the arguments above. In general, certainly in the UK, and without the complications that arise from ICT, the notion of teaching as a profession has been under threat.

Professionals, such as lawyers, doctors and teachers, have a number of factors which contribute to their sense of being professional, which include specialist bodies of knowledge, an agreed understanding of identity, a philosophy of reasoning and judgement, their expertise incorporated in independent professional bodies and associations. In varying degrees, governments have sought to erode this independence. Teachers in particular have become vulnerable. Governments are increasingly imposing their definition of teaching, by involving themselves in the nature of the curriculum, defining outcomes to be measured, and identifying the means whereby it is to be 'delivered'. And this government-sponsored definition is characterised by a series of competencies – for both teachers and learners. This characterises the teacher as a technician, with narrow and specific goals.

Such a characterisation leaves no room for a teacher's expertise. And yet it is this expertise that underpins a teacher's sense of identity, voice and self. Over time their growing expertise and wisdom contributes to their personal commitment as professionals. Teaching, as with other professions, is a very personal endeavour. The literature about teachers refers to their endeavours not simply as purveyors of pedagogic knowledge. We also know them as holders of tacit knowledge built up through experience, as professionals with a range of styles to suit circumstances. People embark on change for a number of reasons, but reasons that invariably have a resonance with their personal philosophy about teaching. Teachers are thinkers, with emotions, beliefs and enthusiasms – and it is this that characterises them as much as their professional expertise. Teachers have a professional voice – and it is that voice and style which pupils often remember long after they have left their formal education.

The axis of tension that appears to surround teachers is I believe in part because the significance of the personal in teaching – the individual voice of the teacher - has been sidelined in the recent push for performativity through definitions of competence. Teaching is an intellectual pursuit, which embraces ideas, reasoning, thinking and communicating. It is also a human pursuit, where individuals draw upon attributes such as humour, metaphor, and emotions in the pursuit of effective teaching. Serious problems arise in the medical profession when doctors treat the disease not the person. Equally serious problems arise if teachers strive to know their pupils only by their cognitive capabilities, without concern for their individual characters, foibles, concerns and circumstances.

The professional development of teachers based on a competency approach would appear to have a limited chance of succeeding. Practice is more likely to be transformed by an approach that meets their intellectual and emotional needs as professionals. Change, a deep process of restructuring, is likely to occur when there is a strong personal involvement in the matter in hand.

## 6. CONCLUSION

And so the teacher as professionals appears to me to lie at the heart of the stacking boxes – the core of what makes a teacher. Current discussions place useful emphasis on theories of learning and models of teacher knowledge. I would argue that the teacher has often been a relatively absent figure. For this reason I am characterising the teacher as the forgotten stakeholder.

The analysis in the papers in this book, often very pertinent and always informative, contributes to the conception of the teacher of the future. There have been lots of words like cognition and learning; but few about responsibility and the act of teaching. What has been missing is I believe a greater understanding of the sociology and philosophy of teachers. Teaching is an emotional and intellectual business.

## REFERENCES

Anderson, R. (2002). Guest editor, special issue. *Journal of Computer Assisted Learning, 18*(4).

Barrow, R. (1984). *Giving Teaching back to Teachers*. Toronto: Harvester Wheatsheaf.

Becta (2002). *NGfL Pathfinders Report*. London: Department for Education and Skills.

Becta (2002). *ImpaCT 2 Reports*. London: Department for Education and Skills.

Bowers, C. (1988). *The Cultural Dimension of Educational Computing*. New York: Teachers College Press.

Bryson, M. & de Castell, S. (1994). Telling tales out of school: Modernist, critical and postmodern "true stories" about educational computing. *Journal of Educational Computing Research, 10*(3), 199-221.

Collis, B. (1998). New wines in old bottles? Tele-learning, Telematics and the University of Twente. In F. Verdejo & G. Davies (Eds), *The Virtual Campus*. Boston: Kluwer.

Collis, B. & Moonen, J. (2001). *Flexible Learning in a Digital World*. London: Kogan Page.

Cuban, L. (1986). *Teachers and Machines: The Classroom Use of Technology since 1920*. New York: Teachers College Press.

Cuban, L. (2001). *Oversold and Underused*. London: Harvard University Press.

Denning, T. (2001). Guest editor, special issue. *Information Technology for Teacher Education, 10*(1&2).

Dwyer, D. C. (1996). The imperative to change our schools. In C. Fisher, D. Dwyer, & K. Yocam (Eds), *Education and Technology: Reflections on Computing in Classrooms*. San Francisco: Jossey Bass.

Erault, M. (1994). *Developing Professional Knowledge and Competencies*. London: Falmer Press

Fullan, M. (1991). *The New Meaning of Educational Change* (second edition). London: Cassell.

Fullan, M. & Hargeaves, A. (Eds) (1992). *Teacher Development and Educational Change*. London: Falmer Press.

Hargreaves, A. (1994). *Changing Teachers, Changing Times*. London: Cassell.

Hargreaves, A. & Fullan, M. G. (1992). *Understanding Teacher Development*. New York: Teachers College Press.

Huberman, M. (1993). *The Lives of Teachers*. London: Cassell.

Lehtinen, E. (2000). Information and communication technology in education: Desires, promises and obstacles. In D. M. Watson & T. Downes (Eds), *Communication and Networking in Education: Learning in a Networked Society*. Boston: Kluwer.

Loveless, A. & Ellis, V. (Eds) (2001). *ICT, Pedagogy and the Curriculum: Subject to Change*. London: Routledge Falmer.

Morin, E. (2001). *Seven Complex Lessons in Education for the Future*. Paris: UNESCO.

OECD (2001). *Learning to Change: ICT in Schools*. Paris: OECD.

OFSTED (2001). *ICT in Schools: The Impact of Government Initiatives. An Interim Report*. London: Office for Standards in Education.

Olson, J. (1988) *Schoolworlds/Microworlds: Computers and the Culture of Classrooms.* Oxford: Pergamon Press.

Olson, J. (1992). *Understanding Teaching.* Milton Keynes: Open University Press.

Ragsdale, R. (1988). *Permissible Computing in Education.* New York: Praeger.

Sarason, S. B. (1990). *The Predictable Failure of Educational Reform.* San Francisco: Jossey Bass.

Shulman, L. S. (1987). Knowledge and Teaching: Foundations of the New Reform. *Harvard Educational Review, 57*(1).

Stevenson, D. (1997). *The Future of Information Technology in UK Schools.* London: McKinsey & Company.

Sandholtz, J. H., Ringstaff, C. & Dwyer, D. C. (1997). *Teaching with Technology.* New York: Teachers College Press.

Watson, D. M. (Ed.) (1993). *The ImpacT Report: An Evaluation of the Impact of Information Technology on Children's Achievements in Primary and Secondary Schools.* London: King's College.

Wood, D. (2002, November). *The THINK Study (first draft).* Retrieved from http://www.eun.org/insight-pdf/think_report.pdf

# Section 2

# The Teacher of The Future as a Professional

# ICT, National Policies, and their Impact on Schools and Teachers' Development

Rosa Maria Bottino
*Consiglio Nazionale delle Ricerche Istituto Tecnologie Didattiche, Via De Marini 6-16149, Genova, Italy, bottino@itd.ge.cnr.it*

## 1. INTRODUCTION

This paper briefly sketches Italian public policy in promoting the use of ICT (Information and Communication Technologies) in school education (primary and secondary level). It tries to identify aspects that appear to be supporting the development of pedagogically 'sound' approaches to technology, enhanced teaching and learning, as well as some of the problems that are in evidence.

The objective is to contribute to the discussion on the ways in which public policy can facilitate the development of appropriate forms of technology use in school, considering it in the wider perspective of the information society.

## 2. ITALIAN POLICY FOR THE DEVELOPMENT OF TECHNOLOGY ENHANCED LEARNING

For some years the Italian government has put in place programmes to equip educational institutions with the necessary ICT infrastructure and to train teachers.

In 1997 the Ministry of Education launched a Programme for the Development of Educational Technologies (PSTD) having as its main stated goals: the provision of infrastructure to schools (PCs, internet connections, etc.); the improvement of teachers' professional skills in using ICT; the improvement of effectiveness of learning and teaching methods and content; and the promotion of the use of ICT and multimedia tools among students.

Moreover the Italian government, in line with the eEurope Plan (www.europa.eu), adopted an Action Plan for the Information Technology Society on June 2000 with the aim of further completing and strengthening the educational technologies development programme.

The programme offered funding to individual schools for the creation of equipped laboratories and for organising autonomous basic ICT courses for teachers. A total of 13,300 schools were involved between 1997 and 2001. The situation is quite different from school to school with regard, for example, to school level, school typology, and school geographical location. Table 1 briefly summarises the average current situation regarding technology infrastructure in schools (Fierli, 2002). It can be noted that technological equipment is mainly located in laboratories, and access is seldom available from classrooms.

*Table 1.* Average situation in Italy regarding technology infrastructure in schools

| School level | PC/students | Schools with Internet connections (%) |
|---|---|---|
| Primary school (age 6-11) | 1/50 | 80% |
| Lower secondary (age 11-14) | 1/25 | 80% |
| Upper secondary (age 14-19) | 1/10 (from about 1/5 of technical schools to 1/25 of lycei) | From 100% of technical schools to 80% of lycei |

As far as teacher training is concerned, the first widespread initiative of the Government was the National Plan for Informatics (launched in 1985). This was a centralized plan for in-service mathematics teacher training whose aim was to provide basic computer science literacy. This training plan was enacted through courses for teachers in which traditional lessons alternated with computer practice. The method used was a 'pull-down' one (i.e. the training programme is operated through trainers who are in-service teachers specifically trained for this purpose).

These training initiatives had been funded by the Ministry, but their organisation and content had been left to schools. Between 1997 and 2001, 43,300 refresher courses for teachers were organised as a consequence.

Currently it can be said that approximately half of the Italian primary and secondary school teachers have been involved in training initiatives related to the use of information and multimedia technologies. Quality and depth of training have been very variable.

Now the Ministry has launched and financed the development of on-line services for training support. On-line training at present involves approximately 60,000 teachers.

For the next year a new initiative (funded with UMTS license incomes) will involve 180,000 teachers. This initiative will provide 12 hours of training for each teacher (six hours face to face and six hours online).

In addition to the great effort of the Government in providing schools with ICT infrastructure and teachers with a basic knowledge in ICT, the Ministry has recently promoted initiatives to support the use of ICT in classroom practice. Some projects have been launched to provide teachers with examples of practice in which technology has been used to support the teaching of discipline topics. Such projects (SET projects, INDIRE documentation of experiences) are aimed at publishing on the Internet didactical itineraries (both at primary and secondary school level) on curricular topics integrating ICT. These projects have had positive aspects (such as the involvement of both teachers and educational researchers in the implementation of the educational itineraries) and have represented interesting experiences for the teachers directly involved in the work, but still they have not had a significant impact on a wider basis.

## 3. IMPACT ON SCHOOL EDUCATION

Despite the efforts made in the field of training and in the equipping of schools, to date the results at the school level are still relatively limited. There is not a wide integration of ICT use as tools to enhance teaching and learning in curricular topics.

Even when the use of ICT, though with differing modes and characteristics, enters into teaching practice, one often observes purely superficial changes that do not impact upon the effective renewal of the syllabuses and methods, i.e. the modification of the methodological approaches, the content and relational dynamics in classes and schools, and the organisational aspects within schools (Bottino & Furinghetti, 1999). This situation is not substantially different from that in other European countries (Mallon, 2002).

One can observe that the government programme for the development of educational technologies has achieved significant results in providing schools with technology infrastructure and a considerable number of teachers with ICT basic skills. Nevertheless this has not led directly to an improvement of teaching and learning methods and to a change in approaching discipline subjects. A direct relationship cannot be established between provision of infrastructure and ICT training, and the effective pedagogical use of technology in schools. This last goal is less clearly supported by governmental polices and needs a careful consideration of related difficulties and possible interventions.

Difficulties that can be shown are of a different nature and can be related both to technical and structural problems and to more general organisational and pedagogical aspects (Prometeus Position Paper, 2001).

It is a fact that the resistance on the part of many teachers to using ICT in class can be ascribed to technical and structural problems such as, for example, the lack of technical personnel to help manage laboratories, the fact that the substantial time dedicated to preparation of materials and lessons which integrate technology use is not acknowledged in teachers' current work time, and the limits imposed by the overall scholastic system (the ever increasing number of subjects and topics present in syllabuses, the limited time available, the question of individual assessment of students, etc.). The often poor quality of educational software available, with a predominance on the market, especially at primary and secondary school levels, of substantially drill and practice systems, have often reduced the initial enthusiasm of teachers towards the use of technology as a means to renew and improve teaching methods.

Moreover, ICT training often has been confined to the development of product-related skills rather then being aimed at the promotion of more general and critical skills (such as, for example, how to choose among different products, how to develop capacities of finding proper and meaningful information on the web, how to use available products in discipline teaching, etc.).

Nevertheless, even if all the preceding considerations are true, one will miss the point if he or she does not consider that, from a pedagogical point of view, it is pointless to make ICT based tools available if the educational strategies and the activities the learners engage in are not suitably revised. Technology can influence learning by fundamentally changing both the content of a subject and the way in which that content can be taught and learnt.

It is widely recognised that the professional development of teachers in the field of ICT has to be carried out through the development of competencies both in their use and in their integration in discipline teaching. In the initial pioneering period the influence of the 'computer anxiety/appeal' has strongly pushed towards the necessity of teachers acquiring a practical knowledge about computers and computer related products. After a number of experimentations, it has been recognised that to confine teachers' knowledge only to this level is not fruitful and could be dangerous.

These considerations bring with them the problem of the policies that can be enacted to promote such changes.

## 4. FROM 'TECHNOLOGY PUSH' TO 'DEMAND PULL'

Policies should move from technology push (i.e. actions that are driven by the necessity to make the technology available and usable) to 'demand-pull' (i.e. actions that are driven by users' needs and pedagogical opportunities).

Politicians should be convinced that ICT is not, by itself, an easy and cheap solution to educational problems. The successful introduction of ICT in schools is determined not only by money invested, but also by a change of mental habit.

Until fairly recently the use of ICT tools such as word-processing, graphics packages, database and spreadsheet applications, has often been proposed as evidence of technology uptake and integration into learning and teaching. While many worthwhile uses have been made of these tools, their integration has largely been as an optional addendum to an unchanging traditional teaching environment.

When reflecting on the design and use of technology for education we need to consider the whole teaching and learning situation; not only how technology can be applied but also the needs of the teachers who will use it, the ways in which it will be used, the curriculum objectives, the social context and the way in which learning is organised.

This means that consideration needs to be given to the definition of meaningful practices through which technology can be used effectively. The design itself of educational technology should include examples of meaningful pedagogical processes based on a widespread consensus derived from appropriate pedagogical research. These considerations can have an impact on policies to promote technology enhanced learning.

The next stage for policies should be to concentrate on the provision of a network for disseminating good practices, research results, discussions, and exchange of ideas and perspectives in order to promote a true synergy among the different actors. In other words, it is necessary to intervene in the school context to promote a paradigm shift in ways of looking at teaching and learning processes, considering the innovations and needs brought about by new technologies not only in schools but in the society as a whole.

Even if it is not possible to define a single strategy for promoting such change, some general indications can be outlined:

- Promoting co-operation among teachers, researchers in educational technology and in discipline subjects, administrators, trainers, parents, etc. This could be done by increasing investments in research and development and in the creation of new learning environments for working together. In particular, it should be considered that any partnership for change in the relationship between research and classroom activity must include teachers as equal partners. As a matter of fact, what has not yet taken place sufficiently is the co-operation of experts across the diverse disciplines in research and practice networks. The essential enabling mechanism for such networks is the implementation of mutual exchange and verification of practicable results. As an example: educational concepts of IT support for education have to undergo technological implementation, and technological concepts of IT support for education have to undergo educational verification.

- Promoting the collection, documentation, and diffusion of good practice examples. There is a mounting interest in aspects related not only to software design, but also to the definition of ways of use suited to exploiting software features in order to accomplish meaningful teaching and learning activities. It is therefore not enough to establish collections of best practice, or to codify knowledge about e-learning, since the knowledge will only be of use to teachers and learners who are new to e-learning if it is made suitable for people in their position, rather than for experts. Moreover, the study of models for effective dissemination of successful pilot projects is needed to ensure teachers are aware of the potential of technology-supported learning.
- Promoting curricular change, shifting the focus from knowledge as a set of content to knowledge as an integration of processes and skills. The changing global context due to the impact of ICT is redefining the type of literacy and skills that are needed. Such skills are not only technical (e.g. how to access and use distributed and continuously changing information), but also cognitive (i.e. how to integrate different knowledge), relational (i.e. how to foster interpersonal capacities, responsibility, co-operation, adaptability, flexibility, etc.), and concerning high-order thinking (such as problem solving, creative thinking, decision making etc.). The crucial importance of new skills has started to receive considerable political interest throughout Europe. Several actions have been launched by the European Commission such as the Action Plan for skills and mobility (European Commission, 2002) and the establishment of the European ICT Skills Monitoring Group (2002).
- Rethinking teachers' training as a life-long learning perspective. Even if the aim of training, at a first level, has been to give teachers sufficient levels of confidence, competence and flexibility in the use of new technologies, this is not enough to significantly affect the process of innovation. Teachers need to be given the training to operate effectively in ICT-rich environments and the 'space' within their school based

work, to take advantage of the potential it offers. The integration of ICT use into pre and in-service programmes for teachers will need to support them not in the automation of traditional process, but rather to use ICT to support active engagement, problem solving, group learning, interactions, feedback and connections with the 'outside' world. Training should be based on planning and reflection on classroom practice and potential new practice, including a reflection of their own roles as teachers and of learners' roles. Some recent UNESCO reports can be considered as reference in this regard (see UNESCO 2001, 2002).

## REFERENCES

Bottino, R. M. & Furinghetti, F. (1999). Mathematics teachers, new technologies and professional development: Opportunities and problems. In N. Ellerton (Ed.), *Mathematics Teachers Development: International Perspectives* (pp. 1-11). Australia: Meridian Press.

Bottino, R. M., Kearney, N., Lefrere, P. & Lindquist, K. (Eds) (2001). Position Paper. *Open Consultation Process.* PROMETEUS Report. Retrieved from http://www.prometeus.org/E_gatekeeper.cfm?FileID=148

European Commission (2002). Retrieved from http://europa.eu.int/comm/employment_social/news/2002/feb/ap_en.html

European ICT Skills Monitoring Group (2002). Retrieved from http://europa.eu.int/comm/enterprise/ict/policy/ict-skills.htm

Fierli, M. (2002). *Le Tecnologie Didattiche Nella Scuola: Stato Dell'arte e Prospettive,* Italian Ministry of Education, Atti multimediali del Convegno. TED2002, Genova, maintained by D. Persico, L. Ferlino, G. Olimpo, M. Tavella & C. Tirendi. Retrieved from http://www.ted-online.it/atti2002/index.htm

Mallon, M. (Ed.) (2002). *Addressing Change in the Role of the Teacher in ICT Based Learning: Uptake and Integration Considerations.* PROMETEUS Report. Retrieved from http://www.prometeus.org

UNESCO (2001). *Report on: Teacher Education through Distance Learning: Technology, Curriculum, Evaluation and Cost.* Retrieved from http://unesdoc.unesco.org/images/0012/001253/125396e.pdf

UNESCO (2002). *Report on: Teacher Education Guidelines: Using Open and Distance Learning.* Retrieved from htpp://unesdoc.unesco.org/images/0012/001253/125396e.pdf

# Using an Educational Consensus to Reach Educational Technology Tipping Point

Roger Carlsen
*Department of Educational Leadership, Wright State University, Dayton, Ohio, USA, roger.carlsen@wright.edu*

## 1. INTRODUCTION

In the United States, the use of educational technology is mandated by accredited teacher preparation programs and by state accrediting departments of education. Yet the majority of teacher education faculty fail to infuse educational technology procedures into their courses at substantial levels (Mitchell, Dipetta & Kerr, 2001), and teachers fail to infuse technology into their teaching (Anderson & Speck, 2001). For educational technology to become firmly entrenched in our educational systems, educational technology must become a part of the culture of our schools. This paper reports the attitudes and opinions gathered from interviews, questionnaires, and classroom artefacts from two groups of practicing teachers (n=31) enrolled in a 'teacher leader' graduate program. This paper represents only the first phase of a census-like assessment of a much larger group of undergraduate (n=133) students, graduate level teachers (n=92), information technology directors and college faculty (n=32) from twelve colleges and universities.

## 2. NEED

During initial class discussions no pervasive plans for the ubiquitous infusion of technology into education were reported in any of the schools from which a group of Teacher Leader graduate students (n=31) hailed. In a follow-up session the teachers were asked to complete an educational technology questionnaire indicating their experiences and opinions related to the use of educational technology and the Internet. The Tipping Point, a theory put forth by Gadwell (2000), appeared to be an appropriate model for educational technology development in all the schools from which the participating teachers came. The teachers' positions were evaluated for preparedness to teach using technology. Secondly, a determination was made relative to each teacher's ability to play one of Gadwell's leadership roles as Connector, Maven, or Salesperson.

Malcolm Gadwell's basic principle for achieving the Tipping Point in a learning community is based on the idea that a social epidemic will take place when there are sufficient or strong enough individuals to bring about change. He viewed this as being a critical point akin to critical mass when a culture changes. His idea of the Tipping Point differed from critical mass somewhat because he believed that the Tipping Point need not be arrived at gradually. Gadwell also identified three roles that would contribute to this change, the Connector, Maven, and Salesperson. The Connector was an individual with special talent to bring people together to work well in teams. Mavens were pivotal because they, unlike geeks or gurus, possessed both knowledge and social ability. Mavens give freely to colleagues. Mavens mentor and work alongside those with less developed knowledge and skills. Finally, Gadwell identified Salespeople who usually exhibit the characteristics of exuberance and enduring optimism. Salespersons, however, often fail to succeed without Mavens and Connectors.

## 3. RESULTS

Teachers were asked if they could provide a metaphor for the use of technology or the Internet in their educational programs. Ninety-three percent (n=29) of the respondents produced neutral or positive metaphors such as technology offers students "windows to the future" while two (7%) offered dismal metaphors. The most negative metaphor was that, "computers are the root of all evil and computers are the future."

Eight teachers (26%) had personal web pages while only five (16.67%) reported that their students had access to either personally developed or school maintained resource pages. These percentages with access to such resources were substantially lower than those reported by Levin and Arafeh (2002). The older their students, the more frequently teachers felt that the students knew more than the teachers. These findings were especially interesting because 18 (60%) felt more knowledgeable than their colleagues.

All but four teachers replied to the request that they report how they use computers or the Internet creatively. The two most common responses were as a word processor (n=7) and to create PowerPoint presentations (n=3).

Several individuals did mention activities such as morphing digital pictures, creating maps, going on scavenger hunts, and creating poetry art.

There was wide agreement (96.7%) on using Internet filters, with only two secondary teachers reporting that filters should be used only with young students. Three teachers did not answer this question because their students were not permitted on the Internet. It is interesting to note that this position, at least at the secondary level, is contrary to that of the American Library Association (2002).

Most teachers (n=28, 90.3%) used e-mail on a daily basis. Five teachers (16.1%) used e-mail for communication with friends or their college professors, but not in their schools or with their students. Only one teacher did not have access to the Internet outside school. Twelve teachers (38.7%) used instant messaging software, while only 4 (12.9%) participated in chat. Overwhelmingly, most teachers (n=30, 96.7%) felt that the Internet benefited them greatly, while far fewer (n=19, 63.3%) reported that their students benefited from using the Internet.

The feelings that these teachers reported towards using technology and the Internet were positive. Only six (19.4%) reported feeling frustrated or uncomfortable with technology. Four teachers (12.9%) reported feeling moderately comfortable but they felt that they needed more time and training. Twenty-one (67.7 %) reported feeling that they were comfortable or very comfortable with their use of technology and the Internet in their educational programs.

Only one teacher from this group possessed sufficient knowledge, skills and inclination to be identified as a Maven. Other teachers demonstrated potential Connector or Salesperson traits. Such traits may only be visible when classrooms are constructivist rather than traditional. Two teachers exhibited negative responses and thus might be viewed as being negative Salespersons.

## 4. CONCLUSIONS AND FUTURE ACTIVITIES

This paper examined practicing teachers who reported feeling comfortable with their technology and Internet use, but who appeared, in many cases to lack knowledge, skill, or in many cases the ability to use technology creatively. Few teachers were ready to accept the roles of Maven or technology Salespersons. This report appears to confirm a recent report identifying a digital disconnect between schools and their students (Levin & Arafeh, 2002). This disconnect gap appears to grow wider based on the age of the students. Few practicing teachers that we evaluated, however, saw their technology or Internet abilities deficiencies as being sufficiently inadequate for a call to action.

Several current teachers reported feeling frustrated and confused. Thus it would appear that a small core of teachers remains reluctant to participate and may view technology with hostility. When Carroll (2000) asked the question, "If we didn't have the schools we have today, would we create the schools we have today?" one wonders if he perhaps should have also referred to teacher preparation, teacher in-service, school administrators, and school infrastructure.

This is only a preliminary investigation to help identify issues and questions for a larger census of education graduate and undergraduate students, college faculty, and information technology directors. Because of our current investigative schedule we are limited to what we can add relative to this larger study. It does appear as though undergraduate preservice teachers' knowledge and skills relative to technology and the Internet will differ substantially from those of current practicing teachers.

## REFERENCES

American Library Association (2002). *Plain Facts About Internet Filtering Software.* Retrieved from http://www.pla.org/publications/technotes/technotes_filtering.html

Anderson, R. & Speck, B. (2001). *Using Technology in K-8 Literacy Classrooms.* Upper Saddle River: Prentice-Hall.

Carroll, T. G. (2000). If we didn't have the schools we have today, would we create the schools we have today? *Contemporary Issues in Technology and Teacher Education, 1*(1). Retrieved from http://www.citejournal.org/vol1/iss1/currentissues/general/article1.htm

Gadwell, M. (2000). *The Tipping Point: How Little Things Make a Big Difference.* Boston, MA: Little-Brown.

Levin, D. & Arafeh, S. (2002). *The Digital Disconnect: The Widening Gap Between Internet Savvy Students and Their Schools.* Pew Internet & American Life Project. Retrieved from http://www.pewinternet.org/reports/toc.asp?Report=67

Mitchell, C., Dipetta, T. & Kerr, J. (2001). The frontier of web-based instruction. *Education and Information Technologies,* 6(2), 105-121.

# Path to the Future: Generative Evaluation for Simultaneous Renewal of ICT in Teacher Education and K-12 Schools

Niki Davis, Mari Kemis and Natalie Johnson
*Center for Technology in Learning and Teaching, Iowa State University, N108 Lagomarcino Hall, Ames, IA 50011-3192, USA, nedavis@iastate.edu*

**Abstract:** Educational organizations, teachers and teacher educators are challenged to renew their practice and to respond to changing community and national demands, including changing technologies. This requires 'simultaneous renewal' of teacher preparation and collaborating K-12 schools. The ongoing development of effective models of ICT-enriched learning and teaching environments in both universities and schools will remain a challenge. There is also the need to develop appropriate methodologies and approaches for researching simultaneous renewal of education across interconnected educational organizations. Two universities and partner elementary schools in the USA have been working on simultaneous renewal of teacher education to develop exemplary practice technology under the initiative to Prepare Tomorrow's Teachers to use Technology (PT3). Iowa State University started first with their project called 'Technology Collaboratives', followed two years later by the University of Florida Technology Initiative project, which draws upon TechCo's approach, strategies and evaluation. The innovative 'generative evaluation' is a key overarching strategy within each project to support their simultaneous renewal and also the inter-project collaboration. This paper proposes that generative evaluation may also inform regional and international collaborations to renew ICT in teacher education thus develop organizations and programs better suited to the teachers and the learners in our future.

## 1. INTRODUCTION

Educational organizations, teachers, and teacher educators are challenged to renew their practice and respond to the changing community and national demands, especially from accreditation agencies. This paper takes the case of the notable challenges posed by the integration of (ICT) into teacher education and K-12 schools simultaneously. This can be seen as a world-wide phenomenon. In the USA the two major societies for teacher education commissioned working groups to advise the organizations and their memberships on ICT. In Europe, over the last decade, there have been significant national and international efforts to incorporate new technologies in teacher education (Davis, 2001). Additionally, colleagues in Australia reported similar initiatives across their states and more widely in the Pacific region. Most recently, in 2001, the United Nations Education, Scientific and Cultural Organization (UNESCO) appointed a task force to produce guidance for teacher educators integrating ICT in their curriculum, and their guidance document from the task force is starting to be disseminated (UNESCO, in press).

Guidance for the appropriate adoption of ICT to improve education as a whole and teacher education specifically cannot be simple because educational organizations and systems are complex and often chaotic. Education is made up of a number of interacting complex systems, forming an ecology. Change within one group of participants or in the curriculum will be accompanied by complementary changes within and beyond the systems with which it interacts. Leaders will be well advised to appreciate their educational organizations as complex and complicating systems that can only be interpreted though multiple perspectives with a variety of complementary frames (Davis, 2002).

The major complicating factor to the renewal of education is the location of such changes. There is no one location, and so change agents frequently experience a dilemma in choosing where to start. Goodlad (1994) encapsulated this dilemma as follows:

> What comes first, good schools or good teacher education programs? The answer is that both must come together. There are not now the thousands of good schools needed for the internships of tens of thousands of future teachers. The long-term solution—unfortunately, there is no quick one—is to renew the two together. There must be a continuous process of educational renewal in which colleges and universities, the traditional producers of teachers, join schools, the recipients of the products, as equal partners in the simultaneous renewal of school and the education of educators. (p. 2)

Goodlad (1994) called for 'simultaneous renewal' of practice in both teacher education and in collaborating K-12 schools where the beginning teachers gain experience and undertake their internships. However, good practice with ICT in teacher education is probably at least as patchy as what takes place in K-12 schools.

The National Council for Accreditation of Teacher Education (NCATE) Task Force on Technology found that in most teacher education programs, technology is considered an addendum to curriculum and not a cognitive learning tool that is infused throughout the entire teacher education program (National Council for Accreditation of Teacher Education, 1997). Teacher educators reported the following problems when using technology: (1) lack of time to learn about new technologies; (2) lack of technology and technical support; (3) limited number of faculty technology training opportunities; and (4) an academic reward system that does not provide incentives for technology innovation. Several expert groups strongly suggest that colleges and universities must take a leadership role in preparing preservice teachers to use and integrate computer-related technology in schools (Espinoza & McKinzie, 1994; International Society for Technology in Education, 1998; Office of Technology Assessment, 1995). Since 1999, the USA has been investing in ICT in teacher education through the federal initiative Preparing Tomorrow's Teachers to use Technology (PT3) and significant patches of excellence have developed across the USA.

This paper addresses two of the significant patches of excellence using research and evaluation of simultaneous renewal in two teacher education programs in the USA. These universities faced up to the challenge of simultaneous renewal using ICT as a catalyst to develop good practice and enhance teacher quality in both the universities and strategically chosen K-12 schools. The K-12 schools chosen welcome student teachers and aim to provide technology-rich field experiences and internships for preservice teachers. Careful attention to in-depth research and development is necessary to find a path to the future. This paper describes the 'generative evaluation' approach that was developed to guide leaders of educational renewal so they, in turn, may guide participants through the chaos of change catalyzed by ICT in university programs, teacher education, and collaborating K-12 partner schools.

## 2. THE CONTEXTS

Two universities in the USA have been working on simultaneous renewal of teacher education with ICT using federal funding under the initiative to Prepare Tomorrow's Teachers to use Technology (PT3, see http://www.pt3.org). Iowa State University (ISU) started first in 2000 with their project called 'Technology Collaboratives' (TechCo). This was followed two years later by the University of Florida Technology Initiative Project (TIP), which draws upon TechCo's approach, strategies, and evaluation techniques. The innovative 'generative evaluation' is a key overarching strategy within each project to support their partnerships and also the inter-project collaboration. Both projects are developing their organizational structures, teachers, teacher educators, and leaders in the participating organizations (Thompson, Schmidt & Davis, 2003).

Both projects work with multiple organizations because teacher education does not take place in one location. Each project's participating organizations include discipline-specific colleges within the universities (Engineering at ISU, and Science at the University of Florida), K-12 partner schools, as well as their teacher education department. ISU also works closely with the local education authority (AEA). Together, all of these organizations collaborate in the development of courses and field experiences that model good practice with infusing new technology for beginning teachers, along with relevant professional and organizational development for the teachers involved. This extensive collaboration is very challenging. In addition, both projects require and welcome collaboration with other PT3 projects, the national PT3 organization, and professional societies.

This paper will not describe the strategies that were developed, shared, and adapted by project leaders. These strategies are described on the web sites and in the academic papers of the projects. As in previous projects, the successful strategies were intensive and eclectic, responding to individual, discipline, and organizational needs that developed over time (Thompson, Schmidt & Davis, 2003).

## 3. GENERATIVE EVALUATION

The purpose of this paper is to share the successful approach taken to inform and assess simultaneous renewal of education, referred to by us as 'generative evaluation'. It was created to answer the need to develop an appropriate methodology that could be applied to inform a holistic perspective in complex systems. In a separate article the lead author describes the characteristics of complex systems and identifies teacher education as one example (Davis, 2002). It provides examples where an assumption that change is occurring in a simple system has increased the challenge (turbulence) experienced by participants and leaders. We understood that research and evaluation of simultaneous renewal of education across complex and interconnected educational systems is complex and messy. We used our understanding of educational change models (see Ellsworth, 2000, and Sherry, 2002, for surveys of change models) to provide a well-researched structure through which to interpret the repeating patterns and pathways through the chaos evidenced in complex systems striving for renewal.

The approach draws upon Davis' (2001) discussion of the active involvement of participants in the process and related developments in evaluation. Experts on program evaluation (House, 1993; Schorr, 1997; Shadish, Cook & Leviton, 1991) all indicate that program evaluation has undergone a major transformation in the last three decades. There is now recognition of the influence of multiple interests at work. Evaluation has changed from single external views of objective judgments to pluralist conceptions, with multiple perspectives, audiences, measures, methods, and criteria. Implementation analysis becomes particularly important under these conditions. Evaluation must take into account all the different organizations, constituencies, and individuals in different phases of technology integration, including:

- Acquisition and installation of hardware and software;
- Training of teacher educators, teachers, their leaders, support staff, and communities;
- Integrating technology into the curriculum and instruction, especially into discipline specific (content) methods courses;
- Evolution of the institutions and the academic programs within and beyond their traditional boundaries; and the
- Transferring of good practice across institutions and educational systems.

The education of the project leaders was recognized as an important part of the 'generative evaluation' process. An approach that educates participants to become more effective professionally as well as to become members of the evaluation or research teams has been successfully implemented in previous ICT projects. For example, Bridget Somekh, as leader of the Pupil Autonomy and Learning with Microcomputers (PALM) project, explicitly set out to support teachers to change practice in their classroom by educating them to adopt action research as well as skills and knowledge with ICT (see Somekh & Davis, 1997, and Somekh in the Educational Research Forum http://telematics3.ex.ac.uk/erf). In a simpler approach, Davis et al (1997) used examples of ICT in teacher education to survey the needs of teacher educators across Europe with an additional objective of raising their awareness of the potential range of ICT applications.

Generative evaluation educates each project leader at several levels as it gathers both formative and summative data on the structures, undergoing renewal, and related activities. The process is informed by theories of change in education. The process often results in leaders generating and adapting strategies and actions to expedite change and educational renewal, hence, the name chosen. This is illustrated in the next section.

## 3.1 The interview process

The generative evaluation technique takes the form of a structured interview of a project leader conducted by two researchers well versed in educational change. This intensive interview took place in a room with a whiteboard upon which one interviewer developed a very messy version of figure 1, annotated with labels and descriptions provided by the interviewee. The second interviewer provides additional depth to the explanation of the change models in use and managed the time spent on each section.

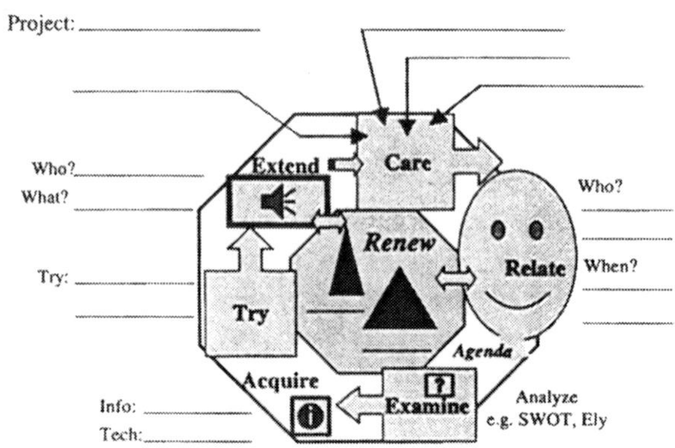


*Figure 1.* Planning change with CREATER+
(after Havlock & Zlotolow, in Ellsworth, 2000)

First, the interviewer captured the leader's personal view of the organizations involved in educational renewal and their relationships. An adaptation of Steve Bosserman's model of institutional change was used to interpret the leader's perception of the educational systems undergoing educational renewal under her shared leadership. Bosserman encourages us to think in terms of formal structures (denoted by triangles), but also in terms of the larger environment in which we function (Bosserman cited in Silag & Fields, 2001, p. 68).

Once the arena for simultaneous renewal was established, the six steps for a change agent postulated in Havelock and Zlotolow's (1995) CREATER model (Ellsworth, 2000) were then explored and points added to the white board one by one, starting with Care. The six steps in the CREATER model replaced Bosserman's five stages, and were similar. Where relevant, other models of educational change were introduced. For example, Hall, George and Rutherford (1985) focus on the Concerns of the individual in their Concerns Based Adoption Model (CBAM) and in our generative model Concerns accompanies Care because there were commonalities between these stages. Ely's (Ellsworth, 2000) environmental conditions of change and tenets of Rogers' (Ellsworth, 2000) 'observability' stage in his diffusion of innovation model were often used at the Examine stage of our model. Each element of the model was explained to the interviewee. Following the explanation, the interviewee was requested and encouraged to provide examples or give suggestions based on personal experience with an individual project.

The interviewer sketched the examples and suggestions into the developing image on the whiteboard. This process allowed for verification and occasional corrections when necessary. Each interview ended with an invitation for interviewees to reflect on and respond to the value of this type of interview. The interviews were conducted twice, and each was scheduled for an hour. During the first round of interviews more time was spent on the early stages of the model. However, the second interviews were timed so that adequate time was spent for the important final stage Extend. This is the stage where the lessons learned are uncovered with reflection on the educational renewal that had taken place. Having ninety minutes for the interviews would allow us to better explore the issues, had it been available.

## 3.2 Data analysis

The analysis of data started at the time of the interview with the construction of a current personal perspective of the system undergoing educational renewal and the stages of action in the CREATER cycle. This was constructed and verified between the leader interviewed and the two researchers as interviewers. As noted above, modifications to the content on the whiteboard were made when necessary during the interviews. This data on the white board were photographed, 'transcribed' and presented into a graphic form. The details of the interview were also transcribed, verified with participants and analyzed against the diagram to provide a full, rich, and holistic picture. Both pairs of leaders were interviewed for both projects during their first year. The two leaders of the TechCo project were also interviewed in the third year of their project (2002). In addition, the generative evaluation technique was modified and developed into a worksheet for use in three conference workshops to assist leaders and change agents think strategically about planned change.

## 4. FINDINGS

On every occasion the interviewees indicated that the interview experience was valuable and energizing, with the exception of the interview we conducted with both the Dean and assistant Dean together. These leaders were not project managers leaders and we also feel that the joint interview resulted in confusion between two individuals' perceptions.

On all other occasions the intensive interview generated strategies that the participants felt led to improvement of their project management and leadership. The first intensive interview for Ann Thompson in year 1 of the project showed that she was intuitively strong on the **R**elate process early in the project, with few activities planned to move into the **T**ry phase and into lessons learned for **E**xtend. This was a common finding in all the interviews early in the project. Ann recognized this and adjusted the agenda for project meetings, conference presentations and papers for dissemination that encouraged partners across the consortium to share their '**T**rys' plus the lessons that they learned.

Denise Schmidt generated additional faculty participation in partnering K-12 schools focusing on '**T**rys' to encourage the extension, transfer and reciprocating of those lessons learned into university courses in the teacher education program. The leaders of the UFTIP project also generated additional collaborative activities between more schools and their teacher education program. Participants in the four workshops generated new plans as well as an overarching view of their project, and on all occasions at least one participant remarked on how the process helped in the re-conceptualization of planned change and their role in the process.

To date, only two rounds of interviews with project leaders have been conducted that permit us to examine the data for evidence of simultaneous renewal. In each case, comparison of the central circle of renewal for interviews one and two shows a significant change in the renewal taking place in each university and partnering K-12 schools as these organizations move simultaneously.

The use of a schematic diagram to depict organizational structures shows the close collaboration and partnership that have developed during the project (developed from Bosserman in Silag & Fields, 2001). During educational renewal the process is not static and changes within collaborating organizations move closer or overlap their boundaries indicating that simultaneous renewal is underway and likely to succeed in the longer term.

Denise Schmidt, TechCo's second leader, produced a similar perspective in year 3 of the project. During her second interview she explained relationship building as one of the major lessons learned (**E**xtend):

> ...building relationships and trust is one of the things that I learned....to do things right, you need an audience is manageable....just being able to organize or even able to provide leadership for a project....they know you won't lead them down the wrong path and I think that's important. So building those are huge. (DS interview October, 2002)

The building of these relationships with the four K-12 schools and their local educational agency (AEA) led to many collaborative activities and support. As a result, these partners were pulled together more closely. This view stands out at the forefront of Denise and Ann's perspective of renewal taking place in teacher education with ICT.

In summary our novel 'generative evaluation' technique has developed successfully over two years to address six objectives:

- To inform both projects' management as the projects evolved
- To educate the project leaders about appropriate and timely models of educational change
- To encourage and support action research by project participants
- To inform leadership of simultaneous renewal in education across multiple organizations
- To provide formative evaluation assessment of simultaneous renewal that took place in both projects that took place, if any
- To research and further develop the technique of 'generative evaluation'.

# 5. CONCLUSION

A path to a future in which well-prepared teachers can effectively deploy ICT in K-12 schools and good practice is modeled in teacher education can be hard to find. We know that good practice and effective integration of ICT must include simultaneous renewal across many organizations. Our collaboration across organizations involved in two PT3 projects and across PT3 projects has been successful in further embedding ICT into systems and organizations in one university and establishing that process in the second. We learned that pockets of excellence in teacher quality could be developed. However, we also recognize that simultaneous renewal is complex and fragile, requiring sustained and well-informed leadership (Sherry, 2002). The development of 'generative evaluation' for simultaneous renewal of ICT in teacher education holds promise for the transfer of a robust approach that is transferable and applicable to other projects and partnerships.

This paper provides early evidence that 'generative evaluation' can guide leaders and change agents on their pathway to the future. We believe that the intensive support of leaders who heroically struggle for simultaneous renewal of education is important. There are also indications that leaders will benefit from this approach and technique even when ICT is not involved as a catalyst for change. It is proposed that this innovative approach to formative and summative evaluation of change in the complex systems that make up teacher education will be valuable to other cultures and contexts. Generative evaluation as an approach may also inform regional and international collaborations to renew ICT in teacher education, further developing organizations and programs that are better suited to meet the needs of change agents, teachers, and the learners of the future.

## ACKNOWLEDGEMENTS

The participation and support of colleagues at Iowa State University and the University of Florida are acknowledged. Specifically, thanks to Ann Thompson, Denise Schmidt, Kara Dawson, Colleen Swain, and ISU's TechCo coordinator Clyciane Michalini. The contents of this paper were developed in association with two grants from the Fund for Improvement of Post Secondary Education (FIPSE), and the US Department of Education. However, the contents do not necessarily represent the policy of the Department of Education, and you should not assume endorsement by the Government.

## REFERENCES

Davis, N. E. (1997). Telematics applied to the training of teachers: A survey via video conferencing across Europe. *European Journal of Teacher Education, 20*(1), 49-60.

Davis, N. E. (2001). International contrasts of information technology in teacher education: Multiple perspectives on change (Editorial). *Journal of Information Technology for Teacher Education*, *9*, 139-147.

Davis, N. E. (2002). Leadership of information technology for teacher education: A discussion of complex systems with dynamic models to inform shared leadership. *Pedagogy, Education and Technology*, *11*(3), 253-272.

Davis, N. E, Hawkes, M., Heineke, W. & Veen, W. (2001). Multiple perspectives on evaluation of new technology in education and teacher education. In W. Heineke, L. Blaise & J. Willis (Eds), *Research Methods in Educational Technology* (Vol. 1: Methods of evaluating educational technology). Greenwich, CT: Information Age Publishing.

Ellsworth, J. (2000). *Surviving Change: A Survey of Educational Change Models.* Syracuse, NY: ERIC Clearing House on Information and Technology.

Espinoza, S. & McKinzie, L. (1994). Internet activities open new worlds for educators. *Technology and Teacher Education Annual*, 666-670.

Goodlad, J. (1994). *Educational Renewal*. San Francisco: Jossey-Bass Publishers.

Hall, G., George, A. & Rutherford, W. (1979). *Measuring Stages of Concern about the Innovation: A Manual for Use of the SoC Questionnaire*. The University of Texas at Austin.

House, E. (1993). *Professional Evaluation*. Newbury Park, Beverley Hills, CA: Sage.

International Society for Technology in Education (1998). *Survey: Information Technology in Teacher Education.* Retrieved from http://www.iste.org

Lane, C. & Cassidy, S. (1994). The role of technology in the systemic reform of education and training. *ED Journal, 8,* 1-22.

Milken Exchange on Education Technology (1999). *Will New Teachers be Prepared to Teach in a Digital Age?* Santa Monica, CA: Milken Family Foundation.

National Council for Accreditation of Teacher Education (1997). *Technology and the New Professional Teacher: Preparing for the 21st Century Classroom.* Washington D.C.: Author.

Office of Technology Assessment (1995). *Teachers and Technology: Making the Connection.* (Report no. OTA-EHR-616). Washington, DC: U.S. Government Printing Office.

Panel on Educational Technology (1997). *Report to the President on the Use of Technology to Strengthen K-12 Education in the United States.* Washington, DC.

Schorr, L. B. (1997). Common Purpose: *Strengthening Families and Neighborhoods to Rebuild America.* New York: Anchor Books Double Day.

Schrum, L. (1994). First steps into the information age: Technology infusion in a teacher education program. *Journal of Computing in Teacher Education, 10,* 12-14.

Shadish, W. R., Cook, T. D. & Leviton, L. C. (1991). *Foundations of Program Evaluation: Theories of Practice.* Newbury Park: Sage Publications.

Sherry, L. (2002). Sustainability of innovations. *Journal of Interactive Learning Research, 13,* 211-238.

Silag B. & Fields A. (2001). *Creating the Engaged University. Iowa's Model for Change.* Ames, Iowa: Iowa State University Extension.

Somekh B. and Davis N. E. (Eds.) (1997). *Using IT Effectively in Teaching and Learning: Studies in Pre-service and In-service Teacher Education.* Routledge: London and New York.

Thompson, A., Schmidt, D. & Davis, N. E. (2003). Technology collaboratives for simultaneous renewal in teacher education. *Educational Technology Research and Development, 51*(1), 71-87.

UNESCO (in press). *ICT Teacher Education. Guidance.* Paris: UNESCO.

# ICT and Future Teachers: Are We Preparing for E-learning?

Anthony Jones
*Department of Science and Mathematics Education, The University of Melbourne, Victoria 3010, Australia, a.jones@unimelb.edu.au*

## 1. EXPECTATIONS

It is now common for relevant authorities to insist that all newly qualified teachers are able to use a range of ICT applications for teaching and administration (DfEE, 1998; NCATE, 2001; SCTP, 1999). The Australian government has published several papers containing plans and strategies for bringing schools and teachers into the information age (DEST, 2002; DETYA, 2000). The latter, under the title "Learning in an online world" includes:

- Introduce strategic initiatives into teacher pre-service education to improve the ICT competence of commencing teachers.

- Develop teacher competency standards in using ICT in curriculum practice and incorporate teacher ICT standards into human resource management within education authorities and individual schools, including recruitment and promotion practices. (DETYA, 2000, p. 52).

The more recent paper, under the general heading of "Pre-service," states:

> For teacher education institutions to be able to train and graduate beginning teachers who have the necessary knowledge, skills, understandings and attitudes to make effective use of ICT in their teaching practice, a number of capabilities need to be in place. These can be categorised as:

leadership and vision in the use of ICT;
infrastructure providing appropriate access and technical support;
curriculum/programs that integrate the use of ICT;
partnerships with schools to provide appropriate professional experiences for pre-service teachers;
competence in, and understanding of, the effective use of ICT for teaching and learning by teacher education staff. (DEST, 2002, p. 14)

The Department of Education and Training in Victoria (DE&T), in a professional development section of its website, has an outline of ICT capabilities that could be expected of teachers. Included are:

using and managing technology
using basic computer applications
using desktop publishing and presentation software
using multimedia
using communication technologies
using learning technologies in the key learning areas. (DE&T, 2002)

These documents, from both Australia and overseas, make it abundantly clear that every teacher is now expected to be capable of competently and effectively using the ICT and other learning technologies currently available in schools. But what of advances such as e-learning that are not yet widely used?

## 2. WHAT IS E-LEARNING?

The documents referred to previously do not specifically mention e-learning, instead using terms such as online and flexible learning. Depending on the definition chosen, e-learning has been used for training in the business context for many years, although its current significance is due to improvements in web-based communication technology. Business oriented e-learning providers accept that they primarily offer training, as evidenced by definitions such as, "e-learning is online training that is delivered in a synchronous (real-time; instructor-led) or asynchronous (self-paced) format" (KnowledgeNet, 2002). E-learning, digital learning, computer enhanced learning, no matter which tag is applied, all aim to exploit web-based technology to improve learning for students. Improvement is seen as a consequence of enhancing traditional face to face room-based learning through the use of technology that employs different modes of delivery and can cater for thousands of students in geographically different locations, learning at different times, while allowing for inexpensive and on-going updating of content.

## 3. WHY SHOULD TEACHER EDUCATION BE CONCERNED WITH E-LEARNING?

The initial response to this question is obvious when we consider changes in our society, especially changes in schools and universities. New housing developments have cabling for computer use included as part of the infrastructure. Students from these developments live in houses and attend schools that are prepared for the revolution in information access brought about by the world wide web. At school and home, e-learning will be a fact of life for these students, supplementing rather than replacing traditional schooling and life long learning as currently practiced.

Australian schools have already taken on many aspects of computer enhanced learning. However the majority of formal learning still occurs through the sharing of spoken and written words in a room with peers and a teacher. More critically, the majority of web use consists of searches for isolated packets of information for the learner, but directed by the teacher. Most teachers are unable to integrate ICT use into their everyday classroom practice. However, in 2003 Australian teachers can no longer claim that they do not use computer enhanced learning because of a lack of access to appropriate technology.

## 4. A VISION OF THE FUTURE FOR TEACHERS

In the foreseeable future teachers and learners will not be anchored to classrooms as they make appropriate use of various forms of computer enhanced learning. The traditional positioning of teacher at the front of a classroom with students at tables around, but basically facing the teacher, will be only one of many learning situations to be used each day. Similarly, the traditional expository mode of teaching will become just one of several modes learners and teachers will switch between depending upon their particular needs. At different stages of a lesson students might work as a whole class, in small cooperative groups, in pairs, or individually. Life long learning for teachers beginning their careers early in the 21$^{st}$ century will require that they are able to make effective use of all of these combinations.

The use of cooperative or collaborative groups to solve problems appears to be a trend in both work and education. A major difference of course is that work-related problems are real life issues that have to be solved, while education problems are simulations or hypothetical, contrived situations. However the use of problem-based learning (PBL) in schools and universities is becoming more common, and will increase as long as it remains a practice in business and industry. In addition to assessing the work of students for content related matters, teachers of the future will also assess more formally the ability of students to work in groups and to make use of the most appropriate of the technologies available.

Finally, teachers in the future will make even more use of ICT for professional activities including lesson planning and preparation of teaching materials, recording student assessment and other administrative tasks, and their own professional development and continuing education. Teachers already produce design briefs and worksheets using word processing, but this will change to encompass web-based material as the electronic screen slowly replaces printing on paper. Materials for units of work will not be printed, will increasingly not be burnt onto a CD, but will be placed on a public website and will incorporate many links to a wide variety of other relevant web sites. Teachers, working in collaborative groups that might cross school boundaries, will develop this material. A recent decision by Massachusetts Institute of Technology to provide free public access to all course materials is the forerunner to education systems and individual schools following suit.

## 5. BRINGING THE VISION TO REALITY

To a large extent the tools, educational theories and pedagogic constructs necessary for this vision already exist. Unfortunately, mainly because teachers have not been trained to use them, these things are rarely implemented in the same place at the same time. Schools are beginning to make use of wireless technology for computers, especially wireless local area networks (WLAN or LAWN) that enable connection to remote servers without the constraint of cables. Newer laptop computers with more efficient batteries will enable WLAN technology to operate almost anywhere on the school campus. Perhaps, at least for a while, schools will go back to having sets of laptop computers stored on trolleys that can be moved to any part of the school. Eventually laptop computers will be replaced by something even more portable and offering more flexibility, perhaps handheld technology. Jeremy Roschelle and the WILD Team at SRI International have investigated teaching and learning with handheld devices, and report that the benefits far outweigh current limitations (Roschelle & Pea, 2002).

Concepts such as 4MAT (About Learning, 2001) will be used to help teachers devise learning experiences that don't just allow for different learning styles, but instead actively encourage students to learn to learn in a variety of modes and groupings. When using a model such as 4MAT teachers follow a series of steps that ensure different learning and teaching styles are seamlessly interconnected into practice. To assist future teachers it is necessary that education systems, the employers, indicate to teacher education providers which models they would expect teachers to follow. Australian schools currently make use of a diverse collection of theories and methods, including all or part of Bloom's taxonomy, Gardner's multiple intelligences, de Bono's thinking hats, constructivism and 4MAT. While all of these have been adapted to include student and teacher use of ICT, technology is in reality an "add on" rather than one of the fundamental building blocks. However a more significant problem relates to the inconsistent use of these ideas across education systems. It is impossible to properly prepare new teachers, and to offer professional development to existing teachers, when there is no systemic agreement on which ideas will be used at what levels.

In England there is already a curriculum for beginning teachers that specifies skills and processes related to each subject and each level. Teachers are expected to be able to teach the ICT content and skills their students will need to use, as well as develop and implement lessons making effective use of ICT (DfEE, 1998). Such a curriculum can allow for different approaches in different subjects.

## 6. CONCLUSION

The future of teaching is largely in the hands of the teacher education providers. Teachers are still the portals through which students are given opportunities to incorporate appropriate forms of computer enhanced learning. No matter what educational systems mandate and expect, in the end effective learning is very dependent on the competence and will of the teacher. Preparing teachers for a technologically rich future is difficult because new teachers have not only to acquire proficiency in using technology for educational purposes, they also have to undergo a revolutionary revision of the practices of classroom teaching and learning. Chalk and talk will never be replaced while teachers and learners meet face to face. However future teachers will spend less time with a piece of chalk in their hand and more time with a handheld electronic device or a mouse.

## REFERENCES

About Learning (2001). *What is 4Mat?* Retrieved from http://www.aboutlearning.com/

DEST (2002). *Raising the Standards: A Proposal for the Development of an Information and Communication Technology (ICT) Competency Framework for Teachers*. Retrieved from http://dest.gov.au/schools/publications/2002/raisingstandards.htm

DETYA (2000). *Learning for the Knowledge Society: A Training and Action Plan for the Information Economy.* Retrieved from http://www.dest.gov.au/edu/edactplan.htm

DE&T (1998). *Learning Technologies Teacher Capabilities.* Retrieved from http://www.sofweb.vic.edu.au/pd/tchcap/tchcap.htm

DfEE (1998). *Initial teacher training curriculum for the use of information and communications technology in subject teaching. Annexe B of DfEE Circular 4/98.* http://www.dfee.gov.uk/circular/0498.htm

KnowledgeNet (2002). *What is e-learning?* Retrieved from http://www.knowledgenet.com/corporateinformation/ourhistory/elearning.jsp

NCATE (2001). *Program Standards: Educational Computing and Technology.* Retrieved from http://www.ncate.org/standard/programstds.htm

Roschelle, J. & Pea, R. (2002). *Take a Walk on the WILD Side: How Wireless Handhelds may Change CSCL.* Retrieved from http://www.stanford.edu/~roypea/RoyPDF%20folder/roschPeaWild.ppt.

SCTP (1999). *Guidelines for the Evaluation of Teacher Education Courses.* Retrieved from http://www.vit.vic.edu.au/pdfs/Guide99.pdf

Spender, D. & Stewart, F. (2002). *Embracing e-Learning in Australian Schools.* Retrieved from http://www.commbank.com.au/about/education.asp

# Developing a European Pioneer Teacher Community for School Innovation[1]

*Vittorio Midoro, *Stefania Bocconi, **Allan Martin, *Francesca Pozzi and *Luigi Sarti
*Istituto Tecnologie Didattiche, CNR, via De Marini, 6, 16129 Genova, Italy, midoro@itd.ge.cnr.it, bocconi@itd.ge.cnr.it, pozzi@itd.ge.cnr.it, sarti@itd.ge.cnr.it
** The University of Glasgow, e-mail: a.martin@compserv.gla.ac.uk

**Abstract:** ULEARN is a project that aims to create a stable community of 'pioneer teachers' in Europe through a system that supports teachers' lifelong learning, knowledge sharing and cooperation. Herein we call 'pioneer teachers' those who are keen to use ICT in the classroom and who can be seen as the early adopters of ICT-based innovation in education, already having had some experience in this field. They play a key role in the diffusion of innovation since the majority of teachers learn about new ideas from peers via interpersonal channels. To achieve our aims, U-LEARN.IT has being developed – a system that can be thought of as a virtual lifelong learning system of excellence for European pioneer teachers adopting ICT in education. It is based on the different needs of educational systems in European countries and involves three main functions: lifelong learning on ICT in education, the sharing of knowledge, information and materials, and cooperation within this community. As far as the pedagogical approach is concerned, the project focuses on lifelong cooperative learning supported by a networked infrastructure. The key pedagogical idea is that learning is the result of social interaction within a community of practice. The learning process is mainly based on asynchronous communication within a computer conferencing environment. The same environment supports cooperation among teachers and the sharing of knowledge, information and materials.

[1]This project has been carried out with the support of the European Community. The content of this project does not necessarily reflect the position of the European Community, nor does it involve any responsibility on the part of the European Community.

# 1. INTRODUCTION

The 'Report to UNESCO of the International Commission on Education for the Twenty-First Century' (UNESCO, 1996) identifies some strong tensions between society and school systems, such as conflicts between global and local realities, tradition and modernity, long and short terms, competition and concern for equality of opportunity, the extraordinary expansion of knowledge and the human capacity to assimilate it, spiritual and material values, etc.

The report of the French National Commission for UNESCO (Cornu, 2001) adds more elements to this picture, posing some questions raised by globalisation, which affect all areas of human activity and not just economics.

Closing the gap between school and society requires that the dynamics of school change become comparable to those of evolution in society. Up to now, school systems have been characterised by strong inertia. School should be rethought of as an evolving body, whose rapid modification is similar to that of society's. This implies that the school needs both to understand the evolution of the external world and to equip itself with a conceptual and structural repertoire, in order to match its aims to social evolution and to change.

The school system is a complex one and innovation should take into account all its components and the relationships between them, holistically. These include aims, curriculum areas, ways of learning, ICT pedagogical applications, school structure, resources and teachers.

While the 20th century school focused on teaching, the 21st century school may well focus on learning, and the teacher's role will change to reflect this. Consequently, teacher training processes will also need to change: teachers will become managers and facilitators of learning. To enhance children's learning, they will design, adapt, manage and evaluate learning environments.

This paper focuses on ULEARN, a project carried out in the framework of the European program 'e-learning'. The partnership involves:

- C.N.R. Istituto Tecnologie Didattiche, Italy (prime contractor)
- Uni–C Danmarks It-Center For Uddannelse Og Forskning, Denmark
- Ivlos Institute for Education, Universiteit Of Utrecht, The Netherlands
- The University Of Glasgow, UK
- Departament De Didactica Y Orgnizacion Educativa - Universidad De Barcelona , Spain

Following the recommendations formulated in the 'IFIP International Conference on the School of the Future' in Chile 2000 (Focus Group 2,

2000), which suggests defining measures to encourage the creation of teacher communities, ULEARN aims at creating a stable community of 'pioneer teachers' in Europe through a system which supports teachers' lifelong learning.

The project's main assumption is that teachers play a key role in ICT-based innovation in schools. According to Everett Roger's theory of diffusion of innovation (Roger, 1995), members of a social system are classified on the basis of innovativeness in 5 categories: 1) innovators; 2) early adopters; 3) early majority; 4) late majority; 5) laggards.

Herein we define as 'pioneer teachers' those who are keen to use ICT in the classroom and already have some experience; these are teachers who can be seen as the early adopters of ICT innovation in education. They play a major role in the diffusion of innovation since the majority of teachers learn about new ideas mostly from peers via interpersonal channels.

In this paper a profile of the pioneer teacher is identified and a report is made of the measures taken to develop a community of these teachers at a European level.

## 2. A MODEL OF THE PIONEER TEACHER

ULEARN is founded upon the following assumptions (ULEARN, 2002):

- in any educational context, there is a body of individuals who might be identified as *pioneers*;
- these persons are the main agents of innovation in their schools;
- their ability to carry out the role of pioneer can be enhanced by participation in a community of practice;
- this community can act at a pan-European level.

A pioneer teacher may be characterized by:

***i. Pedagogical expertise.*** The pioneer teacher is first and foremost an accomplished teacher, one who can practise, demonstrate, advise and train others in pedagogy in the context of current developments in learning and teaching.

***ii. Collaboration and co-ordination.*** He/she can participate in, initiate and co-ordinate collaborative activities within the institution, or with other institutions.

***iii. Monitoring and evaluation.*** He/she can monitor and evaluate educational developments within his/her institution and contribute to organisational change, and can critically reflect upon his/her own professional practice and development.

In the context of ULEARN, the concept of the ICT pioneer teacher has been defined: on the basis of a matrix initially proposed by Martin (ULEARN, 2002), describing the pioneer teacher competencies and levels of mastery, all partners[2] have worked co-operatively to refine the concept herein presented.

## 3. THE ICT PIONEER TEACHER

The ICT pioneer is a sub-type of the pioneer teacher characterized by the following aspects (ULEARN, 2002).

### 3.1 Effectiveness in pedagogical implementation of ICT

The ICT pioneer teacher demonstrates effective pedagogical implementation of ICT. This effectiveness will have been developed through personal experimentation, involvement in collaborative activities with other ICT-using teachers, or participation in continuing professional development: often a combination of these routes has been followed. ICT usage is characterised by appropriate and creative application, which is not necessarily complicated or 'high-tech'. Often the simplest uses of ICT are the most effective in enhancing learning because they are rooted in templates of learning activity with which teachers and students are already familiar. The ICT pioneer teacher will also be aware of the ICT skills of his/her students, and know how much further they can be taken before difficulties begin to interfere with the intended learning. In his/her own use of ICT in enhancing his/her teaching, then, the ICT pioneer teacher already forms a role-model for other teachers, for they will see that what he/she does is successful in enhancing learning without being complex or arcane. The ICT pioneer teacher is also aware of ICT applications and courseware that are available and most appropriate for his/her curriculum area, as well as the sources of information regarding pedagogical use of ICT. Such sources will include official agencies, interest groups, publishers and other suppliers, and online sources.

[2] Partners involved in the definition of 'pioneer teacher': W. Admiraal, S. Bocconi, J. Dixon, U. Gjorling, I. Lam, A. Martin, V. Midoro, M. Morales, L. Poulsen, F. Pozzi, J. Sancho, A. Thomson.

## 3.2 Advising on use of ICT

The ICT pioneer teacher trains other teachers in ICT skills and advises them (sometimes formally in in-service settings, but often in informal situations) in appropriate and effective use of ICT in the classroom. The ability to teach colleagues successfully is achieved by a minority of teachers who can adapt their teaching styles so as to impart new skills to colleagues without threatening their self-perception as leaders in the classroom. Teachers' awareness of the ICT pioneer as a good teacher is an important foundation for their willingness to ask for and to listen to advice. A second foundational element is that the ICT pioneer does not challenge colleagues' mastery of their own subject specialisations. He/she only offers guidance on how ICT might be employed by them in the context of their own objectives and styles, and the final decision on the adoption of any ICT enhancement is for the subject teacher rather than the ICT pioneer. The process of advising will be two-sided and follow a conversational model. The implementation of ICT by those who have taken advice will be supported appropriately by the ICT pioneer, and may at times take the form of collaborative teaching. The role of the ICT pioneer here is to respond to requests for advice.

## 3.3 Collaboration and co-ordination of ICT activities

The ICT pioneer teacher is happy to get involved and collaborate with colleagues within the same institution, as well as with those in other institutions. For some teachers, collaborative activity is problematic, either because it challenges the model of a single teacher commanding the classroom, or because it obliges them to admit that there are areas where others might have more expertise; there is also the fear that "I will do most of the work and the others will reap the benefits." However, most teachers who have participated in successful collaborative ventures attest to the value of such activity. They are also aware of the significance of collaboration as a mode of learning. The ICT pioneer teacher may participate in an ICT-focused collaboration, or provide an ICT perspective to a collaborative project involving a range of other inputs. The ICT pioneer teacher will also be able, where appropriate, to co-ordinate collaborative activities, and if necessary to provide a leadership element. This will require a range of skills, including project planning and social interaction. It will also include the use of a range of ICT-based means of collaboration. This activity may well be formalised, with the ICT pioneer teacher being given responsibility for monitoring and co-ordinating ICT within a department or other administrative unit, or even, for a small or medium-sized institution, across the whole institution, earning the title of 'ICT Co-ordinator' or something similar. This job will be defined in educational terms, and will be distinct from that of an ICT support technician.

## 3.4 Monitoring and evaluation of ICT Activities

The ICT pioneer teacher is willing and able to monitor and evaluate ICT developments within his/her institution. In a secondary school, this may begin within a department, but an ICT pioneer teacher might well be given cross-institutional responsibility for ICT co-ordination, which could involve developing a whole-institution picture of ICT developments. The skills of monitoring and evaluating are partly organisational, partly administrative, but also involve more personal qualities such as respect for others and mutual trust, and the ability to evaluate without being judgemental: these are qualities which take time and experience to develop. But as well as being able to monitor and evaluate the activities of others, the ICT pioneer teacher must also be able to monitor and reflect upon his/her own development, as a user of ICT in an educational context, and also as one who aspires to being identified, by colleagues and managers, as a specialist in this area.

## 3.5 Perspective and awareness of current trends

The ICT pioneer teacher has the quality of perspective, the ability to stand back and view the landscape from a distance, and see how the foreground relates to the background. He/she will be aware of current trends in ICT and its application in education, and will be able to place these in the broader context of movements in the areas of ICT and education. He/she will also seek to evaluate the implications of new technologies for his/her teaching, and, where appropriate, adopt them and adapt them to his/her needs. This will make the ICT pioneer teacher a valuable contributor to strategic discussions and to policy formation within the institution.

## 3.6 Competence in using ICT

The ICT pioneer teacher demonstrates familiarity, confidence, knowledge, understanding and skill in the use of ICT hardware and applications. This skill may have been developed through personal interest in the use of ICT in the classroom, personal use of ICT at home, or attendance at a course, either for personal interest or as continuing professional development. Often, skills have been developed through a combination of all these. Some teachers will become very highly skilled in particular aspects of ICT use, such as programming, web page construction, desktop publishing or electronics. For some, this specialization can become their only ICT interest; such a teacher may be identified in the staff room as a 'techie' or 'geek', perhaps useful on occasions when technical skill is required, but not perceived as a model to emulate (such teachers will often leave teaching in order to pursue their ICT specialization). The ICT pioneer teacher, on the other hand, may also have some very highly developed skills, but also displays a broad competence and ease with the range of ICT equipment and applications encountered within the institution. He/she would be willing to offer guidance on simple hardware or software problems, but would be aware of his/her limitations and know at what point to refer to expertise elsewhere (e.g. technician or external specialist). For the ICT pioneer teacher, ICT expertise is a means to greater effectiveness as a teacher rather than an end in itself, and this effectiveness includes preparation and administrative activity as well as the use of ICT in the classroom. We should not overlook the fact, however, that the ICT pioneer teacher enjoys using ICT, will probably have a personal computer at home, and may include ICT use amongst his/her leisure interests.

## 4. THE PROFESSIONAL DEVELOPMENT MATRIX OF THE ICT PIONEER TEACHER

Drawing on the qualities outlined above, it is possible to develop a matrix for representing the professional development of the ICT pioneer teacher. In constructing the matrix, two hypotheses are adopted:

- that all six of the qualities listed are necessary to the formation and maturation of the ICT pioneer teacher; and
- that progression in each of the qualities is possible, and that it can be mapped in broadly comparable stages.

The assumption is also made that the matrix is no more than a window opening onto an individual's professional development: there is much that has come before, and much that will come after. Individuals do not enter the window's frame as *tabulae rasae*, nor do they leave it as 'completed' professionals.

In stating that progression is possible in each quality, however, we should not assume that easily defined thresholds can be postulated; the difference between the levels may be fuzzy at the edges, and may only be discernible well into each stage.

## 4.1 Matrix functions

The matrix enables the starting point to be fixed (following a needs analysis process), the subsequent professional development of any individual to be mapped, and a professional development profile to be generated at any point in time. This will enable the individual to formulate and modify at intervals a personal development plan, and to maintain a professional development file and portfolio, in which the dynamic of his/her development as a professional may be encapsulated. On the basis of an initial needs analysis and subsequent personal development planning, each individual can select courses and collaborative and sharing activities appropriate to his/her strengths, needs, and intentions.

The elaboration of the curriculum for the professional development of ICT pioneer teachers is made clearer and more consistent through the process of mapping onto the matrix. This process will enable identification of the level at which courses are targeted, and the extent of coverage of the desirable characteristics, and therefore the applicability of the course to any particular individual. In this way the matrix provides a form of mediation between the needs of teachers and the repertoire of courses available. Note that while courses need not necessarily be derived directly from the matrix, they should be mappable onto it. This would suggest that any course should only map onto one level of the matrix, although the content may straddle more than one of the characteristics.

The matrix enables certification thresholds to be defined in terms of the broad definitions of levels. This will facilitate the process of mapping on of local certification standards, and help to achieve consistency in defining the level of applicability of any course, which is necessary for the development and maintenance of a pan-European certification scheme. It will also facilitate the mapping on of the requirements of national certification structures, so that pan-European courses or national courses derived from pan-European models or from national courses in other states may become accepted for purposes of achievement of professional qualifications or recognition of the right to practise.

The general definition of levels will assist in the clarification of developmental progress. A question arises here. Should a teacher be required to achieve all elements at the aspirant level before moving on, and similarly at the practitioner level, or should a certain level of 'peaking' be permitted whereby a teacher may move rapidly ahead in some characteristics while leaving others relatively undeveloped? This is an important issue, since the ICT pioneer teacher has been conceived here in holistic terms, i.e. as an individual possessing a broad range of complementary skills.

The matrix is also important in mapping the community of ICT pioneer teachers. This community includes all individuals at all stages from aspirant to consultant. However it is useful for members to be able to develop a realistic image of their own development within the community, and to feel confident that that perception is based on concepts shared by other members of the community.

## 4.2 ICT pioneer teacher community

ULEARN aims to develop a community of practice of pioneer teachers. According to Wenger (1998), a community of practice is characterised by three elements:

- a set of members mutually engaged
- a common enterprise
- a shared repertoire.

### 4.2.1 A set of members mutually engaged

The mutual engagement of members of a community of practice derives by working co-operatively, which implies acting together to develop a product, a service or the accomplishment of a function of whatever nature (Schmidt & Bannon, 1992). Building an environment for cooperation and making it available for pioneer teachers facilitates the accomplishment of a joint enterprise and induces the development of functional relationships among ICT pioneers.

### 4.2.2 Joint enterprise

The 'glue' that binds a community of practice is the joint enterprise. This enterprise can be thought of at different levels of granularity. At a higher level, the main aim is school innovation, while at lower level specific common projects can be conceived as articulations of the main joint enterprise. Making things explicit through a negotiation process, creating a 'regime' of mutual accountability, and creating a shared repertoire all help the development of this community.

### 4.2.3 Shared repertoire

The shared repertoire consists of both conceptual and physical objects and procedures.

Creating an environment in which materials, best practices etc. can be shared among ICT pioneers contributes to growth of a common language, shared approaches and methods, which constitute the repertoire of this community.

ULEARN cannot achieve all of these things, but it can set up structures which will enable the European community of ICT pioneer teachers to develop a conception of itself, and initiate appropriate activities. However in this process it is important to involve members of the community from the very earliest stage, and to seek the involvement of the community in its activities.

This does not necessarily mean following the model of what is already established or accepting uncritically the models which may be espoused by governments or by other powerful interests. While we must offer a model and a structure on which existing national or even local structures can be mapped, in accordance with the terms of the EU funding award we are to apply the experience and expertise of the ULEARN partners to the tasks we have identified.

## 5. DEVELOPING U-LEARN.IT, A SYSTEM FOR THE COMMUNITY OF ICT PIONEER TEACHERS

ULEARN aims to develop a community of practice of ICT pioneers through the implementation of U-LEARN.IT, a complex distributed system composed of several national systems, harmonised by a coordination unit. U-LEARN.IT can be thought of as a 'system of systems'.

It involves a *European Coordination Unit (ECU)* and the *national systems,* which reflect the structures of current educational and training contexts within partner countries.

U-LEARN.IT's main functions are:

- lifelong learning in ICT in education
- the sharing of knowledge, information and materials
- cooperation among pioneer teachers.

These functions are interrelated to ensure that new competencies are developed and then transferred into the classroom and maintained over time through systematic interaction among the community members. U-LEARN.IT is based on an interactive integrated web environment which is accessible via a portal that delivers the above mentioned functions.

The U-LEARN.IT portal contains:

- the European curriculum for pioneers on ICT in education

- links to the available courses (as far as the *learning function* is concerned)
- links to the available sources (as far as the *information sharing function* is concerned)
- links to the available tools such as forums, newsgroups, cooperation areas (as far as the *cooperation function* is concerned)
- links to the 5 national systems, each containing:
  - the curriculum translated into the national language
  - links to the available courses (in the national language)
  - links to the available sources (in the national language)
  - links to the available tools (in the national language)
  - links to local systems, each containing its own services.

## 5.1 European level

The main task of the ECU is to harmonize national branches of the system. ECU doesn't impose an extra structure; it co-ordinates and harmonizes the whole system, in order to perform its 3 main functions: learning, information sharing and cooperation.

During the project, the *European Coordination Unit (ECU)* is made up of the ULEARN partnership. ECU activities are:

- defining a common European curriculum on ICT in education;
- specifying how the system functions are to be performed and handling design of the overall system, i.e. the online training environment, contents, learning strategies, methodologies and techniques, online tutor training, the knowledge environment, sharing information and materials, the cooperation environment and so on.
- designing a core of common online courses with the related learning materials
- defining criteria to implement the online environments and the related activities at national level
- defining methods to evaluate the quality of the overall system and to monitor its activities.
- the ECU members interact in an ECU cooperation area, based on a Computer Mediated Communication system (in ULEARN FirstClass® by Centrinity). The structure of this virtual environment reflects that of the cooperative work performed by the ECU. During ULEARN, this work consists in the development of the project activities, and the cooperation area is structured to reflect the breakdown of the project's general activities.

## 5.2 National levels

A national system is composed of a *National Coordination Unit* and a number of *Local Systems*, spread throughout each country.

Generally speaking, the *NCU* functions are:

- designing and implementing the national system (according to the specifications of the ECU)
- running and monitoring the national system. This implies:
  - identifying and developing the local systems within the country;
  - defining a national certification system for the acquired competencies;
  - choosing the software tools and platform to accomplish the specified functions;
  - implementing the specified environments (for learning activities, knowledge sharing, cooperation etc);
  - localising to the national context the learning materials of the courses related to the curriculum;
  - training the online tutors;
  - supervising and supporting tutors' activities;
  - evaluating the quality of the overall activities according to the methodologies suggested by the ECU.

A *Local System* consists of:

- a service centre, which provides the infrastructure (for example it implements the computer conference system locally, provides the administration of this system, gives technical support and general assistance to the local agencies, gathers data on the activities of the local agencies etc.);
- a series of related local agencies which recruit groups of pioneer teachers for online courses, deliver these courses through online tutors (trained at national level), provide assistance for cooperative projects, stimulate discussions inside the community of pioneer teachers, facilitate information sharing, and so on.
- Each national system reflects the structure of the current educational and training context within a given country.

During the pilot phase, each ULEARN partner will act as a *National Coordination Unit* in its own country.

# 6. CONCLUSIONS

In the paper we have described the key ideas, approaches and ongoing achievements of the ULEARN project. A definition in the form of a matrix that captures the concept of the ICT pioneer teacher has been produced and assumed as a definition. The matrix enables mapping of initial and subsequent professional development of any individual, and represents the basis for elaborating the curriculum for the professional development of ICT pioneer teachers.

The U-LEARN.IT system has been specified and designed. It involves a *European Coordination Unit* and *several national systems. A national system* is made up of *a National Coordination Unit* and a network of local systems. Each partner has produced a description of his national branches.

The U-LEARN.IT portal has being designed and its implementation initiated.

U-LEARN.IT can be seen as a laboratory of innovation in learning. The new concept of pioneer teacher provides an effective basis on which to build systems at national and international level, one that can support the growth of a community of expert teachers, and bring about innovation in the school system. The work done so far has made it possible to identify pioneer teachers, has allowed them to meet one another and will help them to grow from aspirants to consultants by means of tools made available via ULEARN.IT. Furthermore, the cooperation environment developed for ULEARN has proved very effective and can provide the basis for a network-based system which supports the collaboration inside *European and National Coordination Units.*

The next steps are: full implementation of the pilot U-LEARN.IT, delivery of the online courses and activities related to the pilot, evaluation of the overall project carried out both at international and national level, definition of a transferability strategy to extend the pilot to a larger scale and to make the system evolve into a stable structure, and implementation of dissemination products (a video and a website) and initiatives including 5 national seminars and an international event.

## REFERENCES

Cornu, B. (2001). *Winds of Change in the Teaching Profession.* The report of the French National Commission for UNESCO. Paris: UNESCO.

Focus Group 2 (2000). Changing roles of the teachers and pupils with ICT. *The School of the Future.* Boston: Kluwer Academic Publishers.

Rogers E. (1995). *Diffusion of Innovation* (4th edition). New York: The Free Press.

Schmidt, K. & Bannon, L. (1992). Taking CSCW Seriously. *International Journal of Computer Supported Cooperative Work,* 1(1-2), 7-40.

ULEARN (2002). *ULEARN Report 1,* internal report.

UNESCO (1996). Report to UNESCO of the International Commission on Education for the Twenty-First Century. Paris: UNESCO.

Wenger E. (1998). *Community of Practice.* Cambridge: Cambridge University Press.

# A New Qualification and Certification for Specialist ICT Teachers

Sigrid Schubert
*Didactics of Informatics and E-learning, University of Siegen, D-57068 Siegen, Germany, schubert@informatik.uni-siegen.de*

**Abstract:** Student teachers qualify as specialist ICT teachers. This paper discusses selected objectives of informatics, the development of appropriate e-learning modules and some social and ethical requirements of such a contribution to teacher education. In 2001 and 2002 initiatives of IFIP and EU and self-reflection led to more collaborative learning and certification scenarios.

## 1. INTRODUCTION

Teachers worldwide have been surprised at the dramatic changes in their profession. When ICT first emerged in schools they expected a new learning and teaching medium which could be integrated with traditional pedagogical concepts. But the recent IFIP conference on the school of the future held in Chile (Taylor & Hogenbirk, 2001) showed that the informatics core of ICT gave rise to new ways of learning and teaching. Therefore appropriate pedagogical concepts were to be created and evaluated. The contribution of the research group 'Didactics of Informatics', chaired by the author, is a verifiable suggestion for new ways of qualifying and certifying specialist ICT teachers. Members of the group were informatics scientists, teacher trainers, educationalists, students of informatics and student teachers. They were involved in a process over a period of four years:

- developing guidelines and curricula in Germany (section 2),
- training student teachers and evaluating courses at the Universities of Dortmund and Siegen (sections 3 and 4),
- designing e-learning material in national and international communities (sections 4 and 5),

- exchanging experiences at the IFIP conferences in Copenhagen 2001 and Dortmund 2002 (section 6).

In this paper, obstacles and recommendations are discussed.

## 2. EDUCATIONAL GUIDELINES FOR SPECIALIST ICT TEACHERS

Publications of IFIP (Mulder & van Weert, 1998; van Weert & Tinsley, 1994) inspired the development of educational guidelines for ICT teachers issued by the German Informatics Society in 1999. All student teachers were to have the opportunity to choose such certified courses of 300 training units (60 minutes each). The following six fields of informatics were compulsory:

1. The students should know social and ethical criteria and be able to evaluate connections between the Information Age and the impact of ICT.
2. They should know the process of modelling in informatics and be able to create and to evaluate such modelling solutions.
3. They should know how to solve problems with the help of informatics to achieve reliability, extendibility, reusability and portability.
4. They should know the basics of algorithms, data structures and programming languages, and be able to develop and to evaluate software.
5. They should know the basic concepts of information security and of data protection laws, and be able to apply this knowledge.
6. They should know the fundamental principles of informatics systems.

These aims are characteristic of a lot of extended training programmes in informatics. But in this case the time available was only 120 training units. Appropriate educational experiences and learning materials were not available. It was clear that we could not use the traditional learning and teaching methods. The courses were expected to provide the opportunity to study the subject areas in a learner-centred, interdisciplinary and project-oriented way with the right mixture of lectures, exercises, practical training periods and examinations.

On the basis of this curriculum the qualification started in October 2000 at different universities. At the University of Dortmund all student teachers were offered two new courses, 'Computing Systems' and 'Modelling in Informatics'. The first course enables future teachers to understand the functionality, architecture, application and administration of highly complex ICT systems in education. The second course was designed and held by the author's group. It helps teachers to be fully responsible members of an interdisciplinary collaborative working group for the evaluation, implementation, modification and creation of ICT systems in education.

## 3. MODELLING IN INFORMATICS

The participants in this course were experienced teachers from schools and student teachers from universities. They started with a discussion and choice of a project theme, for example an ICT-based learning aid for English lessons. Parallel with the introduction to fields 2-4 (section 2), they developed their project programme and carried out its various phases. Each participant had his or her own project, but experienced teachers and student teachers worked together in mixed groups. This cooperation provided the opportunity to exchange the views of schools and universities and to test some ideas in the classroom practice. The educators made two decisions about the learning matter, one concerning the design strategy and the other concerning the programme language:

1. The introduction to modelling and problem solving is based on object-oriented design (OOD), which is suggested by cognitive aspects and which is state of the art in informatics.
2. The programme language was to stay in the background as a mere aid, easy to understand and to apply. That is why the script language Python has been chosen for object-oriented programming (OOP) as it offers a rich library of ready modules for the construction of software and brings the logical structure of solutions into focus.

But both of these decisions have also caused difficulties in the learning process.

The first problem is to learn OOD. Students start with easy tasks related to an ICT project 'library' and such object-oriented solutions are easy to discover and to describe but difficult to implement. An author, for example, normally writes more than one book. And a book may have more than one author. Beginners have no trouble identifying the informatics objects 'authors' and 'books' and to connect both with a correct relation, called association. But they can not cope with the creation of classes to produce the objects and the Python representation of association between the objects.

The second problem is to learn formalisation. This course brings various student teachers together. This results in the encounter of scientific cultures that are very different from the ways of creative thinking that are specific to informatics. Arts students, for example, get a shock when confronted with a formal language of informatics. Students of linguistics, on the other hand, are well able to read and write in such a formal language. In interdisciplinary teams both groups stand to gain from the wide range of previous knowledge and talents.

In the early stages an additional problem cropped up. On account of the complicated content and difficult methods of informatics a strong lobby argued that teachers need no deeper understanding of informatics to manage ICT at schools. Part of this lobby in Germany were influential enterprises which trained teachers to use their products. But the web-based learning and teaching approach at schools failed because specialist ICT teachers were not adequately educated (Watson & Andersen, 2002). So it is necessary to explain the relation between modelling in informatics and web-based learning in more detail. Discussion with experienced teachers shows that the following tasks will have to be tackled by specialist ICT teachers in cooperation with the school administration:

- informatics consultation and training of colleagues,
- careful choice of applications for web-based learning and teaching,
- infrastructure decisions from pedagogical and informatics points of view,
- responsibility for information security and data protection at their schools.

Therefore modelling in informatics must be understood as the complete process of specification, design, programming and evaluation of informatics applications. This has to happen with an ICT developing environment for editing, saving, loading and executing individual software solutions.

Easy learning objectives are extended to more complicated ones. Students will, for example, discover the power of the concept of data structures step by step as the first ICT project, 'library,' requires numerous names of authors and titles of books modelled as strings. And someone must input all these data. Then the user can make inquiries to which the system can display the response. But there can be an emergency when the system loses the huge collection of data called data structure of records. The records can not be permanently saved in the main memory. So a storage medium is necessary to save the records in a more complex data structure called a file. In this way students understand the key concept of each database application and learn to control the access to files. Every file is connected with basic operations such as opening, reading, closing, creating, writing, deleting. A lot of files are not well protected. Many schools have no reliable concept of information security and privacy and no efficient backup mechanism as they have no specialist ICT teachers (Passey & Kendall, 2002).

Software designers and users lose track of things without the highly successful principle of reducing complexity, the principle of modularity. Modularisation improves the flexibility and comprehensibility of an informatics system. The design of classes to create informatics objects, for example books and readers, is an opportunity to develop one's own modules. But modularisation also requires the ability to import existing modules of partial solutions from an informatics modules library. This sounds very easy, but the students have to learn how to prove the correct functionality of each module interface before they can use it. The module ensures information hiding of all internal data and access over the interfaces with parameters. The control and connection of parameters is difficult to understand, so that students need special support, for example with learning aids for exploration (Brinda & Schubert, 2002b).

Records or, in general, all sequences of informatics objects can build up the more complex data structure list. The list is an important cognitive tool for problem solving, and the library software also needs some lists, like, for example, a list of books and a list of readers. Extendibility and reusability are two criteria for evaluating the quality of informatics systems that can be realised with the concept of inheritance. All special lists, for example, inherit attributes and operations, also called methods, from an abstract class list (Figure 1). The concept of inheritance is easy to understand but difficult to apply. Here the students need further learning aids.

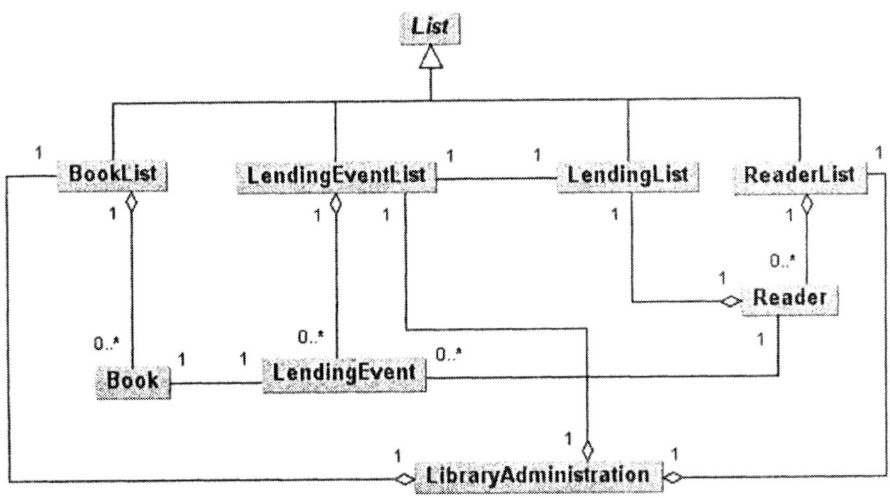


*Figure 1*. Class diagram of the library

# 4. EXPLORATION MODULES FOR OBJECT-ORIENTED MODELLING

The students can successfully learn the development process of ICT solutions through approaches based on theories of constructivism. This requires learning material that allows a lot of student errors without a system collapse. The author has introduced the expression 'exploration modules (EMs)' for such a special learning software. EMs are basic components of the 'Didactic System for OOM', which has been implemented at the University of Dortmund (Brinda & Schubert, 2002a). EMs allow the students to learn by discovery. EMs are difficult to programme and not available for all the basic skills in informatics which are connected with the process of OOM, like:

a. a deeper understanding of object-oriented problem solving,
b. OOD with the Unified Modelling Language (UML),
c. programming of OOD with the script language Python,
d. evaluation of educational results and self-assessment.

EMs support the objectives a. and b. while c. and d. have to be learned in the traditional way. Learners can design a class diagram in UML with different lists. EMs can examine the existence of the main classes and the relations among these classes. EMs do not show the tutor's solution but the results of the student's solution. So students have to discover the difference between their aims and their results. In difficult cases EMs give recommendations, such as to move the joint attribute 'number of elements' to the abstract class list (Figure 2).

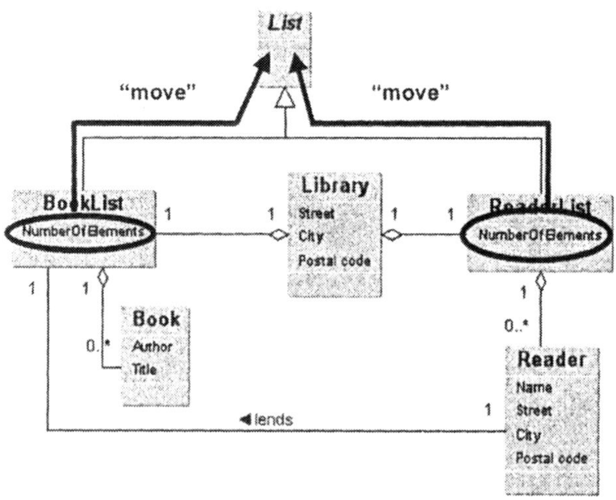


*Figure 2.* Exploration of inheritance

A project team of informatics students has developed a collection of EMs and integrated them into a 'Learning Environment of OOM (LEO)'. With LEO the student teachers can start application scenarios, for example 'library', and watch different 'views'. There is a view of typical administration procedures represented by icons for service staff, readers with user cards, shelves with books, computers with catalogues and databases. The learners can switch over to more abstract views like object diagrams and class diagrams with UML to discover the process of informatics modelling through formalisation step by step. A big problem for beginners is to ensure completeness and consistency of an object-oriented model because in the past only programmes could be tested by computer. But EMs show the results of the model during the OOD stage. The learners are able to correct their errors immediately and do not have to stabilise the faulty structure until they reach the OOP stage. The complexity can be controlled when details are hidden or stressed. The learners can watch how messages are exchanged among objects, objects are created, used and destroyed. The change of object states and the execution of methods are monitored. EMs make the hidden processes of synchronisation and transformation of model parts visible, thus supporting the evaluation of models by the learners themselves. Empirical studies show the increasing interest of student teachers in presenting and discussing their models in groups.

# 5. EUROPEAN CONSORTIUM OF INNOVATIVE UNIVERSITIES

While other subjects have a long tradition in learning by discovery with suitable learning aids, informatics had first to develop high-quality learning aids. Such a complex task could be better solved with partners. So we have become part of national and international networks for cooperation, for example the European Consortium of Innovative Universities (ECIU, 2002). In cooperation colleagues from the Universities of Aalborg, Aveiro, Barcelona, Dortmund, Glasgow, Joensuu, Siegen and Twente began to develop web-based learning aids for informatics education. The author was project manager of the informatics track. She was responsible for the successful running of two workshops, the stimulation of the cooperative work for half a year, and the delivery of the final product. Starting in March 2002 with a first workshop discussing realistic aims, the team decided to work on two themes, recursion and programming paradigms. The group developed a joint statement for the design and structure of further e-learning material. A second workshop was held in July 2002 at the IFIP Conference on 'Social, Ethical and Cognitive Issues of Informatics and ICT (SECIII)' to share the e-learning experience with a wider international community.

We wanted to have e-learning support for programming paradigms because specialist ICT teachers need the ability to evaluate different paradigms but have time to learn only one paradigm in depth. The examples developed by the ECIU team were integrated in the course 'Modelling in Informatics'. The student teachers in Dortmund and Glasgow used them to discuss the pros and cons of different problem-solving strategies of informatics, for example the functional and the object-oriented programming paradigms. They also compared the given e-learning material with the results of their own ICT project. The students from Dortmund were encouraged to continue the course when they realised they were not behind the educational aims, as their international partners had to overcome the same obstacles and problems.

With members of the ECIU team, students discussed the recommended design approach to the creation of appropriate e-learning components as features within hybrid courses typical of schools. We reviewed the methodological process with the group of learners. The colleagues from Glasgow knew best how to produce animated components to be used with learning materials from the project called 'Scottish Teachers On-line Modules'. The animations afford learner interaction with scope to explore the behaviour of the represented example and allow the students to make some processes visible that cannot easily be discerned. This experience was stimulating for our students. Smaller learning components that could be used widely within existing course structures and across differing schools could be developed by students and ICT teachers.

## 6. SOCIAL AND ETHICAL REQUIREMENTS

In 1998 we entered upon group communication and annual meetings of students and ICT teachers to set up a social network of mentors to guide the classroom practice of beginners. During the following years examples of transferring first-rate practice experience were collected and evaluated. But how to implement social and ethical requirements within the educational process with ICT was an open question. Therefore we expected a paradigm shift from the results of the IFIP Conference SECIII which was held in Dortmund in July 2002 (van Weert & Munro, 2003). We invited ICT teachers to participate in this conference and to set us thinking about the evolution of privacy over the course of centuries. The results of working group discussions (SECIII, 2002) were very helpful in redesigning courses at the University of Siegen. Now the students are responsible for the planning of their collaborative work with experienced teachers. Most of our students know mentors from their previous classroom practice terms. Students make a great effort in the social embedding of their ICT solutions. This has a long-term effect on the linking of cognitive and social aims. When a study group decides to develop web-based exercises for German lessons, including the assessment of students, they normally face a lot of social and ethical problems, such as the protection of privacy and the danger of masquerading. The mentors insist on security by means of encryption and authentication, together with control of access. This reality-based application has motivated the students to study the basic concepts of information security very carefully.

Today all institutions require a high level of infrastructure with complex computer networks and distributed systems. But the installation and management of such complicated informatics systems are not pedagogical tasks. Often school administration can not cope with these problems. So experienced teachers and student teachers have to face up to increased stress through the application of ICT in schools. The SECIII results helped us to understand that this problem can not be solved with new ICT devices but only with a new level of social and ethical relationships. Future specialist ICT teachers must be educated as producers rather than as consumers. The students have a certain impact on their partner schools because they do not insist on traditional procedures and have much more time for innovations. In all institutions the proper management of knowledge is a source of progress which can be made accessible only with difficulty. Human aspects of collaboration have to be taken into account, like the question of motivating successful teachers to support their colleagues. Their responsibility for the next generation of teachers should result in such a motivation. Therefore the joint training of students can help to promote knowledge management at schools and universities and between them, so that student teachers will become equal members of such a learning community.

The borderline between fact and fiction is fuzzy in ICT-supported learning environments and a lot of dangerous situations are hidden under colourful surfaces. Learners need orientation for their behaviour, decisions and responsibility that only social and ethical rules can provide. But such rules are learned when they are lived. Student teachers should have learned to avoid exaggeration. Not all e-mails, for example, need encryption, but in some cases encryption is the only reasonable way. If student teachers do not put this into practice in their daily lives they should not teach it. The change in the professional situation of teachers is extremely difficult because scientific content and pedagogical strategy are only effective in combination with the social and ethical behaviour of teachers appropriate to the Information Age. We have changed the subject content to promote the critical understanding of software agents as an attack on informational self-determination, an elementary human right. The students have acquired the ability to fight off cookies and user profiles successfully and to protect private data like photos and certificates. They have learned how to shield ICT environments with firewalls from software agents and to develop devices to demonstrate dangerous attacks to learners. They are convinced that learners need free access to web-based material to assume ethical responsibility.

We also changed the procedure of certification. New abilities are important and there is more flexibility of time management. It is no longer the product of an ICT project that is the focus of attention but the design process and the effectiveness of methods. This is why exams take place as group discussions with presentation, self-reflection and assessment of social integration of ICT and the impact on learning and teaching. The students present examples of ICT-supported learning environments that are theoretically well-founded and have been tested in classroom practice. This requires sufficient time for empirical studies with learners, which can be obtained either by putting the provisional results to test at school and redesigning them continuously, or by appending the empirical studies to the university courses.

## 7. CONCLUSION

The students were satisfied with their qualification as ICT teachers. They received excellent job offers and are involved in the continuous training of their colleagues. They use ICT to maintain their collaborative efforts in social networks after finishing their university training. Quite a number of them have become active members of professional communities of the German Informatics Society, to improve learning conditions with ICT in schools.

The course 'Modelling in Informatics' has met the objectives. The students were able to learn and teach in different age groups with teachers, parents and children and with students and teachers of school partnership programmes with different countries. The demand for such courses will increase. A lot of interdisciplinary research is necessary for better professional strategies of teachers in general and ICT teachers in particular. Today student teachers have to become involved in this change of learning and teaching paradigms step by step without being given a ready-made blueprint.

We plan to offer additional workshops for e-learning. They will provide opportunities for presenting and discussing new results and for developing methodologies among researchers, students and partners. Partners can present results of e-learning processes and new requirements. Students can choose themes, tasks and partners for their project work or diploma.

## REFERENCES

Brinda, T. & Schubert, S. E. (2002a). Didactic system for object-oriented modelling. In D. Watson & J. Andersen (Eds), *Networking the Learner. Computers in Education* (pp. 473-482). Boston: Kluwer Academic Publishers.

Brinda, T. & Schubert, S. (2002b). Learning aids and learners' activities in the field of object-oriented modelling. In D. Passey & M. Kendall (Eds), *TelE-Learning: The Challenge for the Third Millennium*. Boston: Kluwer Academic Publishers.

ECIU (European Consortium of Innovative Universities) (2002). *Web-supported learning pilots*. Retrieved October 6, 2002 from http://cvu.strath.ac.uk/eciu/

Mulder, F. & van Weert, T. (Eds) (1998). *Informatics in Higher Education*. London: Chapman & Hall.

Passey, D. & Kendall, M. (Eds) (2002). *TelE-LEARNING. The Challenge for the Third Millennium*. Boston: Kluwer Academic Publishers.

SECIII (Social, Ethical and Cognitive Issues of Informatics and ICT). *Working group discussions*. Retrieved October 6, 2002 from http://wwwedu.ge.ch/cptic/prospective/projets/ifip/workarea/dortmund/welcome.html).

Taylor, H. & Hogenbirk, P. (Eds) (2001). *Information and Communication Technologies in Education. The School of the Future*. Boston: Kluwer Academic Publishers.

van Weert, T. & Tinsley, D. (Eds) (1994). *Informatics for Secondary Education – A Curriculum for Schools*. Paris: Unesco. Retrieved October 6, 2002 from http://wwwedu.ge.ch/cptic/prospective/projets/unesco/1994/

van Weert, T. & Munro, B. (Eds) (2003). *Social, Ethical and Cognitive Issues of Informatics and ICT*. Boston: Kluwer Academic Publishers.

Watson, D. & Andersen, J. (Eds) (2002). *Networking the Learner. Computers in Education*. Boston: Kluwer Academic Publishers.

# In Service Teacher Development Using ICT: First Step in Lifelong Learning

José Armando Valente
*Department of Multimidia and Nucleus of Informatics Applied to Education (NIED) – UNICAMP, Graduate School of Education Curriculum – PUCSP, Brazil, jvalente@unicamp.br*

**Abstract:** What should the teacher of the future be? Among other things this professional should be able to practice and promote the development of lifelong learning skills. The question is how to prepare teachers to be able to reach this goal.

The process of preparing teachers to use ICT in their pedagogical activities, carried out in two main courses in Brazil, is an attempt to move in this direction. These are on-line courses on the Internet, designed to prepare teachers respectively from special education, and from basic education, to be able to use ICT in their classroom activities. These courses use the *virtual being together* approach to Distance Education, promoting the development of the reflective teacher, emphasizing reflection-in-action and reflection-on-action and working with contextualized and decontextualized knowledge.

Since the course emphasizes the development of reflective teachers and provides a means for them to understand ICT activities as windows into peoples' thinking processes, teachers are acquiring ways to interact with their students, discussing the concepts involved in their activities as well as how knowledge is constructed. These are the first steps in mastering important ideas about how to become lifelong learners and how to create learning situations to help their students to develop lifelong learning mindsets.

## 1. INTRODUCTION

The increasing amount of information available today and the need to know how to process and attribute meaning to it indicates that we are living in an intensive knowledge-based economy. In this new economy people need to be critical, creative, with the capacity to think, to make decisions, and to solve problems. In fact, these are the most desired characteristics indicated by owners or high executives of 1,500 industries (small, medium and big), in the São Paulo state, Brazil, in a survey conducted by the University of São Paulo (USP) in 1998, as part of the study "Engineers of New Times" (Engenheiro dos Novos Tempos). The six most desirable characteristics listed were: the ability to work in teams, commitment to the quality of what is done, the ability to live with changes, the ability to take initiative in decision making, a clear vision of the client-producer's role, and the ability to use knowledge of information technology.

From this list it is clear that professionals in the knowledge-based economy must learn how to learn, to deal with an increasing number of information sources and to collaborate with people locally or around the world by using new information tools. The emergence of a knowledge-based society is demanding a more comprehensive framework for human resource development, and human development is becoming too important and diverse to be left only for schools. Changes are taking place so fast that it is unthinkable that teachers and the school can provide all the knowledge we need in our lifetime. People should become lifelong learners and schools have an important role in helping them to develop lifelong learning skills. This applies to everybody, including teachers and students.

However, schools and teachers have to be prepared to cope with these changes. Providing more of the same traditional education that emphasizes transmission and memorization of information will not contribute to solving the human development bottleneck. The kind of "education" necessary in order to be effective in the knowledge economy should be one that leads to learning as a process of constructing knowledge of concepts, of strategies about how to use these concepts in problem solving, as well as of how to learn.

One of the solutions schools have adopted to change their educational approach is the introduction of information and communication technology (ICT) as a pedagogical tool. Similar to what has happened in other sectors of society, the introduction of these technologies implies changing certain procedures and the preparation of people to be able to explore the resources ICT provides.

Regarding the preparation of teachers to be able to use ICT in their practice, there are two different solutions that have to be implemented. One is the preparation of undergraduate students who are going to be teachers. The other is the preparation of teachers who are already working in schools. The work that is described in this article is related to the latter situation.

The preparation of teachers already in the classroom poses interesting problems, especially in large countries as Brazil, with about 1.2 million teachers. The solution that has been adopted is in-service training courses, via the Internet, using the ICT facilities that are being installed in schools.

These courses have the advantage of keeping teachers in their work settings, of using the technology available in the school, of helping teachers to solve idiosyncratic problems they find in their school that prevent the integration of ICT into their practice, and of helping teachers not only to acquire knowledge about ICT but also about learning to become lifelong learners. The main objective of these courses is to convey a construction of knowledge mindset and an understanding of how ICT can help students and teachers in this process.

ICT can play two fundamental roles as a learning tool: to make thinking processes explicit and to allow the establishment of a virtual learning network. In the first, computer activities create a window into the learner's mind (Valente, 1995a; Weir, 1987) so the teacher can engage and interact with the student in a Socratic mode to discuss her/his knowledge construction; in the latter people are allowed to present and discuss via the Internet the product of their learning process with a larger audience and with depth that is almost impossible to do in a face-to-face situation. In both cases, the objective is to help people to become better learners and to give them tools to become lifelong learners.

## 2. ICT ACTIVITIES AS WINDOWS INTO THE LEARNER'S MIND

ICT can be used in education in many different ways. It can be used to help students to acquire information, as a way to deliver information in an organized way, such as is achieved with tutorials, or to present tasks to be solved by the student and automatically corrected. In all these ICT has been used to enhance the teaching process in the sense that it can help fill up the learners' mind with information – a computer version of the banking approach to education, as pointed out by Paulo Freire (Freire, 1975).

However, ICT can do much more than this. It can function as media to be filled with information by the learner as s/he uses these technologies to solve problems. Now the learner has to use the knowledge s/he has in order to instruct the ICT about how to solve a particular task, making explicit what s/he knows. In this sense, ICT activities become a window into the learner's thinking and knowledge. In order for this to happen, the learner has to use open-ended software such as programming languages, word processors, spreadsheets, systems to create database, or systems to construct Web pages. This way, ICT presents important features, functioning as tools for students to construct new knowledge.

The analysis of computer activities using open-ended software (Valente, 1999a) shows that the user-computer interaction can be seen in terms of a sequence of actions – description-execution-reflection-debugging[1]-description, each having an important role in the process of acquiring knowledge such as:

- Description of the problem solution using the learner's knowledge (concepts involved in the problem, concepts about the computer and about the software, and strategies about how to apply these concepts) to represent and describe steps of the problem solution in terms of the software;
- Execution of this description by the computer, producing immediate and accurate feedback;
- Reflection on results given by the computer, leading the learner to compare what was achieved with the originally intended ideas and to take one of the following alternative actions: do nothing, since the problem is considered resolved; or debugging the description, since the result is different from what was intended;
- Debugging the learner's original description by thinking over or searching for new information. Once the description is changed, the sequence description-execution-reflection-debugging-description can be repeated.

However, the description-execution-reflection-debugging actions do not happen by simply putting the learners in front of the computer. A teacher who knows a great deal about how to foster learning – a learning agent – must mediate the learner-computer interaction. In addition, the learner is a social being and is part of a social and cultural environment that can be a source of ideas and information, or a place to find projects to be solved.

The sequence of actions description-execution-reflection-debugging provides important ingredients for the knowledge construction process. First, it shows the importance of description and execution. What the learner passes to the computer is an explicit expression of her/his reasoning, in terms of a specific piece of software. However, it is not enough to describe thinking. It is necessary to execute it. In this sense, it is as if the computer were executing the learner's thinking. The immediate and reliable feedback allows the confrontation of the learner's original ideas with the results obtained by the computer and this comparison is the first step in the

[1] Debugging is a term introduced by Artificial Intelligence (Sussman, 1975), meaning the process of eliminating "bugs" that prevent computer programs from working. In this case, programmers do not ask whether the program is correct or wrong but if it has bugs and if is possible to fix it or "debug" it. Bug and debugging were adopted by Papert (1980) as a way of looking at intellectual activities as having bugs rather than errors for which to be punished.

reflective process, to be aware of what s/he knows and what should be debugged.

Second, reflection and debugging are engines of the construction of different types of knowledge process. While reflecting, the learner has to think about the development of the project, concepts and strategies. If necessary, s/he has to look for new information, transform it into knowledge and apply it to improve the original problem description, thus creating opportunities to discuss the strategies used to develop the project, about concepts involved in the project and about learning strategies. All these are facilitated by the existence of the problem description, making possible the analysis of the problem solution so the learner can find her/his mistakes (bugs) and the teacher can understand what the learner is doing and thinking.

Thus, each of these actions creates opportunities to increment knowledge, contributing to its growth in a crescent spiral – the learning spiral – that takes place as the user interacts with the computer to solve a particular project (Valente, 2002).

This learning spiral is a theoretical construct and does not mean that each action takes place one at a time and in the sequential order as was presented. However, the possibility of using ICT and of engaging learners in this learning spiral helps to create rich, flexible and optimal learning environments, in the sense of Csikszentmihalyi's flow theory (Csikszentmihalyi, 1990). The desire to have the project solved, the fast and faithful feedback provided by ICT constitutes a stimulating situation, challenging people's intellectual capacities. In this situation people can feel deeply immersed, learn a great deal, and feel empowered. This feeling of empowerment has been observed in different populations of different ages and capabilities, such as in special education (Valente, 1991), in regular school situation (Valente, 1993), with disadvantaged children (Valente, 1995b) and with the elderly (Valente, 2001).

However, as pointed out before, the teacher has a very important role in keeping the sequence of actions running so the learning spiral can happen. This means that the teacher needs to be prepared to know how to take advantage of each situation to help the knowledge construction process. This implies knowing about ICT and how to use it pedagogically.

## 3. THE PROCESS OF PREPARING TEACHERS

The process of preparing teachers should be based upon knowledge construction, through the learning spiral, as discussed above. These teachers should experience exactly what they will provide to their students. As mentioned by Torres (2001) nobody can promote development of something that was not developed in herself/himself. Thus, the objective is to help teachers to learn about ICT so they can integrate these technologies into their practice. The idea is not to deal with the content of their specific subject area but to allow the construction of the following types of knowledge that overlap and do not happen necessarily in this sequence:

- To understand the potentials of ICT as resources to construct new knowledge. This understanding will be constructed as the professional reflects upon her/his own learning experience using these technologies to develop their own projects;
- To know how to use ICT in pedagogical project activities. This implies two types of knowledge: one, about how to develop her/his own projects using these technologies; the other, about how to interact with learners and help them to develop their projects through the use of ICT;
- To know how to act with her/his own classroom. The knowledge the teacher is constructing has to be contextualized in the community in which s/he acts. This happens as the teacher works with her/his students, helping them to learn and to become better learners. Thus these teachers will learn how to be learning agents not only by thinking but by acting as learning agents;
- To understand her/his actions as learning agent. Each teacher has to reflect upon her/his performance as learning agent and to debug it. This has the function of helping the development of knowledge about learning, about the learner's style, about how to encourage the learner's reflective and critical capacities, and about how to promote social relations so that learners can learn from one another and can work cooperatively;
- To confront the teacher's approach with other teachers. This has the function of decontextualizing the knowledge the teacher has acquired in her/his community, broadening it, comparing pedagogical ideas with other teachers, understanding that there are many different ways of approaching a learning experience;
- To be aware of and to use lifelong learning ideas herself/himself and in her/his practice, integrating them into all the activities developed with other learners.

From this perspective, preparing teachers to be able to use ICT cannot be based upon courses to pass on information, but upon the establishment of learning spirals about these different types of knowledge. A specific learning experience is taking place with respect to each of these different types of knowledge. Each of these experiences has to be used as an object of reflection and of knowledge construction about technical and pedagogical issues, about learning and about lifelong learning.

Another component of this preparation strategy is that these teachers cannot be removed from their work place or interrupted in their classroom activities in order to learn. This would leave too many classrooms without teachers. The solution is an in-service training by creating a virtual learning environment, via the Internet. This will help teachers to become learning agents as well as create opportunities for them to become familiar with tools for continuing learning throughout their lives. They will not only be able to help other people to become lifelong learners but they will be lifelong learners themselves. However, the distance education approach used has to be one that emphasizes the process of knowledge construction.

# 4. A DISTANCE EDUCATION APPROACH THAT ALLOWS KNOWLEDGE CONSTRUCTION

The idea of the learning spiral has been used also to establish a methodology for distance education, via the Internet. Briefly, distance education has changed the temporal and spatial relationship between the learner and the source of information (teachers or printed material). Different media and possibilities made available by the Internet have changed the ways education is taking place today, creating real opportunities for lifelong learning independently of time and space.

In the Web it is possible to find courses that are based upon different educational methodologies, although they can be categorized in three major groups: broadcast, consisting of making information available by means of mass media such as TV, radio or Internet, with no interaction between users and provider; virtual school, on-line courses using a pedagogy that is very similar to what happens in a face-to-face classroom today, with a certain degree of interaction between users and provider; and the virtual learning environment (Valente, 1999b).

The virtual learning environment allows teachers and the course docent to be together, side by side, although via the Internet. It is highly interactive and the interaction teacher-docent is established in order for the docent to help the teacher to solve particular problems s/he encounters in her/his practice. Thus, in order to be effective in this course, the teacher must be engaged in a project or in a problem to be solved. For example, implementing ICT in her/his discipline or developing interdisciplinary projects with students involving other colleagues. In this situation s/he is producing results and reflecting upon them. If a difficulty emerges, the teacher sends information (problem description, video, pictures) to the course docent. The docent reflects upon the information received and sends back questions, articles, and examples of activities or specific support material so the teacher can use this information to debug her/his project. New results can be obtained, new difficulties can emerge and the sequence of actions can be repeated.

These interactions take place not only between one teacher and the course docent, but all teachers can interact among themselves and with the docent. This helps to constitute a learner's network. Everybody can see and comment on everybody's work, exchange experiences, present different points of view for deeper levels of reflection. This network encourages collaborative work since learners can identify and jointly develop projects that have common backgrounds. At the same time it creates the conditions for the teacher to construct knowledge, fulfilling each participant's needs and interest. Each teacher can use her/his working reality as a context to know more and to improve her/his practice. Thus, the learning spiral is taking place at different levels and with respect to different types of knowledge being constructed (Prado & Valente, 2002).

In this approach teachers' preparation happens without their leaving their work environment. In this sense, it creates the opportunity to bring work experience to the learning environment that is much more difficult in a face-to-face situation. However, this opportunity for higher quality learning does not happen without extra cost. The implementation of the virtual learning environment is much more costly than the broadcast or virtual school approaches. The course docent cannot effectively work with more than 20 learners and it is necessary to maintain a good team of experts to prepare support materials almost under demand.

## 5. EXAMPLES OF TEACHER PREPARATION COURSES

The process of preparing teachers to use ICT in their pedagogical activities, via the Internet, was carried out in two main courses in Brazil. These were Distance Education courses, to prepare teachers from special education and from basic education respectively, to be able to use ICT in their classroom activities. These on-line courses used the virtual learning environment approach, promoting the development of the reflective teacher, emphasizing reflection-in-action and reflection-on-action and working with contextualized and decontextualized knowledge. These different reflections and knowledge were elaborated at different levels: about technical aspects of ICT, about the use of ICT to develop their own projects, about how to use

ICT with their students, and about the product of their learning process through discussion, via the Internet, with a larger audience and in great depth than is usually possible in a face-to-face situation.

One course was part of the *Projeto de Informática na Educação Especial – PROINESP* (Project of ICT in Special Education), sponsored by the Special Education Secretary from the Ministry of Education Office and by the National Federation of APAEs (FENAPAEs). The objective was to prepare special education teachers from APAE[2] and other special education institutions in different regions in Brazil to be able to use ICT in their classroom activities.

The PROINESP course happened twice and the latest version was administered by two groups of docents, one from the Nucleus of Informatics Applied to Education from the State University of Campinas (UNICAMP) and the other from the Nucleus of Informatics in Special Education from the Federal University of Rio Grande do Sul (UFRGS). This was a 210-hour course, divided into two modules. One of 90 hours, involving face-to-face activities, taking place at the local participant's region, about introductory aspects of ICT (Windows operating system, Word and the Internet). Its objective was to give the participants the minimal knowledge necessary to be able to communicate via the Internet. The other module was a 120-hour on-line course, about 12 weeks, via the Internet. At the end of the second module there was a three-day face-to-face seminar.

The 120-hour on-line course consisted of activities about the computer language Logo, the pedagogical uses of Internet, educational software available to special needs children, integration of different software in project development, devices to increase ICT accessibility and about the development of a plan regarding the use of ICT in the institution. The on-line course used the TelEduc[3] e-learning system. Each teacher had to develop ICT activities individually and had to use ICT with her/his students.

There were 389 teachers enrolled in the course, from 95 institutions (four teachers from each institution), divided into 17 groups of about 23 teachers each. From this total, 344 (88.4%) were approved, 11 (2.9%) teachers could not finish the course because of technical damage to the Internet connection and 34 (8.7%) did not accomplish the minimal requirements in the course and did not pass.

---

[2]APAE (Associação de Pais e Amigos dos Excepcionais) is a non-government organization of parents of special needs children.

[3] TelEduc is a distance learning environment for courses through the Internet. It is being developed jointly by the Nucleus of Informatics Applied to Education (Nied) and by the Institute of Computing (IC) of the State University of Campinas (Unicamp). It is a free software under the GNU - General Public License and its site is at teleduc.nied.unicamp.br/teleduc

The three-day face-to-face seminar happened one week after the end of the on-line course and 121 teachers (from 72 institutions) attended it. They presented posters on the work they developed with their students during the course and work they did in terms of disseminating ideas about the use of ICT among their colleagues in their own institution. These posters were visited by docents present in the seminar and commented upon in plenary sections in order to help teachers to debug their pedagogical use of ICT, and to discuss ideas that had important pedagogical contributions and could be implemented in other institutions. The principle results of this course can be seen in the Project site (Proinesp, 2002).

The other course was part of the Graduate Program in Education: Curriculum, from *Pontifícia Universidade Católica de São Paulo* (PUC-SP). Docents and graduate students of this Program administered the *Curso de Especialização em Desenvolvimento de Projetos Pedagógicos com Uso das Novas Tecnologias*, (Specialization Course[4] on Development of Pedagogical Projects Using ICT) financed by the *Programa Nacional de Informática –* ProInfo (National Informatics in Education Program) from the Secretary of Distance Education of the Ministry of Education. This was a 420-hour course and its objective was to prepare teachers from secondary and high schools, from different regions in Brazil, to learn how to be able to know how to develop pedagogical projects using ICT.

This course was divided into three modules. The first, of 60 hours, involving face-to-face activities, taking place at the local participant's region, was about introductory aspects of ICT (Windows operating system, Word and Internet). Its objective was to give the participants the minimal knowledge necessary to be able to communicate via Internet. The second module was a 300-hour on-line course, about 8 months, via Internet and using the TelEduc e-learning system. For the third module of 60 hours the teacher had to develop a monograph, under the supervision of a course docent. This was a reflective analysis of the teacher's own learning throughout the course.

The 300-hour on-line course consisted of activities about the development of pedagogical projects using different open-ended software such as a word processor, the computer language Logo, an authoring system to create Web pages, and the combination of these. Also there were several opportunities to discuss theoretical topics and to reflect upon the student's practical experience, with the purpose of relating practical experience and theory. Each teacher had to develop ICT activities individually and had to use ICT with her/his students. Also the Specialization Course structure

[4] It is equivalent to a Master's program, except that the student does not have to prepare and defend a dissertation.

requires that a student participates in at least 85% of the activities and in each activity the teacher needs to achieve a minimum of 70% to pass.

The second module of the course started with 44 teachers, divided into two groups, with 23 and 21 teachers respectively. From this total, 35 (79.5%) were approved, 9 (20.5%) teachers could not finish the course because of either technical damage to the Internet connection, other professional engagements preventing them from developing the course activities or idiom difficulties as in the case of 2 teachers from Chile and one from Argentine.

In both courses the pass rate can be considered very good compared with traditional distance education courses. Several factors may have contributed to this success. First is the fact that a teacher is part of a network involving other colleagues and docents, functioning as a support net. In this environment ties are created, making it almost impossible for the teacher to abandon the course. Second, the purpose of the course is for teachers to learn about ICT in order to implement these technologies into their school or special education institution. If s/ he fails, this can jeopardize a much larger project. Third, part of the teacher preparation is the work s/he does with her/his students. This is another level of responsibility that contributes to the teacher's continuing the course. In many situations teachers have reported that if it weren't for these different hooks, they would have left the course.

On the other hand, the teachers who were able to successfully complete the course reported that, despite the amount of work they had to do and the fact that they had to become more active learners, the course was worthwhile. They were learning about ICT and how to integrate these technologies into their school practice as the product of a construction process. They were constructing knowledge about ICT and about pedagogical changes, and overcoming several obstacles so ICT could gradually be implemented in their school. The fact that they were taking a leading role in implementing ICT in their schools, using an up to date technology, and observing through the use of ICT that their students were learning and showing themselves to be much better learners than the teachers thought, provided an opportunity for these teachers to feel empowered. As several teachers mentioned, the course meant a lot to them and made a big impact in their lives.

# 6. CONCLUSION

Although the virtual learning environment is not a solution to reach thousands of teachers, as is the real demand for teacher preparation in Brazil, this approach is more effective regarding the kind of learning environment educators should experience and know how to set up for their students. In this environment learners have to change attitude and acquire knowledge not only about particular subjects but how to deal with tools and strategies that help them to continue learning.

Since the courses emphasize the development of reflective teachers and provide means for them to understand ICT activities as windows into peoples' thinking processes, teachers are acquiring means to interact with their students, discussing the concepts involved in their activities as well as how knowledge is constructed. These are the first steps in mastering important ideas about how to become lifelong learners and how to create learning situations to help their students to develop lifelong learning mindsets.

## REFERENCES


Csikszentmihalyi, M. (1990). *Flow: The Psychology of Optimal Experience.* New York: Harper Perennial.

Freire, P. (1975). *Pedagogy of the Oppressed.* New York: The Seabury Press.

Papert, S. (1980). *Mindstorms: Children, Computers and Powerful Ideas.* New York: Basic Books.

Prado, M. E. B. B & Valente, J. A. (2002). A Educação a Distância Possibilitando a Formação do Professor com Base no Ciclo da Prática Pedagógica. In M. C. Moraes (Org.), *Educação a Distância: fundamentos e práticas* (pp. 27-50). Campinas, SP: UNICAMP/NIED.

Proinesp (2002). http://www.nied.unicamp.br/~proinesp

Sussman, G. J. (1975). *Computer Model of Skill Acquisition.* New York: American Elsevier Publishing Company.

Torres, R. M. (2001). *Itinerários Pela Educação Latino-Americana: Caderno de Viagem.* Porto Alegre: Artmed Ed.

Valente, J. A. (1991). *Liberando a Mente: Computadores na Educação Especial.* Campinas, SP: Gráfica Central da UNICAMP.

Valente, J. A. (1993). *Computadores e Conhecimento - Repensando a Educação.* Campinas, SP: UNICAMP/NIED.

Valente, J. A. (1995a). Logo as a window into the mind. *Logo Update*, 4(1), 1-4.

Valente, J. A. (1995b) The use of computers with disadvantaged children in Brazil. In A. J. Artiles & D. P. Hallahan (Eds), *Special Education in Latin America* (pp. 77-114). Greenwood's Editor.

Valente, J. A. (1999a). *Computadores na Sociedade do Conhecimento.* Campinas, SP: UNICAMP/NIED. English version retrieved from http://www.nied.unicamp.br/oea

Valente, J. A. (1999b). Diferentes Abordagens de Educação a Distância. *Coleção Série Informática na Educação – TVE Educativa.* Retrieved from http://www.proinfo.gov.br.

Valente, J. A. (2000). Criando Oportunidades de Aprendizagem Continuada ao Longo da Vida. *Revista Pátio,* IV(15), 8-12.

Valente, J. A. (2001). Aprendizagem continuada ao longo da vida: o exemplo da terceira idade. In Vitória Kachar (org.), *Longevidade: um novo desafio para a educação* (pp. 27-44). São Paulo: Cortez Editora.

Valente, J. A. (2002). A Espiral da aprendizagem e as tecnologias da informação e comunicação: repensando conceitos. In M. C. Joly (Ed.), *Tecnologia no Ensino: implicações para a aprendizagem* (pp. 15-37). São Paulo: Casa do Psicólogo Editora.

Weir, S. (1987). *Cultivating Minds: A Logo Casebook.* New York: Harper & Row Publishers.

# Raising the Standards: ICT and the Teacher of the Future

Ian Webb and Toni Downes
*Technology Education Federation of Australia, P.O. Box 1255, ACT 2616, Australia, ian.webb@dicksonc.act.edu.au, t.downes@uws.edu.au*

## 1. INTRODUCTION

The last five years in Australia have seen the intensification of activity around teacher standards. There have been a number of initiatives at the national level, including the development of standards for accomplished teachers of Mathematics, Science and English. A number of state education systems have also undertaken work in this area – for example in Western Australia (EDWA, 2001) and Queensland (Education Queensland, 1998, 2001). More recently some attention has been paid to the matter of teacher standards and the integration of ICTs into teaching and learning in classrooms.

The national statement *Learning in an Online World: The School Education Action Plan for the Information Economy* (Commonwealth of Australia, 1999) outlines a range of objectives and associated strategies in the application of information and communication technology (ICT) in teaching and learning. One such strategy in the area of 'People' is the development of teacher ICT standards for the use of ICT in the curriculum and incorporation of those standards into human resource management within education authorities and schools. More recently, the *Making Better Connections* report (DETYA, 2001) recommended that governments, systems and teacher education institutions and professional associations work collaboratively to develop standards for beginning and advanced teachers, standards for school-based and system-level capacity and for teacher education programmes and institutions, to support the student outcomes, and the linking of professional development strategies to these benchmarks and standards.

In response to these recommendations and other activities at national and state levels, the Commonwealth Department of Education, Science and Training (DEST) funded a project to develop a proposal for a national framework for ICT standards for teachers - both pre-service and practicing teachers. The project was conducted from July 2001 to January 2002.

The overall focus of the project was the development of a framework proposal, which could be used by teacher education institutions, teacher employers and professional associations to develop ICT standards relevant to their purposes and contexts.

The project was conducted in three phases. The first phase comprised:

- a review of the literature;
- an exercise in mapping current policy and practice in regard to teacher professional standards in Australia (national, state and territories) and selected overseas countries (United States, United Kingdom, Canada, Denmark and New Zealand);
- an analysis of the significant issues relevant to ICT competence in teaching and learning. The findings of this phase were reported in a preliminary report: Literature Review and Mapping document.

The second phase of the project was a two-day national forum of key stakeholders held in Canberra in October, 2001. The purpose of the forum was to seek input on the issues raised in Phase One, and on the direction of the project. A full report on the forum is included as an appendix to the final project report.

The third phase involved further analysis of findings, issues and outcomes from the forum, leading to the generation of a draft ICT Standards Framework proposal.

This final report, *Raising the Standards*, has been published on the DEST website at http://www.dest.gov.au/schools/publications/2002/raisingstandards.htm. The report comprises the following sections:

- a proposal for an ICT Standards Framework including analysis of the important issues and recommendations derived from the first and second phases;
- a proposed structure for an ICT Standards Framework;
- a proposal for ways in which this work can be supported and shared at a national level;
- two appendices comprising a report on the national two-day forum and a forum participant list;
- the Literature Review and Mapping as a third appendix.

A review of the literature and experiences overseas and in Australia revealed that the development of teacher professional standards is not without controversy. There are a number of tensions and contentious issues surrounding both non-ICT specific and ICT specific standards. A key matter of contention was whether there should, indeed, be a separate set of ICT specific standards, or whether a better option is to develop generic standards with rich descriptors that involve the use of a wide range of ICTs.

The final report addresses the following issues, and makes recommendations about each:

- language and the nature of competence;
- importance of context;
- supporting capabilities;
- issues of equity;
- relationships to other standards developments;
- a performance management or a professional development model;
- separate or embedded ICT standards;
- generic or subject specific ICT standards;
- standards for levels of teachers or a continuum of development;
- a minimum set of ICT standards for all teachers;
- dimensions of ICT use and stages of development;
- the relationship between non-ICT specific and ICT specific standards;
- who should develop, implement and assess the standards;
- teacher ICT competence, curriculum and student learning outcomes;
- framework evaluation and review processes.

The following formed the key recommendations of the project.

## 2. TECHNICAL COMPETENCE OR A COMPREHENSIVE VIEW OF ICT COMPETENCE

The notion of competence with regard to the use of ICT in education was regarded as broader than the technical skills needed to use ICT. The report stated that to take a technical view of competence would be to deny the plethora of skills needed by teachers to create meaningful and productive learning contexts for students. Therefore, whilst it may be easy to take a technical view of ICT competence, the report argued that it is not sufficient to equip teachers to understand and make effective use of ICT in the classroom. The type of ICT competence needed by teachers is a collection of knowledge, skills, understandings and attitudes that are inextricably bound up with context and pedagogy. The report recommended that "for the purposes of this framework, and standards that may be developed from it, a comprehensive view of competence is to be taken. That such a comprehensive view includes technical and higher order cognitive knowledge, skills, understandings and attitudes related to professional knowledge, professional practice and professional attributes" (DEST 2002, p. 13).

## 3. BASIS OF STANDARDS FRAMEWORK

The project undertook extensive research of existing teacher professional standards – both ICT and non-ICT specific. The research team concluded that no existing set of standards (either ICT or non-ICT specific) adequately reflected all of the capabilities required of a highly skilled teacher in an ICT rich learning environment. However the project concluded that by modifying the following generic teacher characteristics to include the transformative dimensions of ICT use in teaching and learning, they could form the basis for the development of appropriate ICT specific teacher standards. These generic teacher characteristics are:

- a commitment to students and their learning;
- a deep knowledge and understanding of their subject discipline and of effective pedagogy;
- the ability to implement effective monitoring, assessment and reporting of student progress;
- a commitment to reflect critically on their own practice and to engage in ongoing professional development; and
- a willingness to participate and contribute to the whole educational community at a range of levels.

## 4. SETS OF STANDARDS

A major recommendation of the project was that five sets of ICT specific standards be developed. These standards are not to be specific to levels of education or particular subject areas. The five sets of standards relate to the following recommended target groups:

- pre-service/beginning teachers,
- practicing teachers who are beginning users of ICT,
- practicing teachers who are accomplished/highly accomplished users of ICT,
- school and educational leaders,
- teacher educators.

## 5. SUPPORTING CAPABILITIES

There is substantial evidence in the literature indicating that a multi-dimensional approach is needed to successfully implement the use of ICT in schools. In particular, certain conditions must be present in terms of support and institutional capabilities for both teacher education institutions and schools/school systems. These conditions can be referred to as Supporting Capabilities. These capabilities focus on physical, human and financial resources and policy decisions. The project recommended that as part of any national framework, systemic and institutional ICT capabilities be developed for use as part of reviewing, planning and reporting processes.

## 6. KEY STAKEHOLDERS

Findings from the project recognised the critical role of all stakeholders in the process of the development of teacher professional standards. The key stakeholders are the profession, employees, professional associations and education systems. It concluded that there is a need for significant and authentic collaboration between the relevant stakeholders if the development and implementation of teacher professional standards is to be effective and be accepted by the profession.

## 7. CONNECTIONS WITH STUDENT STANDARDS AND CURRICULUM

The project report argues that concurrent with the development of teacher ICT standards, there need to be explicit student ICT specific learning outcomes embedded in curriculum documents, and that any teacher ICT standards should be consistent with student ICT learning outcomes.

## 8. THE FUTURE

The *Raising the Standards* report was published in July 2002. The recommendations from the report are still under consideration by DEST. The Commonwealth is, however, also undertaking other work in relation to teacher standards and student ICT standards. The MCEETYA Teacher Quality and Educational Leadership taskforce is developing a discussion paper in relation to teacher professional standards. This paper is expected to be released towards the end of 2002. In addition the MCEETYA

Performance Measurement and Reporting taskforce has begun addressing the issue of student ICT standards. It is anticipated that the *Raising the Standards* report will inform this work, and in turn any possible future action in relation to teacher ICT-specific standards will be considered in the context of the MCEETYA deliberations.

# REFERENCES

Commonwealth of Australia (1999). *Learning in an Online World: The School Education Action Plan for the Information Economy*. Retrieved September 9, 2001 from http://www.detya.gov.au/schools/Publications.

Department of Education, Science and Training (DEST) (2002). *Raising the Standards: A Proposal for the Development of an ICT Competency Framework for Teachers*. Accessed October 8th, 2002 from http://www.dest.gov.au/schools/publications/2002/raisingstandards.htm

Department of Education, Training and Youth Affairs (DETYA) (2001). *Making Better Connections—The Models of Teacher Professional Development for the Integration of ICT into Classroom Practice*. Canberra.

Education Department of Western Australia (EDWA) (2001). *Competency Framework for Teachers*. Murdoch University: Centre for Curriculum and Professional Development.

Education Queensland (1998). *Minimum Standards for Teacher—Learning Technology*. Retrieved August 8th, 2002 from http://education.qld.gov.au/2001/mst_int.htm

Education Queensland (2001). *Information and Communications Technology Continua* [draft]. Retrieved November 1st, 2001 from http://www.education.qld.gov.au/tal/2001/cont.htm

# Professional Development Needs of Teachers Managing Self-Guided Learning

Wolfgang Weber
*Department of Information, Documentation and Communication, State Institute for Schools, Paradieser Weg 64, D-59494 Soest, Germany, wolfgang.weber@mail.lsw.nrw.de*

**Abstract**: In the project 'Self-guided Learning in Teaching Mathematics at Senior High School Level' (SelMa), five authoring schools are working out scenarios, media and materials for phases of self-guided learning, which will be tested systematically by 10 trial schools with regard to their everyday suitability. In this paper three approaches to such learning arrangements (independent learning centre, jigsaw classroom and learning at stations) are being outlined and relevant experiences are being made available. Learning diaries prove to be useful for the learners' reflections on their learning processes. The adaptation of such learning arrangements and media to a specific learning group does place new demands on the teachers. In addition, diagnosing and consulting in connection with the individual learning processes require new, or enhanced competencies on the part of the teachers who, in spite of having made available more freedom within the framework of teaching, still cannot make adequate use of their enhanced role. Possibilities for further development are outlined.

## 1. GENERAL INFORMATION

The four-year (1999-2003) pilot project 'Self-guided Learning in Teaching Mathematics at Senior High School Level' (SelMa) is funded by the federal government and by the state of North-Rhine-Westphalia. SelMa is monitored by the LfS (State Institute for Schools). The aim of this pilot project is to show what teaching mathematics at senior high school level can look like if self-guided learning and activities are supported by the use of new media. Special importance is placed on integrating aspects of self-guided learning in everyday teaching. Learning, mathematics and the use of new media - these are the pillars on which SelMa stands. Special emphasis is placed on the delivery of the new curriculum for mathematics, which focuses upon aspects of self-guided learning and must be integrated into everyday school life. The purpose of SelMa is to give teachers orientation and ideas for their own teaching. Scenarios and materials for self-guided learning phases in teaching mathematics at senior high school level are being developed in five 'authoring schools'. These learning arrangements are accessible for teachers for trial purposes on the North-Rhine-Westphalian web-site 'learn:line' (http://www.mathe-selma.de). This website provides an information, communication and co-operation environment for this purpose. Learn:line encourages the exchange of information and experiences between teachers. The development of materials by the authoring schools is to take place in an 'open workshop', so that other schools can also try out them at an early stage and regularly report on their own experiences. A special role is played by ten 'trial schools' that systematically try out and evaluate the materials that have been developed to see whether they work in everyday usage. Their feedback will be incorporated in the on-going development of materials. Furthermore, authoring and trial schools are to disseminate their practice so that networks of schools can be created in the different regions and the materials on learn:line can be further developed. In this way the scenarios will be used in an increasing number of schools. Publishers are to be included at an early stage. This is expected to lead to higher-quality (offline and online) media that will support phases of self-guided learning in teaching mathematics. The SelMa project is being evaluated by the Institute for School Development Research, University of Dortmund.

## 2. OUR VISION OF AN INDEPENDENT LEARNER

Independent learners are able to determine their own targets and are accordingly able to choose the topics for their own learning projects. In school it is therefore of importance to them to be involved already in the planning and structuring of lessons. In order to reach their goals the students have at their disposal sufficient self-motivation, which spurs them on in learning and working. They are not dependent on external motivation. They actively contribute to the learning processes. Self-generated activity is another one of their characteristics. The passive receptive role of a learner is alien to them. They understand how to plan their work in proportion to the problem, to structure, organize and carry it out in a time-effective way. In addition to all this they can fall back upon a wide repertoire of methodical know-how. Thus they are able to investigate in a result-oriented way, to select, structure and evaluate the information obtained in order to construct new knowledge of their own, which is tied to the knowledge already at hand, starting a networking process. Their pronounced media competence assists them in making use of both traditional as well as new media for the purpose of their own learning processes. Independent learners are able to clearly and appealingly document what has been learned and are able to process it in such a way that they can present it to others, using reasoned argument to advocate it. Regarding learning situations at school, the teacher is for them a supporter, advisor, coach or even supervisor - who is addressed by them if required or consulted in the case of learning problems.

In addition to the original goals and work, independent learners at the same time have an eye on their own learning processes. They document their own ways of learning thus making them available for their own evaluation or reflection – or for a joint one together with the teacher. This process of becoming aware of their own learning helps them to abstract from the actual learning situation and to gain insight into the transfer to other learning situations – thus further developing their 'learning training'. Based on this background they are also able to realistically assess their own learning performance as well as communicating it, for example to their teachers.

Independent learners additionally bring their communicative and social competencies, their willingness to co-operate and their team spirit to bear in group-relevant self-learning processes. Namely, they must succeed in coming to an understanding with the other learners inside the group about mutual goals, work plans and, for example, criteria for quality assessment with regard to the output yielded. In the case of actions based on 'job-sharing', the working and learning processes have to be co-ordinated with each other and the partial results so gained have to be applied or be brought together. In particular, the handling of stress or conflict situations requires a social competence, which is quite well developed. In relation to group learning processes, the evaluation has to be handled similarly and in addition to the reflection on the personal learning process. Added to the student's responsibility for the personal learning process is a share of responsibility for the learning process of the group's members.

## 3. THE PROJECT REALITY

At the start of the project the participating teachers found themselves facing the following situation: the majority of those learners with whom the project work is being done are from secondary level I, and mainly familiar with traditional teaching methods focussing on the teacher. With regard to teaching mathematics most of them tend to have little motivation, they are rather passive, receptive and fixated on the reproduction of knowledge or information instead of being geared to their own activity. Most of the teachers lack media and methodological competence – especially with regard to the new media. For many learners it is a particular novelty to render their own learning process into the subject of contemplation. Based on such a background, independent learning can only be striven for as a fairly long-term target. Many intermediate steps are necessary and it is consequently very time-consuming to develop the necessary competences.

# 4. DEVELOPMENT OF SCENARIOS AND MATERIALS

Different scenarios (learning arrangements) and materials for independent learning are being developed and tested in SelMa, with different facets of independent learning being the centre of attention. Each and every approach is geared to approaching closer to the ideal of independent learning. Three approaches are outlined here.

## 4.1 The independent learning centre

Learning in the independent learning centre distinguishes itself quite radically from the other scenarios described herein, insofar as with this approach the learners have no choice but to fend for themselves. In a kind of media centre a variety of traditional and new media are at their disposal - but the teachers, who normally accompany the learning processes, are missing.

The work of this SelMa authoring team is closely related to further developments in their school. In an independent learning centre, pupils work on their own, on mathematical topics specified in the curriculum for Years 11 and 12. The material that is prepared for the independent learning centre consists of courses on the one hand and of collections of problems on the other. Graded aids for learning relating to the pupils' existing knowledge provide both food for thought and initial approaches towards solving the problems. Suggested solutions to the problems allow the learners to check the progress they are making. The computer provides opportunities for simulation and visualisation of mathematics. Pupils normally meet in groups of two or three in the independent learning centre and discuss individual problems. The aim is for the individual pupil to establish as precisely as possible those areas where practice is most necessary.

## 4.2 The jigsaw puzzle classroom

Another group of authors tackled in particular the question of how self-directed activity of learners inside the classroom can be furthered. While searching for such scenarios, which depart from teacher-focussed teaching in order to reach forms of teaching, where at any given time several or even many learners can be simultaneously active, they came across the so-called jigsaw classroom.

It appears that for this scenario a substantial part of the teacher's work is based on preparation. He or she divides a larger topic into several (usually 4-6) sub-topics. For each sub-topic materials for self-learning, which are designed in such a way that they can be handled by the learners individually within a given timeframe, are provided. With regard to its sequence, the jigsaw classroom is comparatively strictly organized. It is divided into:

- Introduction, organization of the work;
- Phase 1: Individual work with the materials for self-study;
- Phase 2: Experts' round;
- Phase 3: Exchange round (learning by teaching);
- Retrospective, reflection of the learning process.

In the phase for individual work, the learners exploit the relevant sub-topic as much as they are able to on an individual basis, with the aid of the materials for self-study. Then all those learners, who have tackled the same sub-topic, meet in a group, the so-called experts' round. Here they settle pending questions, discuss their findings and thus jointly become experts for their sub-topic. In this phase they also prepare jointly how they will pass on the newly acquired knowledge to their fellow learners in the next round.

For the next phase the groups will be re-shuffled like in a jigsaw puzzle, so that experts for each and every one of the sub-topics come together at one group table. The learners introduce the various sub-topics, discuss them jointly and thus handle the whole of the topic in the group.

## 4.3 Learning stations

In this scenario, having pupils study materials at different learning stations particularly supports individual learning. The complete learning circle consists of several (about 20) stations, which are assigned to several thematic areas. The stations are set up in such a way that different background levels of learning, different speeds of learning and working, and different needs in terms of working individually, in pairs or in groups are accommodated. There are compulsory and optional stations. Thus the learners are enabled, if only within a limited framework, to influence the selection of learning content. To help pupils find their way they are given a 'docket', which lists all the stations (number; title; topic; compulsory or additional station; individual, pair or group work). The 'docket' also contains hints as to which aspects might be of significance with regard to the selection decision.

# 5. LEARNING DIARIES

In all scenarios it is central to the teachers' intention that the learners also focus on their own learning process - even if this is quite unusual for most of them. At the beginning this is done by rather small surveying tasks, which offer the opportunity for discussion. During the course of events more and more aspects are added. Everything works towards demonstrating to the learner the advantages of keeping an individual learning diary. Compared with the team-related learning diary, this type has demonstrated two strengths. On the one hand, pupils continuously reflect on their progress in terms of the subject matter, and on the other hand, this method allows very personal diary entries about the pupil's progress in learning - provided only the teacher reads the learning diary.

# 6. INSIGHTS AND EXPERIENCES

## 6.1 The independent learning centre

In the case of the independent learning centre the media used for working by the learners, mostly on an individual or partner-oriented basis, play a key role. When designing such media, it is necessary to balance an openness that permits independent learning and working against a more compelling degree of control that does not leave the learners to cope with their problems single-handed. Special attention must therefore be paid to the help systems, which are integrated into the media. It is extremely time and energy consuming to develop such context-sensitive aids to cover the individual learning situation. This has been successfully mastered in the case of well-defined courses, but becomes more and more complex the more open the learning situation is being designed.

With regard to the learners, working in such an independent learning centre demands well-developed competencies and places high demands on their self-discipline. The longer the phases of individual learning last, the higher are the demands on planning, structuring and organization of their own learning process. Weaker pupils in particular tend to bring in the aids integrated into the media much too early and in a far too intensive manner.

## 6.2 The jigsaw puzzle classroom

The jigsaw puzzle classroom is reacted to with a high degree of acceptance both by the learning and the teaching parties. This is probably due to the fact that during the different phases all learners are firmly integrated into the learning processes. Students and teachers experience the exposure to the prevailing topic as being very intensive. The jigsaw classroom supports co-operative work within a group of learners. Quite evidently the jigsaw classroom can strengthen the self-confidence of the otherwise rather quiet or weaker students. The jigsaw classroom may also lead towards a perceptively higher esteem for each other among the learners.

In the case of good preparation, the teacher has completed a "substantial part of his work", when the jigsaw classroom actually begins. The clear structure of the jigsaw classroom enables the teacher to almost completely withdraw from the teaching process while the jigsaw classroom is executed as such. Should the need arise, he is required in the process of group formation, in case or organizational questions and for time control. By withdrawing from the teaching process, a new kind of freedom is created for the teachers. To make use of this freedom in favour of new tasks (e.g. diagnose, consulting) opens up great opportunities.

## 6.3 Learning stations

According to the concept of learning stations the students first of all have to complete their compulsory tasks in the different sections. Due to the optional tasks they themselves may, within a certain framework, influence the choice of topics and also of goals. Better performing students in particular are very appropriately accommodated by the possibilities offered here. Weaker students, however, are easily and very often challenged too much by the sheer range of decisions demanded from them. They become rather unsettled and seem to feel that they miss out on important things.

Again with learning stations the question of making available adequate aids or solutions arises. In the opinion of many teachers, access made too easy entices the learners to leave their own path of learning too hastily. They therefore suggest planning the aids in areas outside the stations and preferably having access monitored by the teacher.

It is remarkable that the learning stations are rarely adopted by the trial schools in a 1:1 ratio. Teachers are using the possibilities to add to the stations their own, already proven tasks, and to make do without those tasks which they consider to be less suitable or rather too difficult. It can be observed that, in the case of such adaptations, the number of options made available to the students is considerably reduced and that thus the degree of reliability is clearly increased. As with the jigsaw classroom most teachers also succeed here in withdrawing themselves to a significant extent from the teaching process. Also here the newly emerging freedom can be seized to a greater extent as a new opportunity.

### 6.4 Learning diaries

Experiences have shown that the keeping of a learning diary has a permanent and positive effect on the learning process in mathematics at senior high school level if pupils accept this method. The pupils clearly pay more attention to the learning process, try to answer questions immediately (rather than waiting until the last possible minute before the test), and are far more aware of their own strengths and weaknesses when studying mathematics. The personal learning diary encourages pupils to reflect more on their own learning strategies. Without exception, pupils who had been using this method for some time gradually displayed more stable and better performance in mathematics compared to that at the beginning of the school year. The learning diary supports comprehending and solving mathematical problems. It increases medium and long-term retention and can relatively easily be incorporated into normal everyday teaching. But very often it takes the students a lot of will power to approach the teacher as a consultant. Only the strict and clear differentiation between consulting and assessing creates the atmosphere of trust required and enables sustainable behavioural changes. Methodical knowledge in the areas of meta cognition and reflection on learning processes proves to be particularly helpful for the teachers with regard to the stimulation of relevant competencies in the students. Through the learning diaries the teachers additionally gain an important tool for reflection on their own teaching.

## 7. NEW DEMANDS ON THE TEACHERS

At the transition point to self-guided learning, the process of learning and the learners themselves are at the very centre of all observations. Which individual dispositions have to be taken into consideration, which previously gained knowledge and which previous experience can be used as a base, which expectations pupils have with regard to topics and classroom teaching and which goals they have when they tackle the syllabus - all this is being analyzed to a much greater extent.

It is the teacher's responsibility to create the required basic conditions, to initiate the learning process, to motivate the learners and to consult and assist them with regard to their planning and the structuring of the learning process, their time-management, their account and back-up of the outcome of their work, their reflection and the evaluation of their own learning processes. The majority of teachers are inadequately prepared for this extended role. During the relevant teaching phases they often withdraw themselves too much, which results in the pupils feeling being left alone. In spite of the fact that teachers would now have time to diagnose the learning level, which would provide them with important clues with regard to consulting and assisting, for the most part they lack the necessary diagnostic repertoire. In addition, teachers perceive themselves as deficient with regard to competence in the fields of communication, presentation, methodology and media especially, all of which are important prerequisites for the core competence of designing adequate learning arrangements for the different phases of self-guided learning.

For this purpose, teachers must know how learners are working with such learning arrangements, in order to gain insight into didactic and methodological design. The compiling of materials for self-guided learning requires that the developers put themselves into the place of the learners and start thinking in the latters' categories of interests, learning prerequisites and expectations. This is the only way to create materials, which at a later stage can be exploited independently by the learners. During the conceptual stages of such learning arrangements, teachers notice quite often that they actually have only slight knowledge of their pupils' learning conditions. If insights into, for example, different types of learners and varying levels of performance, be they low or high, do exist, then the question still remains as to how all this has to be considered in the light of compiling materials and learning arrangements. Particularly in the case of non-homogeneous learning groups, discussions lead again and again to questions of the extent to which help systems are to be integrated into the materials, down to which level of detail they have to be implemented, and to what extent they may then support or even hamper self-guided learning.

## 8. FUTURE PROSPECTS

Phases of self-guided learning are, contrary to popular opinion, generally more strenuous and labour-intensive than preparing for and conducting traditional teaching, and this is true for both the teacher as well as for the learner. Not least because of this, the learners demand again and again to allow equally for phases of traditional teaching. Also the fear that teachers might become superfluous during phases of self-learning is easy to disprove. Particularly during self-learning phases, teachers are challenged in their capacity as qualified experts and, much more than in traditional teaching, as sympathetic pedagogic consultants and experts for the optimization of individual learning processes.

Regarding their workload the teachers often (to their surprise) find out that their own familiarization with the mostly quite complex media associated with these self-learning phases is at times considerably and additionally time-consuming.

If the teachers really get involved in individualized consulting and accompanying of the learners' individual learning processes, then the time and energy used for this purpose during classes does increase considerably. Teachers can only do this in the long run, if learners are also willing in the future to take over additional tasks themselves. New and different methods of self-evaluation might possibly bring relief to the teachers if they display learning progress and learning obstacles to the learners, at the same time providing information that can serve as a basis for consultation between teachers and students.

## REFERENCES

Landesinstitut für Schule und Weiterbildung. (2000). *Förderung selbständigen Lernens in der gymnasialen Oberstufe.* DruckVerlag Kettler, Bönen.

Mandl, H. Reinmann-Rothmeier, G. & Gräsel, C. (1998). Gutachten zum BLK-Programm: Systematische Einbeziehung von Medien, Informations- und Kommunikations-technologien (Forschungsbericht Nr. 93). Ludwig-Maximilians-Universität, Lehrstuhl für Empirische Pädagogik und Pädagogische Psychologie, München.

# Reports of Focus Group Discussions:

# Group A – The Teacher as a Professional: Fostering Professionalism

**Chair:** Raymond Morel, *CPTIC, raymond.morel@tecfaunige.ch*
**Rapporteur:** Paul Nicholson, *Deakin University, pauln@deakin.edu.au*
**Participants:** Terry Cannings (USA), Valentina Daigiene (Lithuania), Niki Davis (USA), Deborah Goldman (Australia), Leon Guss (Australia), Richard Hogg (Australia), Vittorio Midori (Italy)

## 1. INTRODUCTION

Globally, there is a need to improve the status of teachers in society. The status of teachers depends on a range of political and cultural factors that impact on the way in which teaching is perceived – whether as a trade, craft, or profession — and how these are valued. We argue that all teachers of the future will need to have a high status in their societies if they are to help those societies to realise the potential benefits of an increasingly technological future, and that a key step in achieving this is through the formation of professional associations that foster the development of structures to support a professional community of practice, and which create and enforce national or international standards for membership in a similar fashion to medical and engineering professional associations. By adopting such professional characteristics, and by allowing for the professional recognition of all levels of teachers at all levels of education, the influence and actions of these professional associations will, over time, lead to an increased status for teachers and improved external perceptions of the profession. There are a number of key issues that these societies will need to address:

- How to complement and ensure coherence in teachers' professional knowledge and skills
- How to enhance the status of youth and students
- How to articulate and collaborate with multiple stakeholders
- How to develop didactic pedagogy into adaptive pedagogies

## 2. DEVELOPING PROFESSIONALISM

To make effective and culturally appropriate use of ICT in the curriculum, teachers need to develop competencies in the areas of content knowledge and pedagogy, collaboration and networking, technical issues and social issues (UNESCO, 2003). In recognition of the importance of context and situation in teacher learning (e.g. Putnam & Borko, 2000) these are situated in larger themes such as leadership, context and culture etc. (Figure 1) so that they both draw from, and contribute to, these larger themes. It is this bi-directional interaction between classroom practice and societal and educational issues that is at the core of professionalism — providing a conduit to influence society as well as to operationalise its needs. Informed, evidence-based decision-making is another key attribute of professional behaviour, and for this reason research in learning, teaching, and ICT is a central element of the UNESCO framework. We see the role of professional associations being to both implement this framework with its members, and to adopt it as a basis for defining the professional context of teachers of the future.

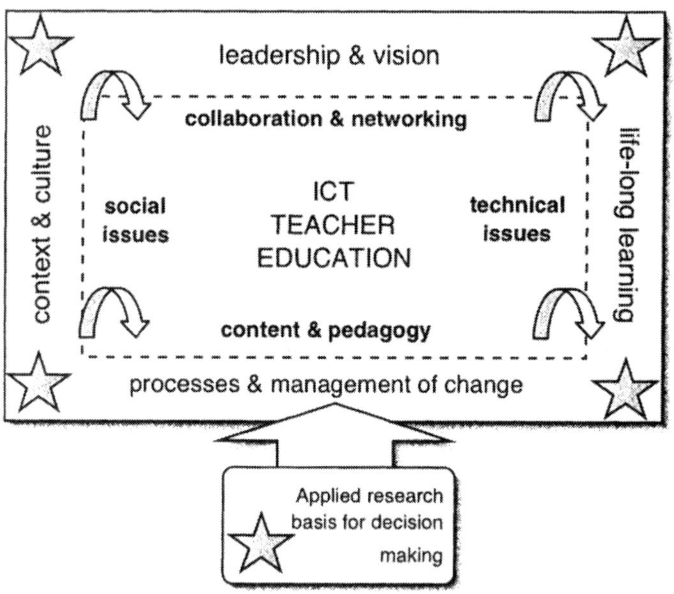


*Figure 1.* Elements of ICT teacher professional competencies (UNESCO 2003)

## 3. RECOMMENDATIONS

The following areas should be given high priority in developing support programmes, practices and policies for increasing teacher professionalism because they underpin key areas of professional practice and behaviour:

- Develop leadership and vision with the profession, underpinned by research. This to include planning and management of change, lifelong learning and the accommodation of relevant contexts and cultures.
- Develop appropriate resources and support for ICT *in* teacher education, and for teachers *of* ICT, in the four areas of the UNESCO framework.
- To apply UNESCO/IFIP recommendations for youth from WCC2002.
- To promote and develop professional communities of practice.

## 4. ACTIONS TO BE TAKEN

To achieve the recommendations above, actions required by IFIP and other organizations are:

- To create professional associations and networks (to coordinate for coherence) to build and enforce international standards for its membership (cf. doctors).
- To create and implement strategies for increasing partnerships with stakeholders.
- To implement communities of practice of early adopters and pioneer teachers to lead and support change.
- To develop related research program(s) with appropriate research strategies.
- To use the research to impact policy and practice.
- IFIP Technical Committee 3 and national bodies to establish incentives for creativity and innovation eg IFIP "Teacher of the future" of the year awards and presentation at WCC/WCCE.
- IFIP Technical Committee 3 and its working groups to incorporate the World Computer Congress 2002 Youth Declaration recommendations in their plan of activities 2003-2007.
- To report activities and progress in the TC3 Newsletter.

# REFERENCES

Putnam, R. T. & Borko, H. (2000). What do new views of knowledge and thinking have to say about research on teacher learning? *Educational Researcher, 29*(1), 4-15.

UNESCO (2003). UNESCO Framework. In *ICT Teacher Education*, Paris: UNESCO.

UNESCO-IFIP (2002). *World Computer Congress 2002 Youth Declaration*. Montreal: UNESCO-IFIP.

# Reports of Focus Group Discussions:

# Group B – The Professional Teacher: Contexts, Capabilities and Competencies

**Chair:** Sigrid Schubert, *University of Siegen, schubert@informatik.uni-siegen.de*
**Rapporteur:** Toni Downes, *Technology Education Federation of Australia, t.downes@uws.edu.au*
**Participants:** Wing-Wah Ki (Hong Kong), Ralph Leonard (Australia), Prathiba Nagabhushan (Australia), Ian Webb (Australia), Trena Wilkerson (USA)

## 1. INTRODUCTION

Within many countries the issue of teachers' ICT competency is on the agenda of key decision makers. The focus group believed that a discussion about competencies with regard to the use of ICTs for teaching and learning, needs to be situated within a broader discussion about the teacher as a professional, the interactions between teachers and colleagues, their workplaces and the broad educational, social and technological contexts which influence their work. The focus group recognised that there are many other issues of importance, especially those relating to equity, but felt that in the time available, it could address only those reported below. Throughout their discussions, the focus group was influenced by the concept of 'collective competencies'. This concept was introduced to the conference in the initial keynote address by Bernard Cornu.

## 2. THE TEACHER OF THE FUTURE AS A PROFESSIONAL

The focus group identified the following characteristics as essential for the professional of the future with regard to ICT use in education. A teacher as a professional should:

- take responsibility for his/her own personal professional learning and that of his/her learners, and contribute to the professional learning of peers;
- be accountable for the individual and collective decisions and interactions they have with students and other stakeholders in designing, implementing and evaluating teaching, learning and assessment activities and selecting resources for these activities;
- analyse and capitalise on the context of their work for the benefit of student learning, and address constraints, requirements and opportunities for change and innovation;
- reflect on and collect evidence with regard to policies and practices and other issues for the purposes of the continual improvement of student learning outcomes;
- be appropriately supported by professional associations and employers and colleagues in the workplace;
- be rewarded for excellence.

## 3. INDIVIDUAL AND COLLECTIVE COMPETENCIES

Individual and collective competencies for teachers need to address ICT use in relation to a range of broader teacher capabilities. These include the three areas of pedagogy and classroom practice professional literacies, as well as knowledge of curriculum (CURRIC) and a deep knowledge of the subject matter (DSK) underpinning the curriculum. A teacher's performance as a professional is the combined result of their capability in the three designated areas. Within each area, a teacher's capability with ICT is a subset of their professional capability in the wider context of each area. As professionals, teachers seek to expand their capability with ICT within each of the identified areas while recognising that the wider context of each area is simultaneously being extended by the profession as a whole. This process is itself impacted upon by the economic, social, cultural and technological changes that continue to transform society. Figure 1 illustrates this environment.

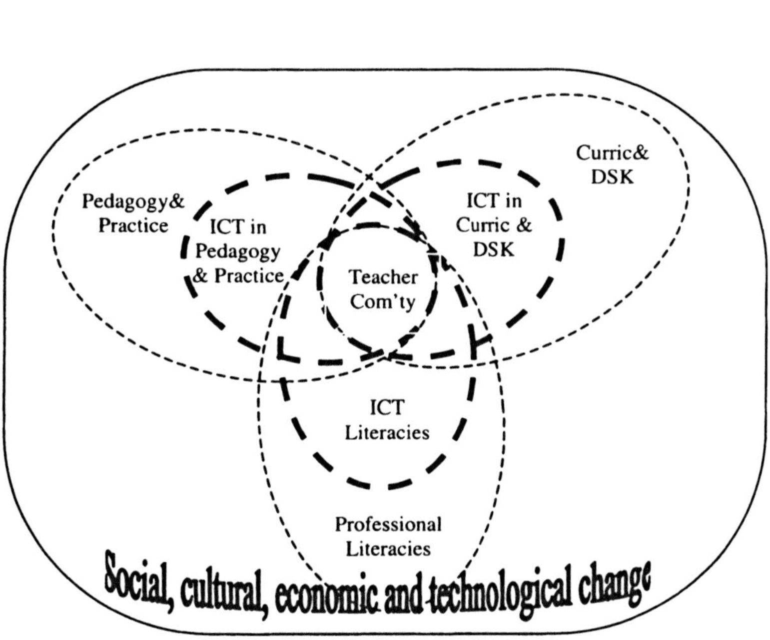


*Figure 1.*The capabilities that constitute competencies in ICT use in teaching and learning

# 4. INTERACTION OF CONTEXTS AND CAPABILITIES

It is important to note that teachers as professionals work within a context, the nature of which impacts significantly on their effectiveness. To effect sustainable change a teacher cannot work in isolation from their community of peers or from the context in which they work.

In particular, in the effective application of ICT in teaching and learning a number of factors need to be in evidence in addition to the personal capabilities of the individual teacher. Figure 2 illustrates these factors. At the school level a range of supporting capabilities need to be in place that include access to effective professional development programs, appropriate access to hardware and software, supportive school policies and practices that reflect and promote effective use of ICT, well articulated ICT rich student learning outcomes and quality curriculum resources. These capabilities are also necessary at the school system level. In order for change to be effective and sustainable such capabilities should be evident in all components of the teachers' professional community.

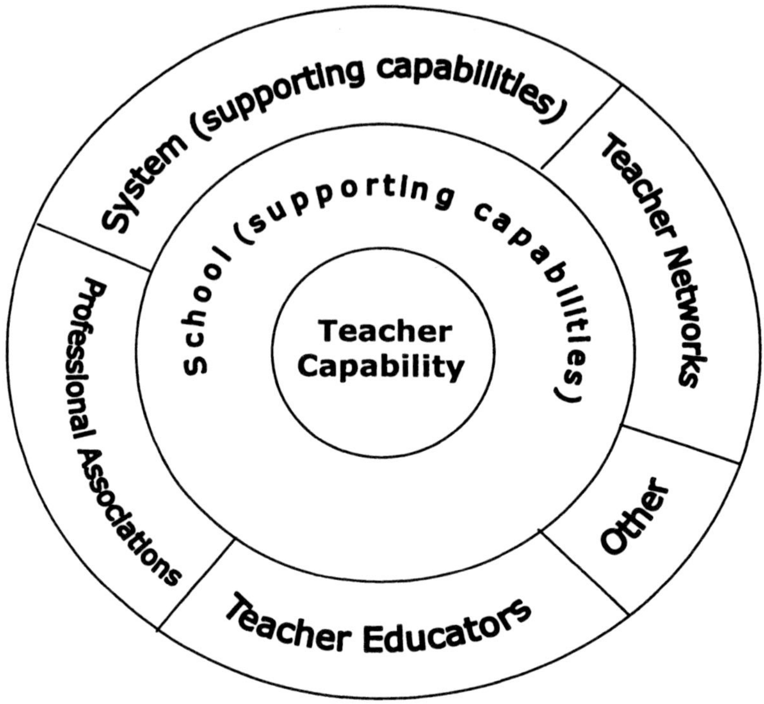


*Figure 2.* Factors that impact teacher competency

Teacher education is a key component of the teachers' professional community. Teacher education institutions need to develop genuine partnerships with teachers, schools and school districts so that teacher educators, classroom teachers and student teachers work together to develop collective competencies in the effective use of ICT in education. To support this development the assessment and certification practices of teacher education institutions need to be consistent with the goals and processes of any partnerships.

## 5. CONCLUSIONS AND RECOMMENDATIONS

Based on the above discussion three significant recommendations follow:

- There should be a shift from over–emphasis on individual competency to a balance of individual and collective competencies. To achieve collective competency it is necessary to create communities of practice and support within schools, within and across districts and nations.

- Standards should be established such that they can guide the flexible creation of professional practice and development and working structures that address the context of work in full integration with the other objectives of education. Teachers should take account of the changing economic, social, cultural and technological society.
- The teacher as a professional must be supported by the school as learning organisation and a wide range of external support structures, comprising resources, policies, curriculum and people.

# Section 3

# Classroom Roles of the Teacher of the Future

# Developing ICT Leadership Skills for Teachers of the Future

Dianne Chambers
*Science & Mathematics Education, The University of Melbourne, Australia, d.chambers@unimelb.edu.au*

**Abstract**: There is a strong demand in schools for capable leaders, in particular in the area of the successful integration of information and communication technologies (ICT) into teaching and learning. This need is addressed by an innovative course *IT in Primary Schools* that prepares our undergraduate students to take on ICT leadership roles in schools. The course is based on a problem based learning approach that utilises the cognitive apprenticeship model. This approach to learning demands that students develop a rich understanding of the complexities of leadership and decision-making about ICT in schools, and the human issues of introducing ICT into a school. Students work in teams, acting as the ICT Committee in a fictional primary school, and solve four large problems over the year. Students develop content knowledge and generic skills, such as information literacy, communication and leadership skills. This approach to learning leads to successful outcomes for students and very satisfying teaching experiences for staff.

## 1. INTRODUCTION

The goal of teacher education is to prepare students to be capable teachers – a Herculean task when one considers the large number of roles a teacher plays within a school! Many teacher education courses focus on developing skills and understandings related to the classroom activities of teaching, and do not address the large number of attributes and skills a successful teacher requires when not in the classroom. We have developed an innovative course *Information Technology in Primary Schools* that is taken by students in the final year of the four-year Bachelor of Education (Primary) degree program. The goal of *IT in Primary Schools* is to develop our students into the leaders of tomorrow, capable of taking on a leadership role in the area of Information and Communication Technology and, through the generic and transferable skills developed, to refine skills for lifelong learning and become a leader in any aspect of a school. We believe that this type of learning cannot be taught through traditional means, and that the PBL approach (Finkle & Torp, 1995; Stover, 1998) with the cognitive apprenticeship model (Collins, Brown & Newman, 1989) is a powerful way to facilitate learning about these complex issues and to develop 'habits of mind' that will be beneficial for the students.

## 1.1 Teacher education and leadership

Not many teacher education courses aim to develop leadership skills in pre-service teachers, nor is leadership an issue that many undergraduate education students think about. It is more usual for issues relating to school leadership to be addressed in postgraduate courses that are usually undertaken by school principals or by senior teachers who are aspiring to a principal's position. However, from even the first year as a teacher, new graduates find themselves in a leadership role in a school because of the increase in the decentralized management of schools in Australia. These roles may include serving as a committee member or as chair of a school committee, often making decisions that impact upon the whole school. The leadership roles that have emerged in Australian schools are less a traditional model with hierarchical authority, but more a shared leadership model where decision-making is done as part of a team (Caldwell, 1993; Walker, 1994).

In addition, because of the common perception regarding the ICT expertise of young people, new graduates are being asked to take on roles within a school relating to ICT that, because of their inexperience in schools, they may not have been asked to take on in other areas for a number of years. This means that new graduates are taking on decision-making roles in this area when they may still be quite inexperienced in many aspects of schools. Leadership roles, whether of the traditional or shared leadership models, require a range of skills that few new graduates have developed.

The skills and attributes needed to be a successful leader are congruent with the goals of developing lifelong learning skills and the goals of problem based learning (PBL). Leadership is not always emphasized in PBL, but is an important aspect of this course. The goals for our students include:

- developing the ability to frame questions from complex scenarios;
- identifying and evaluating suitable resources that may help clarify a problem or be useful in developing a viable solution;
- learning to work with other team members and manage human frailties;
- learning ways to be an effective leader and manager of a team;
- preparing documentation with supporting evidence for proposal; and,

- presenting the essence of the recommendations in a professional and persuasive manner.

In addition to these generic skills the students also learn a vast amount about ICT in schools, including how to effectively include ICT in the curriculum, how to develop and manage an ICT budget, how to design and manage ICT professional development for teachers and for a school, and how to develop a three year ICT plan for a school.

## 2. CONTENT OF THE COURSE

The problems students undertake (in teams) are in the context of decision-making about ICT issues in a fictional primary school – 'Federation Primary School' (named in honour of Australia's Centenary of Federation in 2001). The school and its inhabitants are richly described on the course website. There is a description (with images) of the school, its physical layout, information about the local area, recent school history, children with special needs in the school, staff profile, about the School Council and its members, and other 'factual' information about the school. In addition there is a report from an ICT consultant about current ICT resources in the school, a link to the school's website, and a gossip sheet about the school's staff – the sort of information that would never appear in print (but would be common knowledge in the staff room). Also on the course website are links to readings and resources relevant to the problems and details about required outcomes for the problem. Students have email access to experienced teachers in schools who are in ICT leadership positions. The mentoring of our students by practising teachers is seen to be very beneficial. Through tackling the problems students develop a deep understanding of the issues relating to ICT in the school, the 'mechanics' of implementing ICT in a school, and the intricacies of managing a group of individuals, each with preferences and prejudices (such as resistance to change), strengths and weaknesses.

The course is timetabled for a two-hour block each week over two semesters (total of 18 weeks). Students explore each problem over a four-week period in the following way:

- Introduction to the problem [Week 1]. Teaching staff clarify any issues and respond to questions. Teams start on the problem.
- Student teams work on problem [Weeks 2 & 3]. Staff are available to mentor and coach teams; practising teachers are available via email.
- Student teams present their recommendations to School Council [Week 4]. Guests are invited to attend and teams also take on a role as a member of the School Council and ask questions from that point

of view (such as a parent of a child with special needs). A written document with details and data accompanies each presentation.

The content that students explore is accessed through four problems:

- ICT in the Curriculum,
- Developing an ICT Budget,
- Developing ICT Professional Development Plans, and
- Developing a Three-year ICT Plan for a School.

Nothing is taught about these topics, rather, for each problem a brief introduction to the problem is given and there is the opportunity for students to ask any questions or for clarification. The students then work in teams and decide for themselves what resources they should access to best solve the problem. Staff are available to guide students, and practising teachers are available to contact as mentors. A list of resources is provided as a starting point for the students for each problem. The four topics were decided upon through observation of the issues that many schools were experiencing and, often, struggling with. The four problems were identified as topics of ongoing importance for schools through our observations of schools and discussions with postgraduate students (many of our postgraduate students are the ICT coordinator at their school) and others. Much of the knowledge developed through these problems is also directly transferable to other aspects of a school. For example, if you know how to develop a successful ICT Budget, then you are capable of developing a budget for many other aspects of a school, just as a person who has taken into consideration the issues of developing an ICT professional development program for each staff member can transfer those skills to developing a professional development program focusing on other curriculum areas.

Throughout the course in addition to the domain knowledge that students develop there is a strong focus on developing transferable or generic skills such as information literacy skills, team skills, and leadership skills. As with all areas of learning we do not 'teach' any of these things but rather, through the course's design and implementation, we facilitate the students constructing their own knowledge in these areas.

## 2.1 Constructivist approach to learning

This course is underpinned by a constructivist approach to learning. We support students' learning through a very rich learning environment, an important component of which is the richness and authenticity of the fictional school in which the problems are set. Developing the fictional school was a large undertaking, with contributions from a small team with expertise in the area to ensure that the scenario was adequately complex and reflects a range of issues that are typical in a school. The problems set in this school require that students explore below the surface, engaging deeply with complex issues of the school environment and its personnel.

Very little, if anything, is 'taught' by staff to the students, but a great deal is learned by students who participate in this course. This style of teaching and learning is not usual in the degree program in which this course is situated, so there was much to be learned by both students and staff about this new way of learning. The shared exploration of passing full responsibility for learning to the students and the expression of concerns on both sides helps bond the group and enables further risk-taking in learning. The openness on the part of teaching staff in expressing any concerns they feel also helps model to students how even experienced teachers may feel anxious when trying out new approaches in their teaching.

## 2.2 PBL and the cognitive apprenticeship model

A PBL approach to learning that utilizes the cognitive apprenticeship model developed by Collins, Brown and Newman (1989) is implemented in this subject to support student learning and to help students develop the 'habits of mind' that will benefit them in their professional lives. Collins, Brown, and Newman's cognitive apprenticeship model (1989) of the learning environment includes:

- Modelling
  - an expert carries out the task so that students can observe and build a conceptual model of the processes required to accomplish the task.
- Coaching
  - teaching staff observe students while they carry out a task and offer hints, scaffolding, feedback, modelling, and suggest new tasks aimed at bringing the student's performance closer to expert performance.
- Scaffolding and Fading
  - scaffolding: supports teacher provides to help students perform task.
  - fading: gradual removal of supports until students are on their own.
- Articulation
  - students articulate their knowledge, reasoning, or problem-solving processes.
- Reflection
  - students compare their problem solving (and, in this case, learning) processes with those of other students, an expert, and, ultimately, their internal cognitive model of expertise.

- Exploration
    - students solve problems on their own.

Through these approaches to learning our students gain knowledge, experience, and confidence in tackling the kinds of issues that they are likely to encounter when in a school leadership role. They also develop and practice leadership skills in managing the team to prepare a detailed report and present recommendations to the School Council. Students develop content knowledge relating to ICT in schools, the generic skills expected of a graduate, an ability to frame questions from an ill-defined scenario, an understanding of how to lead a team to achieve an outcome, and confidence in their ability to handle people, new situations, and challenges.

# 3. EVALUATION

## 3.1 End of course evaluation

The End of Course Evaluation (Table 1) was developed by Samford University's PBL Initiative group (Samford University, 1999) based on a review of the PBL literature. As a pilot study, 12 students completed the survey at the conclusion of the course in 2001 and scored each question on a five-point Likert-type scale, where a response of 'Strongly Agree' scored 5 and 'Strongly Disagree' scored 1. This subject scored between 4.8 and 5.0 on a five-point scale for all questions, which indicates that this approach to learning in this subject was very successful for these students.

*Table 1.* Mean student responses to questions from the Samford PBL Initiative's End of Course Evaluation questionnaire (N=12). [Likert-type scale where 'Strongly Agree' scored 5 and 'Strongly Disagree' scored 1.]

| | Mean Score |
|---|---|
| This subject increased my ability to solve real-world problems | 4.8 |
| This subject encouraged me to consider alternatives when solving problems | 4.9 |
| This subject improved my ability to identify appropriate resources | 4.9 |
| This subject improved my ability to work effectively on a team | 5.0 |
| This subject encouraged me to take an active role in my learning | 4.9 |
| I have used knowledge & methods drawn from outside this subject to complete my subject assignments | 4.9 |

## 3.2 Student reflections

The following quotations from students indicate the value that they found in this approach to teaching and learning and how it impacted on them. Of particular note is the number of comments on changes in the student's confidence, both personally and professionally, that were a consequence of this course. Below are some comments made at the conclusion of the course.

> *IT in Primary Schools enabled me to develop as an individual and professional immensely...*
>
> *I thoroughly enjoyed the challenges presented within the subject and have grown a great deal in my professionalism and attitude toward teaching.*

These comments from students' reflective writing indicate the very powerful outcomes when using PBL and the cognitive apprenticeship model are applied as part of the learning process.

At the conclusion of the course students were also asked (among other things) to reflect on the most important things they had learnt in the course. In addition to numerous comments about content knowledge developed, many students commented on the independent learning skills they had developed. The following are some quotations from student reflections:

> *At the beginning, I found that researching for the problems was a real struggle for me but as we did more problems, I gained a lot of independence and confidence in myself and my own capabilities.*
>
> *PBL has also helped me develop research skills which have not only benefited me for this subject but also in other subjects throughout my course and I am sure that these skills will be utilised throughout my entire career.*

As can be seen, students gain so much more than content knowledge when this approach to learning is used. It is believed that, in particular in an area such as ICT where content knowledge is ephemeral, these skills that make a successful leader and life long learner are of great value and will allow students to continue to update and extend their content knowledge.

## 4. CONCLUSIONS

Problem based learning and the cognitive apprenticeship model applied in this course allow our students to analyse authentic situations in the fictional school and consider alternative solutions while working in a team. It is believed that this approach to learning is very suitable for developing a deep understanding of issues, in this case about ICT in a school, and for developing the skills needed to take on an ICT leadership role in a school. Outside the walls of the university new graduates need to be able to continue to learn, to learn from others, to observe how successful role models behave in achieving their goals, and to be reflective about their own practices, both in and out of the classroom. The approach to learning in this subject prepares students for the ongoing learning as professionals as this is how the students learn within the subject. Another very pleasing outcome is that the students are navigators of their own learning. This sense of empowerment is an important aspect for lifelong learning for continued professional development. The approach to learning used in this course expects, indeed demands, that students take responsibility for their own learning and that they hone and refine the skills that will make them successful education professionals and leaders in ICT in tomorrow's schools.

## 5. REFERENCES

Caldwell, B. (1993). *Decentralising the Management of Australian Schools: A Discussion Paper*. Melbourne: National Industry Education Forum.

Collins, A., Brown, J. S. & Newman, S. E. (1989). Cognitive apprenticeship: Teaching the craft of reading, writing, and mathematics. In L. B. Resnick (Ed.), *Knowing, Learning, and Instruction: Essays in Honor of Robert Glaser* (pp.453-494). Hillsdale, NJ: Erlbaum.

Finkle, S. L. & Torp, L. L. (1995). *Introductory Documents*. Aurora, IL: Illinois Math and Science Academy.

Stover, D. (1998). Problem-based learning: Redefining self-directed instruction and learning. *The Forum, 7*(1), 9-10.

Samford University (1999). *End of Course Evaluation. Samford PBL Initiative.* Retrieved October 11, 2002 from http://www.samford.edu/pbl/ece.html

Walker, A. (1994). Teams in schools: Looking below the surface. *International Journal of Educational Management, 8*(7), 38-44.

# The Effects of Attitudes, Pedagogical Practices and Teachers' Roles on the Incorporation of ICT into the School Curriculum

Margaret Cox
*King's College London, Franklin-Wilkins Building, Stamford St, London SE1 9NN, mj.cox@kcl.ac.uk*

**Abstract:** Research conducted at King's College into the attitudes of teachers towards ICT and their motivation for using it in their teaching has shown that these are influenced by their own pedagogies. However when ICT is involved a conflict may arise. This conflict derives from preconceived ideas about what is expected of teachers when using ICT in their lessons, and how this may be alien to their most comfortable pedagogical practices applied in more traditional non-ICT class activities. Attitude theories and empirical evidence lead to an important research question: do the attitudes of the teachers towards ICT, and the types of ICT use, affect the roles they adopt and their pedagogical practices when persuaded to use ICT in the classroom? The paper will present evidence from previous research of the relationship between the types of ICT use, teachers' attitudes to using ICT and the effects on their pedagogical practices.

## 1. FACTORS AFFECTING THE INTEGRATION OF ICT IN THE CLASSROOM

Although much of the earlier research evidence (Cox, 1993a, 1993b; Harrison et al., 2002; Preston et al., 2000; Watson, 1993) showed that one reason for the reluctance of teachers to use ICT was insufficient or inappropriate training, research into the effectiveness of teacher training has shown that many courses did not in fact lead to a change in teachers' practices nor to sustained uptake of ICT in their schools (e.g. see Bliss et al., 1986; Hay McBer, 2000; Passey & Samways, 1997). This is often because teachers do not have a clear and coherent sense of the reasons for educational change (Desforges, 1995; Fullan, 1991; Somekh & Davies, 1991; Underwood, 1988). Additionally, according to the theory of planned behaviour (Ajzen, 1991), human behaviour, including the use of ICT, is guided by beliefs about: the likely outcomes of the behaviour; the normative expectations of others; and the presence of factors that may facilitate or impede the performance. It is also influenced by teachers' perceptions of what ICT means as explained by the definition given in 1.1. The very nature of the ICT medium itself will influence the other major factors affecting the successful integration by teachers.

A very important aspect of ICT regarding how it might influence pedagogical practices and teachers' roles, which is often not addressed by teachers or researchers, is the representations which different ICT environments present to the teacher and the learner. Extensive research by Mellar et al. (1994) and Cheng et al. (2001) has provided a sound theoretical basis for further research into the effects of different ICT representations in education. For example, Cheng et al.'s work into recodifying knowledge has produced a representational epistemology (REEP) which addresses the fundamental roles and functions that representational systems have regarding teaching and learning. In order that teachers can use different ICT environments to teach their pupils they need to understand the scope and meaning of different ICT representational systems (Ainsworth, Bibby & Wood, 1997). For example, in the case of many science topics, using computer graphics would require the teacher to understand the effects of switching from syntactic rule governed notational systems to diagrammatic models. A simple example of this would be when teachers use spreadsheets for modelling in primary schools. At the age of 10 pupils may be able to understand the purpose and structure of a simple table but not the concept of a spreadsheet cell being able to 'contain' text, or a single number, let alone an equation (Cox, 2003). There is an extensive psychology research literature about the problems with different representational systems and the effects they have on students' learning and therefore on teachers' roles.

It is clear from the evidence and discussion presented above that the integration of ICT by teachers and the consequent variation in their teaching roles will be strongly influenced by their attitudes towards ICT and their own pedagogical beliefs. Theories relating to these two factors, which have been developed and evaluated, are discussed in the following sections.

## 1.1 Attitude Theories and Attitudes of Teachers to Using ICT

The theory of planned behaviour, based on the theory of reasoned action was developed by Ajzen and colleagues (1988). According to this theory, shown in Figure 1, behaviour is determined by an intention to engage in that behaviour. In turn, intention to perform certain behaviours is affected by three factors: attitude towards the behaviour, subjective norm and perceived behavioural control.

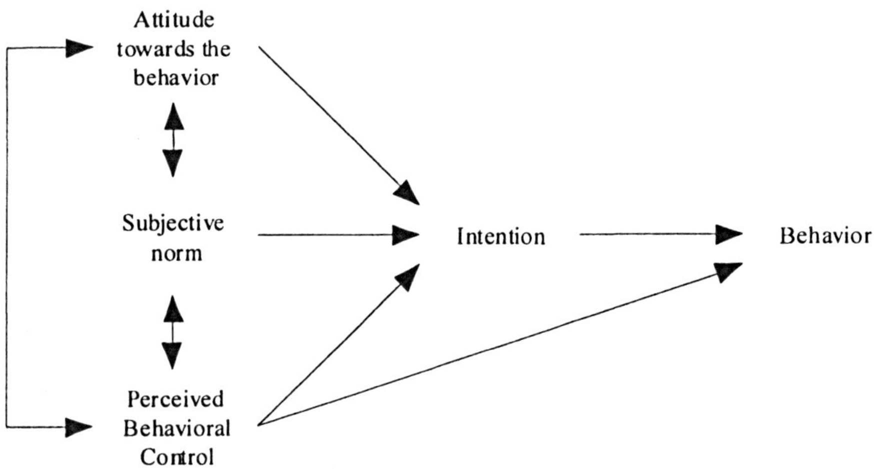


*Figure 1.* Theory of planned behaviour (Ajzen, 1988, p. 133)

Applying this theory to the motivation of teachers to use ICT, the use of ICT in teaching will depend upon the teachers' *intention* to use ICT. This will, in turn, be influenced by the teachers' *attitudes* towards using ICT in their teaching. In relation to teachers, these attitudes might include perceptions concerning the effects on their role as a teacher, the impact on pupils' motivation, the impact on the teachers' influence in the school, how the behaviour might affect other teachers and so on. Furthermore, as was explained above, we might expect that teachers' attitudes towards using ICT will be influenced by their perceptions of what ICT means, the information they have about the value of ICT, their previous experiences and expertise in using ICT and the expectation that it will contribute to pupils' learning.

The second component included in the theory of planned behaviour, *subjective norm*, represents the perceived social pressures experienced by the individual, i.e. people's beliefs concerning others' attitudes towards the behaviour and the perceived importance of these attitudes. Regarding ICT uptake by teachers, this would be the teachers' perception of the social pressure to use or not use ICT. In particular, they may be influenced by the views of their colleagues, pupils, parents or governors. In many previous studies in other domains, attitudes have proved to be more influential than subjective norms (Ajzen, 1988). However, in the case of using ICT in one's teaching, because of the immense and growing pressures from educational reforms, parents, the media, and so on, it is likely that subjective norm will have a greater impact on teachers' use of ICT.

The *perceived behavioural control* component refers to the extent to which teachers believe themselves to be capable of using ICT in their teaching. This "is assumed to reflect past experience as well as anticipated impediments and obstacles" (Ajzen, 1988, p. 132). In relation to the use of ICT in teaching, teachers may feel incapable of using ICT for a number of reasons. For example, they may lack confidence in their ICT skills to be able to help pupils in a lesson, they may not be able to adjust their teaching style to accommodate ICT, or they may not know how to use ICT effectively in their subject.

Davis, Bagozzi and Warshaw (1989) developed a "theory of action relating to reasons", technology acceptance model, based on the work of Fishbein and Ajzen, to explain why some people use computers and others do not. According to their model, shown in Figure 2, the *perceived usefulness* and *ease of use* of the technology will affect a person's *attitude* towards using it. Furthermore, these factors are influenced by *external variables*. As with Fishbein and Ajzen's model, attitudes affect *intentions* to use ICT, which, in turn, affect *actual use*. Davis, Bagozzi and Warshaw tested this model with 107 adult users, who had been using a managerial system for 14 weeks. They found that people's computer use was predicted by their intentions to use it and that perceived usefulness was also strongly linked to these intentions.

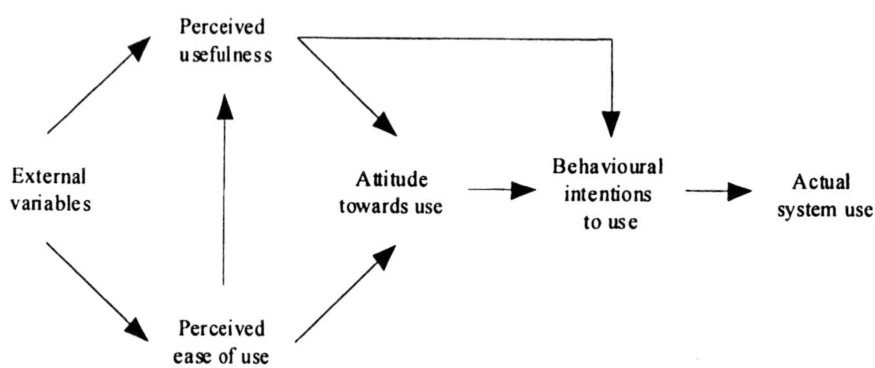


*Figure 2.* The technology acceptance model (Davis, Bagozzi & Warshaw, 1989)

There is a growing body of research evidence showing that ICT makes teachers' lessons more interesting, more enjoyable, and more important to the learners (Preston, Cox & Cox, 2000) and increases self-confidence (Gardner, Dukes & Discenza, 1993). Using evidence from previous research, a number of factors have been identified by Preston, Cox and Cox (2000) that relate to each of the components of this model which are explained below.

### 1.1.1 External variables

In Davis, Bagozzi and Warshaw's model, the external variables represent the many influences on people that may affect their attitudes and behaviour. For teachers these influences may include:

- requirements of the national curriculum or national guidelines;
- local education authority policies;
- school policies on using ICT;
- responsibilities of the teacher;
- training received;
- pressure from parents and pupils;
- opinions of colleagues;
- membership of professional organisations;
- changes in society, including the rapid growth in the use of the Internet and ICT in general.

Other factors, such as the New Opportunities Fund for the training of teachers in the UK and the Teacher Training Agency's requirements concerning the ICT skills for new teachers in England and Wales (TTA, 1999), may have an impact on teachers' ICT use in the future.

### 1.1.2 Perceived ease of use

There are a number of factors that have been identified by previous studies that relate to the perceived ease of use of ICT. Watson (1993), Loveless (2001), Cox (2003) and other researchers have shown that teachers need a wide range of skills and competencies in order to find it easy to use ICT. For example, previous research has shown that teachers who felt confident in using ICT perceived it as being easier to use in their lessons, whereas teachers who experienced technical difficulties using a particular piece of software perceived using ICT in their lessons as being more difficult (Cox, 1997a; Preston, Cox & Cox, 2000; Watson, 1993). The factors identified by previous research relating to perceived ease of use of ICT include:

- ability to use software/hardware;
- confidence in using ICT;

- ability to control the class;
- ability to think of new lesson ideas;
- perceived impact on the content of lessons.

### 1.1.3 Perceived usefulness

If teachers perceive ICT to be useful to them, their teaching and their pupils' learning, then according to the evidence of previous studies (e.g. see Gardner, Dukes & Discenza, 1993; Preston, Cox & Cox, 2000) they are more likely to have a positive attitude to the use of ICT in the classroom. Preston, Cox and Cox (2000) identified a number of factors that relate to teachers' perceived usefulness of ICT:

- whether or not the lessons are made more interesting, enjoyable, or diverse for the teacher;
- whether or not the lessons are made more difficult for the teacher;
- impact on the presentation of materials for lessons;
- perceived contribution to administrative tasks;
- impact on pupils' motivation and learning;
- impact on the teacher's confidence;
- impact on the teacher's prestige;
- perceived effect on career prospects.

As with perceived ease of use, some of these factors add to the perceived usefulness of ICT whereas others detract from it. For example, if a teacher feels that using ICT makes lessons more difficult, then the perceived usefulness will be reduced, whereas if a teacher feels that it makes it more interesting, perceived usefulness will be increased. Teachers' attitudes to many of these factors will depend upon how easy they perceive using ICT to be, both for personal use and for use in teaching. This in turn will be influenced by their perceptions of ICT and how this might affect their ability to use it in their teaching. According to Davis et al's model, the greater the perceived usefulness and perceived ease of use are, the more positive the attitudes of teachers will be to the use of ICT and consequently, the more likely they will be to use ICT in their teaching.

Preston, Cox and Cox's study (2000), which was based on these theories, obtained statistical evidence of the relationship between the ICT abilities of the teacher and their perceptions of the value of ICT to pupils' learning, although they also found that the range of ICT uses by most of the teachers in the study was very limited and did not cover all of those included in definitions of ICT.

The models described above are the most widely used to measure the effects of attitudes on teachers' uptake and uses of ICT, but as yet there is little reported research which delves into the attitudes of teachers to specific uses of ICT as defined in 1.1 above. Extensive empirical evidence has supported these theories described above, and shown that teachers who have taken up the use of ICT in teaching are frequently motivated by their positive perceptions of the value of ICT to their pupils and to their own professional development. On the other hand, for teachers who are reluctant to use ICT, factors such as insufficient resources, lack of confidence and inability to adopt new practices have been identified as important reasons for non-adoption. The evidence from research into the effects of teachers' attitudes on ICT uptake and use discussed above clearly indicates that teachers uses of ICT will also be affected by their perceptions of the pedagogical practices required to integrate ICT appropriately in their teaching.

## 1.2 Theories of Pedagogy and Teachers Practices

The research evidence that has been referred to above into the attitudes of teachers towards ICT and their motivation for using it in their teaching, has shown that these are influenced by their own pedagogies yet when ICT is involved a conflict arises. This conflict arises from preconceived ideas about what is expected of teachers when using ICT in their lessons, and how this may be alien to their most comfortable pedagogical practices applied in more traditional non-ICT class activities, therefore teachers' pedagogical reasoning plays an important part in determining whether or not a teacher will use ICT and the roles he or she may adopt when using ICT.

### 1.2.1 Theories of pedagogy

A review of the literature on how teachers' experiences affect their theoretical knowledge of teaching by Desforges (1995) has shown that the effectiveness of teachers adopting new methods in their teaching is dependent on their attitudes towards improving their professional development, their knowledge of the effects of their teaching on their pupils' learning and the type and extent of teacher training they had experienced. Previous research has also shown that the way in which teachers use ICT depends upon their perceptions of the role and value of ICT and on their other teacher pedagogies (Cox 1997a; Watson, 1993).

Models of teachers' pedagogies have been examined by Loveless (2001) including the model developed by Leach and Moon of professional knowledge (Leach & Moon, 2000) shown in Figure 3.

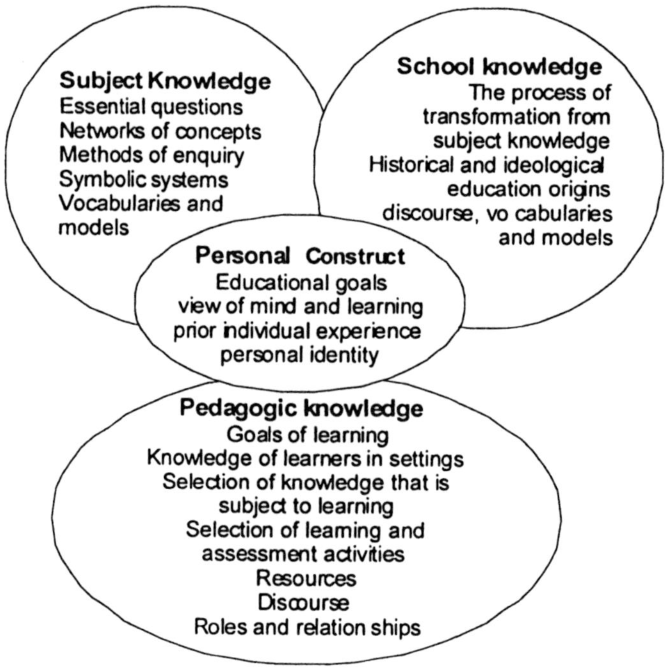


*Figure 3.* Leach and Moon's model of professional knowledge (Loveless, 2001, p. 33)

Loveless supports the arguments of Leach and Moon that "pedagogy can be described as an expression of teachers' professional knowledge in which a number of dimensions interact within a broader socio-cultural context for learning and practice" (Loveless, 2001, p. 30). This model builds on the work of Shulman (1987) whose framework acknowledges the interaction between pedagogic knowledge, subject knowledge, school knowledge and teacher's personal beliefs. Shulman focuses on knowledge rather than ideas and beliefs but, in addition to the large body of attitudinal evidence referred to above, there is evidence that teachers' ideas, beliefs and values may also influence practice (Fang, 1996). These ideas, beliefs and values in turn are influenced as explained earlier by teachers' attitudes, their subjective norms and perceived behavioural control (see Section 1.1 above).

An examination by Webb (2002) of pedagogical reasoning relating to the teaching of ICT as a subject, and the research conducted by Loveless (2001) into teachers' pedagogical practices support the need for researchers and practitioners to distinguish the difference between pedagogy and practice. The conclusion from investigations into pedagogical reasoning confirms the attitudinal psychological research and extensive educational work conducted by Fullan (1991), Desforges (1995) and others that the ability of teachers to adopt ICT in their teaching will depend on a complex range of interrelated factors and will vary according to the types of ICT use being adopted, the subject knowledge of the teacher and the pedagogic knowledge relating to ICT. This applies not only to classroom practices but also to methods of pupil assessment, progression and the interrelationship with other educational experiences and in other educational settings. There have been many research studies investigating the actual practices of teachers when using ICT but most of them have not been able to investigate all these factors for one group of teachers.

### 1.2.2 Pedagogical practices

There are many publications listing different pedagogical practices when using ICT (see, for example, Loveless, 2001; QCA, 2001; TTA, 1999; Webb, 2002). It has been established by these that teachers' practices, including the roles they adopt, will depend upon the following:

- Definitions of pedagogies specifically associated with ICT;
- The types of ICT, as explained in the definition given earlier in 1.1.
- The ICT representations, which are produced by different ICT environments, will be influenced by the hardware as well as the software.
- The level of use of ICT, since this will also influence the pedagogical practices of the teachers; a useful framework for categorisation of level of use is Loucke's Level of Use Model (Loucks et al., 1998), which could be modified for different types of ICT.

The most basic pedagogical practices associated with using ICT are:

- The selection of the ICT resource;
- The organisation of the ICT resource;
- The planning of the lesson;
- The organisation of the lesson, including lesson structure and pupil grouping;
- Teacher interventions, roles adopted;
- Assessment of the pupils;
- Follow up activities.

If we consider the models of pedagogy referred to above and the empirical evidence presented earlier, then these practices listed above are often achieved inadequately because of the limited pedagogical knowledge of the teacher relevant to using ICT. Webb (2002) identified a range of pedagogical issues, shown in Table 1.

*Table 1.* Issues affecting knowledge transformation in the ICT teaching community (from Webb, 2002, p. xxx)

| Categories of Knowledge | Issues affecting availability of knowledge in the ICT teaching community |
|---|---|
| Current knowledge | Some ICT teachers have inadequate content knowledge. Some ICT teachers are expected to comprehend not only content knowledge for ICT but also how this knowledge relates to the content of other subjects so that both can be taught in an integrated way. |
| Pedagogical content knowledge | Less well-defined for ICT than for other subjects. |
| General pedagogical knowledge | Subject specific interpretations are less well-defined for ICT than for other subjects. |
| Knowledge of learners | Limited research base of students' problems and misconceptions in ICT. |
| Curriculum knowledge | The collective curriculum knowledge of ICT teachers is less extensive than for other subjects. The importance of using software in ICT makes curriculum knowledge more complex for ICT than for other subject areas. The scope and possibilities are changing rapidly as technology develops. |

Although these issues have been identified for ICT teachers rather than teachers using ICT in other subjects, they have been shown by many previous research studies, referred to earlier, to apply equally to teachers attempting to use ICT in their teaching. For example, if we consider the use of computer based modelling in physics, then many physics teachers have insufficient knowledge of the advanced physics content which could be taught through computer based modelling at school level, and often have very limited pedagogic knowledge of how computer based modelling could be included in the physics curriculum (Cox, 2000).

## 2. THE EFFECTS OF TEACHERS' ATTITUDES AND PEDAGOGICAL KNOWLEDGE AND PRACTICES ON THE ROLE OF THE TEACHER

Research into the effects of ICT and attainment and the uptake of ICT in education has shown that teachers' pedagogy significantly influences the way in which ICT is used in the classroom and therefore how this will affect pupils' learning. For example, an earlier study by Underwood (1988), who investigated the pedagogies of teachers using information handling packages in twelve primary schools and six secondary schools, found that many teachers believed that when using ICT in their lessons, their role would be more one of classroom manager and facilitator in the learning situation, than the pivotal focus of the classroom. Evidence of this teacher expectation, of withdrawing from a leading role in the classroom when using ICT, has been reported earlier by several researchers including Hoyles, Sutherland and Evans (1986), who found that when pupils were given the task of using LOGO in mathematics, the teachers expected to withdraw from guiding the children in selecting the learning tasks. They found there to be considerable gains in terms of motivation from the pupils deciding upon their own activities. Recent research has confirmed that this is still the practice in many classrooms, although there is now a rapidly growing practice of teachers communicating with pupils through the Internet and thereby engaging with the pupils on a more individual basis, sometimes more frequently than in a traditional classroom (Rees, 2002).

These studies and the empirical evidence presented earlier show that the role of "guide alongside" adopted by some teachers takes no account of the ways in which the ICT learning experience may differ from what is expected due to different ICT representations, therefore teachers may need to adopt many different types of roles according to the types of ICT use, curriculum content and so on. This argument assumes that the nature of the ICT activity should influence the role of the teacher. However the research into attitudes and teachers' practices discussed earlier shows that it may be that many teachers are able to only adopt only certain roles to accommodate their perceptions of ICT and confidence (or lack of it) with particular applications. In other words, the 'guide alongside' role may be adopted by teachers who have little or no idea of what the ICT environment is teaching the pupils. All the evidence presented in this paper and elsewhere clearly supports the argument that teachers need to adopt a very strong leadership role with pupils using ICT in order that pupils can benefit from the experience.

# 3. CONCLUSION

In summary, to address the question: "Do attitudes, pedagogical practices and teachers' roles need to change to enable them to incorporate ICT in the curriculum?" the review of attitudinal and pedagogical research has raised a number of issues that need further research. The evidence from the literature has shown that:

- A positive attitude towards using ICT may depend upon the types of ICT which the teacher feels confident to use with pupils, therefore further research into teachers' attitudes and behaviour involving teachers using a wide range of ICT types needs to be conducted;

- A negative attitude towards using ICT can be caused by a lack of understanding of the pedagogical theories relating to ICT;
- The types of ICT being used may influence the roles which teachers adopt in the classroom which in turn are affected by the teachers' pedagogies;
- Teachers pedagogies may be varied and inconsistent when using ICT, often due to a lack of understanding of the role and function of the ICT activity;
- There can be a conflict between teachers maintaining a positive attitude towards using ICT in their teaching, and pressures to extend the range and uses of ICT in the curriculum.

Evidence from this review of previous research studies shows that teachers' positive attitudes towards ICT in their teaching often exist when the uses of ICT are very limited. Therefore there may be an important relationship needing further investigation, which is the effects of the types of ICT use on teachers' attitudes and practices, and vice-versa. A consequence of this relationship is that for teachers who are whole heartedly adopting the 'guide alongside' approach to using ICT in their lessons, the ICT uses may be of limited educational value and very often all the previous good pedagogical practices go out of the window.

## REFERENCES


Ainsworth, S. A., Bibby, P. & Wood, D. J. (1997). Information technology and multiple representations: new opportunities – new problems. *Journal of information Technology in Teacher Education*, *6*(1), 93-104.

Ajzen, I. (1988). *Attitudes, Personality and Behavior*. Milton Keynes: Open University Press.

Ajzen, I. (1991). The theory of planned behavior. *Organizational Behavior and Human Decision Processes*, *50*, 179-211.

Bliss, J., Chandra, P. A. J. & Cox, M. J. (1988). Introducing computers into a school – Management issues. *Computers and Education*, 12(1), 57-61.

Cheng, P. C-H., Lowe, R. K., & Scaife, M. (2001). Cognitive science approaches to diagrammatic representations. *Artificial Intelligence Review*, *15*(1-2), 79-94.

Cox, M. J. (1993a). Information technology resourcing and use. In D. M. Watson (Ed.), *Impact – An Evaluation of the Impact of the Information Technology on Children's Achievements in Primary and Secondary Schools*. London: King's College.

Cox, M. J. (1993b). Technology enriched school project – The impact of information technology on children's learning. *Computers and Education*, *21*(1/2), 41-49.

Cox, M. J. (1997a). Identification of the changes in attitude and pedagogical practices needed to enable teachers to use information technology in the school curriculum. In D. Passey & B. Samways (Eds), *Information Technology Supporting Change through Teacher Education* (pp. 87-94). IFIP. London: Chapman & Hall.

Cox, M. J. (2000). Information and communication technologies: Their role and value for science education. In M. Monk & J. Osborne (Eds), *Good Practice in Science Teaching – What Research Has to Say*. UK: Open University Press.

Cox, M. J. (2003, in press). How do we know that ICT has an impact on children's learning? A review of techniques and methods to measure changes in pupils' learning promoted by the use of ICT. In G. Marshall & J. Katz (Eds), *Selected Proceedings from Learning with Technologies in School, Home and Community*. Massachusetts: Kluwer.

Davis, F. D., Bagozzi, R. P. & Warshaw, P. R. (1989). User acceptance of computer technology: A comparison of two theoretical models. *Management Science*, *35*(8), 982-1003.

Desforges, C. (1995). How does experience affect theoretical knowledge for teaching? *Learning and Instruction*, *5*, 385-400.

Fang, Z. (1996). A review of research on teacher beliefs and practices. *Educational Research*, *38*(1), Spring.

Fullan, M. G. (1991). *The New Meaning of Educational Change*. London: Cassell.

Gardner, D. G., Dukes, R. L. & Discenza, R. (1993). Computer use, self-confidence, and attitudes: A causal analysis. *Computers in Human Behaviour*, *9*, 427-440.

Harrison, C., Comber, C., Fisher, T., Haw, K., Lunzer, E., McFarlane, A., Mavers, D., Scrimshaw, P., Somekh, B. & Wating, R. (2002). *ImpaCT2: The Impact of Information and Communication Technologies on Pupil Learning and Attainment. BECTa and DfES*. London: DfES Publications.

Hay McBer (2000). *Research into Teacher Effectiveness: A Model of Teacher Effectiveness. Report to the Department for Education and Employment – June*. London: DfEE.

Hoyles, C., Sutherland, R. & Evans, J. (1986). Using LOGO in the mathematics classroom. What are the implications of pupil devised goals? *Computers and Education*, *10*(1), 61-72.

Leach, J. & Moon, B. (2000). *Pedagogy, ICT and Teachers' Professional Knowledge*. Paper presented at the British Educational Research Association Conference, Cardiff, September.

Loveless, A. (2001). An interaction between primary teachers' perceptions of information and communication technology (ICT) and their pedagogy. PhD Thesis, Brighton University.

Mellar, H., Bliss, J., Boohan, R., Ogborn, J. & Tompsett, C. (Eds) (1994). *Learning with Artificial Worlds: Computer Based Modelling in the Curriculum*. London: The Falmer Press.

OFSTED (1995). *Information Technology: A Review of Inspection Findings 1993/94*. London: HMSO.

Passey, D. & Samways, B. (Eds) (1997). *Information Technology Supporting Change through Teacher Education* (pp. 87-94). IFIP. London: Chapman & Hall.

Preston, C., Cox, M. J. & Cox, K. M. J. (2000). *Teachers as Innovators: An Evaluation of the Motivation of Teachers to Use Information and Communications Technologies*. London: King's College/Mirandanet.

QCA (2001). *Information and Communication Technology: A Scheme of Work for Key Stage 3*. London: Qualifications and Curriculum Authority.

Rees, R. (2002). Second year teacher candidates reflect on information technology in Ontario secondary schools: How it is being used and the challenges it presents. *Technology, Pedagogy and Education*, 2, 143-160.

Shulman, L. (1987). Knowledge and teaching: Foundations of the new reform. *Harvard Educational Review*,57, 1-22.

Somekh, B. & Davies, R. (1991). Towards a pedagogy for information technology. *The Curriculum Journal*, *2*(2), 153-170.

Teacher Training Agency (1999). *The Use of ICT in Subject Teaching: Expected Outcomes for Teachers in England, Wales and Northern Ireland.* London: Teacher Training Agency.

Underwood, J. (1988). An investigation of teacher intents and classroom outcomes in the use of information-handling packages. *Computers and Education, 12*(1), 91-100.

Watson, D. M (Ed.) (1993). *The ImpacT Report – An Evaluation of the Impact of Information Technology on Children's Achievements in Primary and Secondary Schools.* London: King's College.

Watson, D. & Tinsley, D. (1995). *Integrating Information Technology into Education.* London: Chapman & Hall.

Webb, M. E. (2002). Pedagogical reasoning: issues and solutions for the teaching and learning of ICT in secondary schools. *Education and Information Technologies*, *7*(2), 237-256.

# From Facilitator to Knowledge-Builder: A New Role for the Teacher of the Future

Elizabeth Hartnell-Young
*Centre for Applied Educational Research, The University of Melbourne, Victoria 3010, Australia, ehy@results.aust.com*

## 1. BACKGROUND

The influence of constructivism and the spread of information and communication technologies (ICT) in classrooms are both expected to change the role of the teacher in the classroom from the expert dispensing knowledge to the facilitator of student learning (Dwyer, Ringstaff, & Sandholtz, 1991; Hadley & Sheingold, 1993; Ravitz, Becker, & Wong, 2000). In such a student-centred classroom the teacher is expected to understand individual learning styles and appropriate means to scaffold learning while social constructivism emphasises student collaboration and interaction with the learning context. The notion of the teacher as facilitator in a student-centred classroom may have been useful to progress pedagogical thinking, but limits attempts to create a knowledge-building community which requires social relations to be reconceptualised. Some suggest that the focus should be on learning-centredness (Marzano, 1992) and many teachers using ICT are happy to acknowledge that they are themselves learners rather than experts. Further, economic and educational imperatives, and the frequent complaint that teachers have "no time" now require that teachers engage in a community of practice where their own learning activities are purposeful and authentic because they are situated within their work (Brown & Campione, 1994; Lave & Wenger, 1994). This community can include teachers and students as co-learners, while technology as a communication medium opens up the possibility for collaboration within and across schools and with other learning partners locally and internationally. (The terms "learning" and "knowledge-building" are used with similar meaning in this paper.)

Scardamalia and Bereiter (2002) argue that where a collaborative knowledge-building approach is adopted, the work to be done in schools becomes the construction of collective knowledge and students become participants in a learning organisation. Similarly it seems that teachers working in a learning organisation cannot operate in isolation, but must model collaboration with other teachers as they reflect on and improve their practice and develop new knowledge. As Hargreaves (1999) suggests, the knowledge teachers bring and create should be better managed to help schools realise their intellectual capital. This paper describes some current examples of teachers and students working together in knowledge-building activities in schools.

## 2. THE SILT PROJECT

The Successful Integration of Learning Technology (SILT) Project consists of qualitative studies over two years in 28 selected state primary and secondary schools in Victoria, Australia. One study aimed to identify the roles and behaviours of teachers using computers in the curriculum areas of Science and Study of Society and Environment (SOSE) in order to assist in future professional development. Teachers used computers in classrooms and computer labs and most had a personal laptop computer subsidised by the Department of Education & Training. Data were gained from conversations with teachers and principals and classroom observations. Transcripts were given to teachers not only for checking but to encourage the documenting of reflective thought. Eight teachers in two primary schools also provided electronic reflective learning journals, which they kept as part of a collaborative classroom project they devised themselves.

Most teachers using computers espoused and implemented a facilitating role in the classroom, generally interacting with individuals and small groups rather than whole classes in both primary and secondary schools. They happily took on the role of learner from, or co-learner with, their students, particularly in relation to learning technical skills, as this teacher describes:

> I find it really stimulating that the students then become my teacher, they teach me things and that's what I found very beneficial. That relationship between the teacher as the provider of the information, student as the person who absorbs it or learns it, then that's completely changed. Everyone is just a learner and just engaging in some sort of exchange, which I find excellent and I think probably some of the most interesting things I have learned about using computers, given that I would describe myself as an early novice in the area, have been things that kids have shown me (secondary teacher).

Some of the teachers in the project had moved beyond the individual facilitator role towards knowledge-building in collaboration with others. These teachers and their students engaged in group-work within the school and communicated with external participants in other schools, industry or the wider community over several weeks. One SOSE class in a city secondary school communicated with a country class to share information about daily life, using email, chat and a face-to-face visit to build up a picture of contrasting environments which was presented on a website. However the potential of this project for knowledge-building was limited as it involved only one teacher in each school. In several schools, teams of teachers and students in Science and SOSE used video conferencing, email and telephone and also engaged in face-to-face interaction to undertake research projects and produce quality products. From planning to realisation, these projects enabled teachers to immerse themselves in continuous professional learning activities as part of their daily work. Two schools using video-conferencing within a mentoring framework for school leaders, teachers and students were able to see the actual operation of classrooms each other's school, stretching their bandwidth capacity to breaking point, but assisting in building a community of practice amongst teachers.

Haslam (2002) found that involvement in these SILT-supported projects gave teachers the confidence to share their learning, an essential aspect of knowledge-building:

> I had a great deal of fun as well as professional development doing this, presenting at a conference, videoing my students (secondary teacher).

She also found that students reported enhanced learning outcomes:

> We were more focused, interested, it sort of made us stay keen, flat out on this work. Pretty much involved all the time. It was probably [pause] doing it this way sticks in your mind better, seems to, this way we got to get more involved. Like I just remember it better. I read the information and trying to put it down into your own little thing, to explain to others that made it stick in my mind better. It is harder work. Perhaps this is not a bad point (secondary student).

The knowledge-building teachers were facilitators, but they displayed additional characteristics that had developed as part of team or school culture over a period of years. They valued social connectedness between people, talked about learning processes with their colleagues as well as their students, planned activities together, linked curriculum areas, invited others into their classrooms, collaborated with and mentored teachers within and across schools, documented their experience in journals, recorded student activities, collected data in their classrooms, participated in email discussion and presented at conferences. The knowledge-building schools were led by principals who displayed leadership in learning and in applications of technology, supported and encouraged the teachers and raised expectations that teachers and students share knowledge. This was modelled from the classroom to a wider scale:

> There is an expectation in this classroom that no knowledge is sacred, everyone shares and if someone moves from one group they'll wander around the classroom and pick up an idea.... kids will come along and say, well why aren't we doing this, why aren't we trying it that way, so we have a go and if it works it's to our pool of knowledge and if it doesn't, we scrap it (primary teacher).

While all the teachers saw themselves as learners, the knowledge-builders had moved beyond learning technical skills from students to regaining a role as mediators of student learning. They used technology to support a range of purposes and made time to reflect on their practice with colleagues:

> I think you have to really reflect on what you are doing and why you are doing it, to make it important, make it worthwhile for yourself and for the people that you are teaching. When you have made those connections and reflections for yourself, it becomes real, like someone discusses it with you, a colleague talks to you about it and you have a real sense of moving in the same direction (primary teacher).

## 3. CONCLUSION

The transition from facilitator to knowledge-builder implies that the teacher acts within a community of practice, which requires collective will and supportive leadership. Where participants take risks, reflect on experiences and share their learning, they build organisational knowledge as well as developing individual skill. The knowledge-building role was well-developed in the primary schools in this study, where collaborative planning, reflective journal-writing and video-conferencing were used by teaching teams. In the secondary schools teachers were experimenting with new applications of technology but were generally not reflecting systematically on their practice or their role, nor collaborating in their daily work, due in part to the pressures they perceived to meet their individual obligations of teaching a range of classes. The projects described in this paper indicate that purposeful, collaborative and supported curriculum projects provide a means of professional development for knowledge-building that can occur through teachers' daily work.

# REFERENCES


Brown, A. & Campione, J. (1994). Guided discovery in a community of learners. In K. McGilly (Ed.), *Classroom Lessons: Integrating Cognitive Theory and Classroom Practice*. Cambridge, MA: MIT Press/Bradford Books.

Dwyer, D., Ringstaff, C. & Sandholtz, J. (1991). Changes in teachers' beliefs and practices in technology-rich classrooms. *Educational Leadership, 48*(8), 45–53.

Hadley, M. & Sheingold, K. (1993). Commonalities and distinctive patterns in teachers' integration of computers. *American Journal of Education, 101*(3), 261–315.

Hargreaves, D. (1999). The knowledge-creating school. *British Journal of Educational Studies, 47*(2), 122-144.

Haslam, F. (2002). *The Apprenticeship Project: Practicability and Value.* Paper presented at the NavCon 2K2 Conference, July, Christchurch, NZ.

Lave, J. & Wenger, E. (1994). *Situated Learning: Legitimate Peripheral Participation.* Cambridge: Cambridge University Press.

Marzano, R. (1992). *A Different Kind of Classroom.* Alexandria, VA: Association for Supervision & Curriculum Development.

Ravitz, J., Becker, H. & Wong, Y. (2000). *Teaching, Learning and Computing: 1998 National Survey. Report #4.* University of California, Irvine: Centre for Research on Information Technology and Organizations.

Scardamalia, M. & Bereiter, C. (2002). Schools as knowledge building organizations. In D. Keating & C. Hertzman (Eds), *Today's Children: Tomorrow's Society: The Developmental Health and Wealth of Organizations*. New York: Guildford.

# Teacher Empowerment and Minimalist Design

Wing-Wah Ki, Albert Ling-Sung Chung and Ho-Cheong Lam
*Faculty of Education, University of Hong Kong, Pokfulam Road, Hong Kong, hraskww@hkucc.hku.hk*

## 1. INTRODUCTION

Although the use of ICT in education has been strongly advocated with a vision of bringing a paradigm shift to education, observational studies and surveys in general indicate that the actual impact of ICT on classroom teaching and learning has been limited. This paper attempts to provide a discussion of the underlying problems, and reports an experience which seems to indicate how the situation may differ if teacher empowerment is taken as a primary concern in the development of ICT in education.

## 2. TEACHER DISEMPOWERMENT

Classroom observation studies provide clear evidence that putting powerful tools in the hands of students does not necessarily imply their powerful usage, and the teacher has a crucial mediating role to play. (Somekh & Davis, 1997; Wegerif & Schrimshaw, 1997). Unfortunately, teacher empowerment studies in general observe that technologizing has brought to most teachers a feeling of deskilling and disempowerment, rather than empowerment. Cuban (2001a, 2001b) points out that underlying most national ICT initiatives is the authorities' agenda to impose educational reforms on teachers, with little consideration of the reasons behind existing practice or innovations in classrooms, and little power is given to the 'frontier soldiers' to decide whether and how things should be done. Alienation and resentment develop, and Cuban contends that if this fundamental issue is not addressed, the whole initiative is going to be self-defeating.

# 3. CRITICAL AWARENESS OF THE NATURE OF THE TECHNOLOGY

Technologies are generally non-neutral. They are created to satisfy our needs, but they also exert an effect on us. Don (1993) points out that it is almost like a law that when one's power gets amplified in a certain dimension, there will inevitability be a reduction in another dimension, both due to the same nature of that technology. Just because a magnifying glass magnifies something, it pushes other things out of your view. From this perspective, Bowers (1988) draws educators' attention to a new way of examining the use of ICT in education.

Fundamental to the nature of computers is that they process representations. Obviously representations can help people's thinking, provided that they can relate these representations (text, diagrams, images) to what are represented. But then the other side of the coin is, how about those who don't see these representations as representations? On almost this same point, Brown and Duguid (2000) remind people of the importance of tacit/implicit knowledge, and warn about 'tunnel visions' in technology developments that focus narrowly on 'information' as if it is an object on its own, leaving out of focus the 'social peripherals', including existing intermediary relationships, and implicit communal knowledge that are essential for the generation and 'reading' of the information.

The notion of ubiquitous usage of computers in classrooms is hence questioned. The computer software at its very best only provides an additional experience. The students and teachers have to make sense of this experience together, and in relation to many other human interactions and physical experiences. And there are also many other valuable and enjoyable activities in the real classroom that don't seem to be replaceable by the technology. The ICT representations can only become rich in meanings as they go along with other concrete contextualized experience.

Immediately pertinent then are the questions: How often do educational software developers take non-ubiquitous and hybrid usage as their objective? And secondly, how much flexibility has been given to teachers in orchestrating the whole range of activities?

Programmability is also fundamental to the nature of ICT. Capitalizing on that, you can prepare rich presentation slides before you teach, but at the same time, it reduces your flexibility in responding spontaneously to feedback from the class. More importantly, the two stages of work can now be undertaken by different people. On the positive side, you have more parties contributing. Yet it is a separation. Is it uncommon to see that the more a developer thinks about and implements his/her desirable flow of a lesson into the software, the less usable the software becomes to the teacher? The separation also implies an issue of power.

## 4. A CONTRASTING EXPERIENCE

In 1998 our research team was sponsored by the Language Fund of Hong Kong to develop a series of computer software packages, called the Dragonwise Series, to enhance children's structural understanding of Chinese characters (Lam, Ki, Law, Chung, Ko, Ho, & Pun, 2001). Based on the theoretical framework of the team, the software was created. After its completion, the software was introduced to over 1,000 local primary language teachers through various teacher workshops. As indicated by surveys done in workshops, the majority of the teachers liked the pedagogic principle and considered the software "very helpful" and "helpful" to their teaching. However, follow up surveys revealed that only limited actual usage of the software can be found.

In view of this, the team decided in 2001, when it received a second phase funding from the Quality Education Fund of Hong Kong, to make a drastic change in its model of development. The resulting classroom impact was dramatic.

## 5. MINIMALIST DESIGN: A NEW STYLE OF SOFTWARE

The idea is borrowed from the theory of Minimalism (Carroll, 1990, pp. 7–10). Simply put, it means to minimise the obtrusiveness of the software to instruction. Our original programs are broken down into a wide range of tiny *learning objects*, each allowing the user to play with a specific concept in a focused context. These learning objects make no assumptions about whether the user is a teacher or student, or whether it is used for presentation, exploration or consolidation. It is just like a piece of rock in a geography lesson, which carries its own properties, but no assumption about how, when, and by whom it is to be used. In this way the software gives maximum flexibility to the teachers in designing their lessons. The learning objects are self-contained and downloadable. They can be run online and offline, or embedded into teacher-produced multimedia materials. Each learning object is simple to use. They are also small; the activity normally takes only a few minutes to finish. If teachers like, they can put several of them together to form a longer activity.

## 6. NEW DEVELOPMENT MODEL: WITH TEACHER EMPOWERMENT

School teachers were given a highly prominent role right from the very beginning of the design of the software. Before any substantial development was done, the team visited 15 schools to introduce prototypes of the learning objects in which are embedded the pedagogic ideas about structural understanding of Chinese characters. Teachers in the schools could choose those types of interactions they liked most, and suggest modifications. After these preliminary exchanges, the team and the schoolteachers went into a partnership for the new software development. Teachers were asked to study their students' work to see if the kinds of errors predicted by the theory did occur, and then to suggest the content of the learning objects they thought most relevant to their students, as well as compatible with the already existing curriculum plans of the school. The research team held discussions with the teachers and produced the agreed learning objects.

With this change of model, the actual classroom impact was dramatic. Within about seven months, a large volume of new software was developed (a total of 1,441 learning objects), and the school teachers were very eager to put them immediately to use in their classrooms (many of them were originally very apprehensive about using technology in classrooms). Some teachers even integrated the learning objects into their school based literacy teaching program, and seven of the 15 schools offered to share their experiences and classroom videos in front of hundreds of other primary school teachers. The materials produced were then put on the web for everybody to share. Within four months, there were over 15,000 hits to the web site (http://www.dragonwise.hku.hk).

## 7. CONCLUSION

It can be seen that, with the principles of teacher empowerment and minimalist design, the teachers not only felt confident and comfortable in using the software, but also they were empowered to synthesize and invent novel and creative ways of teaching their lessons together with the many other traditional means. Teachers' participation in the development process allows praxes of using the software to grow out of the actual needs of the teachers. And ultimately it is the people and the praxes that inject more people into the game.

## REFERENCES

Bowers, C. A. (1988). *The Cultural Dimensions of Educational Computing.* New York: Teachers College Press.

Brown, J. S. & Duguid, P. (2000). *The Social Life of Information.* Boston, Mass: Harvard Business School Press.

Carroll, J. M. (1990). *The Nurnberg Funnel.* Massachusetts: The MIT Press.

Cuban, L. (2001a). *Oversold and Underused: Computers in the Classroom.* Cambridge, Mass: Harvard University Press.

Cuban, L. (2001b). Why are most teachers infrequent and restrained users of computers in their classrooms? In J. Woodward & L. Cuban (Eds), *Technology, Curriculum and Professional Development.* Newbury Park, CA: Corwin.

Don, I. (1993). *Philosophy of Technology.* New York: Paragon House.

Lam, H. C., Ki, W. W., Law, N., Chung, A. L. S., Ko, P. Y., Ho, A. H. S. & Pun, S. W. (2001). Designing CALL for learning Chinese characters. *Journal of Computer Assisted Learning,* 17(1), 115–128.

Somekh, B. & Davis, N. (1997). *Using Information Technology Effectively in Teaching and Learning.* London: Routledge.

Wegerif, R. & Scrimshaw, P. (1997). *Computers and Talk in the Primary Classroom.* Clevedon: Multilingual Matters.

# Innovative Classroom Practices and the Teacher of the Future

Nancy Law
*University of Hong Kong, Pokfulam Road, Hong Kong, nlaw@hkusua.hku.hk*

**Abstract:** The widespread support for the use of ICT to support teaching and learning across the curriculum has been on the grounds that there is a need to equip the younger generation with a new set of competencies required for life in the 21st century. There is also a heightening realization that this will also involve the development of new pedagogies alongside the use of ICT. It is in this context that the Second International Information Technology in Education Study introduced the concept of emerging pedagogical paradigm. The second phase of this study is an international comparative case study of 'Innovative Pedagogical Practices Using Technology' (SITES M2). Altogether 28 countries from around the world participated in this study, and a total of 174 case studies have been conducted and reported. Each of the innovative cases is by definition considered to be a relatively rare and valuable pedagogical development in its own national context and provides a lens for us to have a preview of the classrooms of the future. This paper explores the future roles of the teacher and the consequent demands on teacher professional development provisions based on an analysis of the variety of roles that teachers played in a sample of case studies collected in this study.

## 1. INTRODUCTION

This paper explores the future roles of the teacher and the consequent demands on the provision of teacher professional development based on a study of the variety of roles that teachers played in a sample of case studies collected in an international comparative study of innovative classroom practices using technology.

A main justification for the widespread introduction of ICT to support teaching and learning across the curriculum has been the development of a new set of competencies to prepare the younger generation for life in the 21st century. It is undeniable that there is a growing tendency for education policies on ICT in the curriculum to be linked to or made in the context of a wider educational renewal/reform at a national level (e.g. Ireland, 1999; Korean Ministry of Education, 2000; PCAST, 1997; Singapore Ministry of Education, 1997). It is also in this context that the Second International Information Technology in Education Study introduced the concept of an emerging pedagogical paradigm for the study (Pelgrum & Anderson, 1999) and conceptualized the second phase of this study: an international comparative case study of 'Innovative Pedagogical Practices Using Technology' (hereafter referred to as SITES M2). Altogether 28 countries from around the world participated in this study, contributing to a total of 174 case studies being conducted in 2000 and 2001 (see http://www.sitesm2.org//SITES_Research_Projects/SITESM2/prospectus.html).

As each of the innovative cases is by definition considered to be relatively rare and valuable pedagogical developments in its own national context, the cases provide a lens for us to have a preview of the classrooms of the future. In analyzing the case studies, the Hong Kong research team wanted to address the issue of innovativeness: in what sense can we say that these classrooms are futuristic? What can be learnt from these cases that can help us to transform our classrooms to better prepare students for the challenges of the 21st century? This paper examines in particular the roles played by teachers in the innovative case studies analyzed to provide a better understanding of the changing roles demanded of the teacher of the future and the consequent demands on teacher professional development provisions.

## 2. INNOVATIVE PEDAGOGICAL PRACTICES: A FRAMEWORK FOR ANALYSIS

In order to arrive at a framework for analyzing innovations, the research team found it necessary to examine innovation from the perspective of change and to examine the key dimensions of change that may contribute to classroom practices using technology to be considered as innovative.

Plomp, ten Brummelhuis and Rapmund (1996) discussed the concept of emergent pedagogical practices and the management of change. They introduced two important concepts: 'care for the old' and 'courage for the new'. The basic idea is that in implementing ICT in educational settings, there needs to be a clear focus on bringing about new learning outcomes and new modes of learning, and not just on the adoption of new technologies. However, it is also recognized that schools and schooling cannot be changed overnight and that the process of innovation has to be a gradual one. Thus it was recognized that in the early stages of the implementation process, ICT would most likely be used for the delivery of old classroom practices for the achievement of long existent goals. Plomp et al. (1996) further argued for this kind of implementation to be supported so that the people involved in the process of change can ease into the change. This kind of practice was labeled as 'care for the old'. On the other hand, the same work also pointed out very clearly that it is those practices which bring about new learning goals and new modes of learning that are the most important and any educational institution needs to have courage and determination to bring about such new practices, as these will be the practices that will define and shape the future of schooling.

Adopting this framework to examine the case studies of innovative practices collected in SITES M2, we identify 6 dimensions (or aspects) of classroom practices that might have changed as part of the innovation:

Intended learning objectives of the classroom practice
Pedagogical role(s) of the teacher
Role(s) of the learner
Nature and sophistication of the ICT used
Connectedness of the classroom
Learning outcomes exhibited by the learner

These 6 dimensions of change are key elements in any curriculum implementation involving ICT use. When the features of each case study were examined along each of these 6 dimensions, it became apparent that there was large diversity across these cases. Taking the 'traditional' classroom to be typically one that is isolated, knowledge-focused, teacher-centered, does not use ICT and only assesses students on cognitive learning outcomes, Table 1 lists the features of the practices studied on a 'scale of innovativeness' on the basis of the 'magnitude of change' that has taken place along each of the 6 dimensions of analysis. It is apparent from Table 1 that some of the features observed were very similar to traditional practices, while others may have quite innovative features that are rarely found in current classrooms.

## 3. TEACHERS' ROLES AS A FOCAL DIMENSION AND TEACHERS' CAPABILITIES

While all the 6 dimensions identified are necessarily present in any classroom practice, they are not entirely independent of each other. In fact, the role played by the teacher is arguably the most important dimension since it is the teacher who orchestrates and exerts the greatest influence on the other 5 dimensions. Obviously, it is important to recognize that the

*Table 1*. The six dimensions of change in ICT-supported classroom practices with descriptors for varying degrees of innovation

| Dimension of innovation | Traditional | Some new elements | Emergent | Innovative | Most innovative |
|---|---|---|---|---|---|
| **Intended learning objectives** | • Conceptual learning<br>• Solving well defined problems | • Learn information skills<br>• Self-accessed learning | • Critical thinking<br>• Catering for individual differences | • Inquiry skills<br>• Communication skills | • Solve authentic problems collaboratively |
| **Teacher's pedagogical role(s)** | • Present and explain<br>• Set instructional tasks<br>• Monitor and assess | • Facilitative feedback<br>• Design curriculum and learning activities | • Select ICT tools<br>• Co-teaching | • Support/model enquiry<br>• Liaise with parties outside school | • Facilitate team building and collaborative |
| **Students' role(s)** | • Listen and follow instructions | • Data gathering and processing<br>• Search for information | • Create learning product<br>• Analyzing and drawing conclusions from data | • Collaborate with peers<br>• Engage in enquiry | • Peer tutoring and evaluation<br>• set own learning goals and strategies<br>• Reflect on own learning |
| **ICT used** | • No ICT used | • Tutorials/drill and practice applications<br>• Web browser and search engines | • Web/multimedia production tools<br>• ICT as productivity tool (e.g. office suite) | • Digital communication tools for collaboration<br>• Data-analysis software | • Simulation/modeling, Datalogging software<br>• Purpose designed mindtools |
| **Connectedness** | Parties Involved | | | | |
| | • Isolated classroom | • Teachers and students in same school | • Teacher and students from other schools locally | • Various communities groups (parents, alumni, private sector, etc.) | • Teachers, students, experts, sponsors etc. from other countries |
| | Roles of Collaborating Parties | | | | |
| | • As observers | • Provide administrative/ technical support | • Provide additional information/feedback to teachers/students | • Offer curriculum ideas<br>• Help develop curriculum/ materials | • As teacher/co-teacher<br>• Monitor/assess students' task progression |

teacher operates within the context of the school and is constrained by the vision and goals as well as the resources and priorities of the institution involved, but such factors lie outside the scope of this paper.

In examining the innovative classroom practices collected in SITES M2, the Hong Kong research team observed great diversity across different case studies in the profile of features along the 6 dimensions. It was not common to find classroom practices that possessed highly innovative features along all the 6 dimensions. On the other hand, many of the case studies were highly innovative along one or a few of the 6 dimensions. Another important observation was that even though in some case studies the teachers' pedagogical roles (which encompass the most important aspects of their roles in relation to the pedagogical approach adopted, but not the entire set of roles played by the teachers) remained rather traditional, the innovations that occurred along the other dimensions in those cases also created new demands on the teacher. These new demands then required the teachers to develop new capabilities and competences in the implementation process. Therefore, irrespective of whether there were substantial changes in the pedagogical roles played by the teacher, the teacher had to innovate at a professional level to make the classroom innovation a reality. In the following sections, 3 case studies will be examined to illustrate the diversities in the roles played by the teacher and the range of new capabilities demanded of the teacher in those cases.

## 4. NURTURING LEARNING COMMUNITIES

One of the innovative practices selected for the Hong Kong SITES M2 study was a *Cyber Art Project* in a primary school. The innovation involved the introduction of wireless laptop computers fitted with a pressure pad and associated painting and drawing software for the learning of Art in all classes from grades 4 to 6 in the school. The target was for up to 25% of the Art lessons in these classes to be conducted using this new medium. The aim of the innovation was to promote students' creativity, interest and development of skills through the greater flexibility in the formats and contexts available for art creation offered by the new medium. The pupils were able to experiment with different simulated forms of painting such as graphite sketches, Chinese painting, watercolors and oil painting on the computer. Further, they were able to easily practice drawing outside the Art room: at the school playground, at the Peak, at the Art Gallery, as well as take part in a drawing excursion to the Great Wall in Beijing. The wireless network also allowed pupils to share their artwork with other classmates and the teachers also created opportunities for pupils to discuss and critique each other's work. In addition, the school organized an Art excursion to Beijing that included sharing activities in Art with a Beijing primary school.

This project was led by the 3 Art teachers who taught Art in the 3 target grades (4 to 6), including the Art Panel chairperson of the school who initiated the whole project. Besides these 3 teachers, an additional 14 teachers were also peripherally involved in supporting the Art excursions and took part in some associated professional development activities so as to prepare themselves for playing a more active role in using computers for the teaching of Art when its use became extended to the lower grades in future. These 17 teachers worked closely together to prepare the curriculum materials and the learning activities. They would visit each other's classes to conduct evaluation. Another prominent feature of this practice was that the teachers had to undertake a lot of liaison work with external parties in order to organize the excursions, including parents (who went to Beijing with the students), the Curator of the Art Gallery and the principal and teachers of the partner school in Beijing that hosted their visit.

The pedagogical role played by the teachers in this practice is not considered to be particularly innovative. The practice was still relatively teacher-centered in that the teacher determined the nature and scope of the activity and the pupils largely followed the instructions. The learning outcomes targeted were essentially the same as what one normally finds stated in the Art curriculum. What is outstanding in this practice, however, was the conception of and commitment to extending the pupils' opportunities to learn by extending the learning contexts to beyond the traditional classroom. Here the technology used was not commonly found in Hong Kong schools and the teachers had only marginal knowledge of the technology before the funding for the project was approved. The technology used was specifically designed for creating different Art forms through the digital medium. The teachers had to learn and master this new technology and to creatively design appropriate curriculum activities for the classes concerned using their curriculum development and pedagogical expertise.

Another prominent feature in this practice is the courage that the teachers took in opening up their classroom doors. In so doing, the teachers did not only have to take their pupils out of the classroom, but also greatly increased the range of participants involved in the teaching and learning process. Where traditionally a classroom includes a teacher and a class of pupils, the 'classroom' in this practice extended beyond the school premises and included many more participants such as teachers in the same school other than the class Art teacher, parents, teachers and pupils from another school, as well as people outside the education community such as museum curators. The 'openness' thus created provides a greater opportunity not only for the pupils to learn, but also for the school and the teachers to learn and improve as an organization. This new 'openness' also demanded that teachers be capable of identifying and soliciting collaborative partners to support the planned learning and teaching activities.

A third major challenge that the three core teachers took in their stride was to nurture the establishment of a community of learners within the Art panel team during the innovation process. They worked closely together to tackle the technical and professional difficulties encountered and in so doing created a community of professionals who were capable of identifying their own goals for organizational development as well as individual professional advancement.

In sum, the teachers in this innovative practice have developed remarkable capabilities in helping the school to develop into a learning organization and in bringing extensive community involvement into the learning and teaching process.

## 5. DEVELOPING ACADEMIC PROFESSIONAL EXPERTISE

The second case study to be discussed here, *Computer Assisted Scientific Investigations*, was rather different from the previous one in nature. This innovation involved 3 senior science teachers teaching the three science subjects biology, chemistry and physics respectively in grades 10-13 in a secondary school in Hong Kong. Here, the teachers were not satisfied with the rather didactic and prescriptive way that experimental work in science was generally organized in Hong Kong schools. They very much wished to introduce scientific investigations into the curriculum so that students could generate the problem to be investigated as well as formulate the method of enquiry, in addition to conducting the experiment and interpreting the results to arrive at a conclusion. They believed that the introduction of datalogging in science laboratories would greatly extend the scope of experimentation accessible to the students and would thus enable scientific investigations to be introduced into the curriculum.

Students were recruited voluntarily from grades 10 and 12 into this pilot project and formed into 3 teams, one for each science subject. Each team of students was to further subdivide into 10 groups to develop 10 investigations. First of all, each group had to identify a problem that the members consider to be interesting and/or important to investigate. They then had to work out a method for the investigation, conduct the experiment, and analyze the data collected to determine whether the results so obtained were able to address the problem they started with. In the event that they encountered problems, they might modify or improve their design until they were able to find an answer to their problem. Each group had to produce, as a final product, a laboratory guide for the investigation so that other students could follow the instructions and conduct the experiment accordingly.

While there was some collaboration among the three science teachers in terms of setting up a common structural framework for the pilot project, and in familiarizing themselves with the use of the datalogging equipment, the three teachers worked relatively independently with their own team of students. The greatest challenge was a pedagogical one, changing the role of the teacher from an instructor and evaluator to that of a learning guide to the students. The teachers did not know for sure the answers to the problems to be investigated, as these were authentic ones generated by the students. They modeled the investigation process through sharing and supporting it. However, they did not take over the investigation but rather helped students to clarify their ideas by posing questions and occasionally suggesting possible courses of attack. They also provided resources and technical skills training when required by students.

This pedagogical role change on the part of the teachers brings with it socio-emotional challenges to the teacher as they will no longer be the authority on the subject matter to be taught and will become more like a co-learner alongside the students. In taking up new pedagogical roles, these teachers were also helping students to assume new roles as learners. Students were no longer passive consumers of packaged instruction but learn to become autonomous knowledge workers in a team by contributing productively to the creation of a solution that addresses an authentic problem.

Another challenge that these teachers overcame was academic and professional in nature. The teachers had not used dataloggers at all and only knew about them vaguely through reading in professional journals. They were not particularly technology savvy individuals but took on the professional commitment to keep abreast of the latest developments in their discipline area for the benefit of their students. In so doing, they learnt about the use of rather sophisticated technology that extended the scope of investigations and the extent of knowledge of the discipline areas that they taught in. These teachers, through their own professional conduct and activities, demonstrated clearly that they were practicing lifelong learners.

# 6. ROLE DIFFERENTIATION IN CYBER INSTITUTIONS

The last case study to be discussed here is one drawn from Australia. This involves a *Virtual Schooling Service* in a statewide project. Eighteen teachers were involved in planning the virtual classes and online learning materials in six subject areas for 320 secondary students in 49 schools throughout the state. These 49 schools had difficulty in offering the full range of subjects because of the small student numbers involved. This project was an attempt to extend students' educational opportunities through the use of flexible delivery strategies and a range of synchronous and asynchronous learning technologies. Students were grouped across schools to make up viable virtual classes. Two groups of teachers were involved in this practice: 18 VSS (virtual schooling service) teachers employed for this statewide project and the school teachers from the 49 schools who acted as 'Study Coaches' for students in their own schools.

The 18 VSS teachers were responsible for developing all the curriculum materials for both synchronous and asynchronous delivery. They also played many of the major roles normally assumed by classroom teachers for the students: conducting (online virtual) classes, providing instructions, setting assignments, communicating with students and providing feedback as well as assessing students' learning outcomes.

Students typically had two 'real time' virtual classes of approximately 40 minutes of synchronous lessons and three periods of offline, Study Room activities each week for each VSS subject enrolled. The virtual classes were presided over by a VSS teacher and students were able to interact with the VSS teacher and other students in the virtual class via 'real time' audio teleconferencing and shared computer graphics. During the virtual lessons, students had access to electronic resources, which could be received through emails from the VSS teacher or via some online subject resource repositories. Between lessons, students were able to interact with the remote VSS teacher and fellow students through a range of synchronous and asynchronous technologies, including email discussion lists and 'real-time' chat rooms.

In addition to the virtual classes, independent study time was organized in an online Study Room to engage students in activities and assignments. The Wide Area Network technology used in this project limited the students' access to the online Study Room to allocated asynchronous times of study, before and after school, and at lunch times using the school computers. The participating schools appointed Study Coaches from their own staff to provide assistance and guidance locally to students. Where students were less computer literate or less able to undertake independent learning, the local Study Coaches had to spend much of their time to provide technical support as well as subject-related assistance. The Study Coaches' roles also included supervision and guidance to students on management of their workloads and authentication of assessment items, as well as liaison with the VSS teachers on potential student problems. Student assignment tracking and ensuring assignment completion was a cooperative arrangement between the school-based Study Coach and the VSS teachers. Examinations were set by the VSS teachers and hard copies delivered to the schools' Study Coaches who then supervised the students in the completion of these and sent them back to the VSS teachers for marking.

In one sense, the key innovation involved in this activity was a technological one, using a range of multimedia and course development tools to present course materials, and various forms of synchronous and asynchronous communication tools to support teaching and learning interactions. The goals of the practice were very similar to the original curriculum goals for the subjects when offered in a face-to-face mode. In terms of pedagogical approaches, the VSS teachers were trying their best to replicate the best possible face-to-face approaches that could be used for the teaching of their subjects to the online situation. However, for effective learning to take place, this new mode of learning requires the learners to develop a greater sense of autonomy and self-direction as well as the skills and dispositions for lifelong learning. Furthermore, this activity involved explorations in employing various forms of technology to conduct different kinds of teaching and learning interactions, as well as exploration of ways of supplementing the cyber interactions with a local Study Coach who played roles that cyber interactions could not fully deliver. It is argued here that such explorations are important for generating innovations in learning technologies, in pedagogy, as well as in developing new types of education professionals leading to new ecologies and cultures in education communities.

First of all, the VSS teachers had to master new skills in a range of software (e.g. PowerPoint, NetMeeting) and to determine how to use this software most effectively for various teaching options. While materials and ideas they brought from their previous school-based teaching were useful, they also made adaptations as experience with the technology was gained. As fluency in the use of technology increased, they started to innovate new strategies for teaching and learning in the VSS context. Arguably, much of this courseware development role could be dissociated to a great extent from the actual teaching in virtual classes, leading to the establishment of a new type of education professional who specializes in the development of online course materials.

The physical separation of the VSS teachers from the students also forced them to reflect much more deeply on the strategies they employed and how they orchestrated different forms of communications with students for different purposes in order that they could deliberate more consciously and effectively in their communications (synchronous and asynchronous) with students. These VSS teachers were in fact developing new, specialized pedagogical competencies and capabilities and in the process evolved into a new breed of education professionals for cyber education institutions.

While the Study Coaches did not contribute to the design of the curriculum or to the teaching and assessment of the students, they played important supportive roles in coaching students to become autonomous learners and in liaising with the VSS teachers. Thus one can already observe a differentiation of the classroom teacher's roles into two components, one being played by the VSS teacher and the other played by the Study Coach. It may be possible that, as cyber education institutions grow and develop, Study Coaches will become a new type of education professional with their own unique skills, competencies and capabilities.

The process of differentiation and emergence of new education professionals as described above is an evolutionary process resulting from the process of innovation involving the adoption of new technologies to broaden the education opportunities of learners in remote areas. It is hypothesized here that such innovations will create pressure on the learning technologies to innovate as well, since the education professionals engaged in extensive use of technology will make demands on the technology to support the new pedagogies that they will in time innovate. The differentiation of teachers' roles into a number of different education professionals also makes it imperative that these professionals communicate and collaborate effectively, and it is expected that in time a new professional ecology may develop as a consequence of the emergence of cyber education institutions.

# 7. INNOVATIONS AND TEACHERS' ROLES

In conclusion, we have found analyzing the case studies of innovative pedagogical practices using technology selected from the SITES M2 study along the six dimensions, intended learning objectives, teacher's pedagogical roles, student's roles, nature and sophistication of the ICT used, the connectedness of the classroom and the learning outcomes exhibited by the learners to be very fruitful. The different case studies were found to exhibit particularly innovative features along some of the dimensions only, which may not include prominent innovations in the pedagogical role of the teacher. However, our study found that all the innovations were making new demands on the teacher, who had to be continuously engaged in lifelong learning as well as working collaboratively with other teachers in order to realize the innovative practices studied. The richness and success of these practices is not simply a result of the implementation of ICT in the teaching and learning process, but a consequence of the case selection criteria used in

SITES M2. One important criterion for case selection was that the practice had to demonstrate evidence of significant changes in roles of teachers and students, the goals of the curriculum, assessment practices, and/or the educational materials or infrastructure. It is the author's view that it is through such kinds of pedagogical innovations that the teaching profession renews and recreates itself into a variety of education professionals who will lead schools into become learning organizations of the 21st century.

## REFERENCES

Ireland, I. S. (1999). *Building a Capacity for Change: Lifelong Learning in the Information Society.* Dublin: Stationery Office, Government of Ireland.

Korean Ministry of Education (2000). *Adapting Education to the Information Age: A White Paper.* Seoul: Korea Education & Research Information Service.

PCAST (President's Committee of Advisors on Science and Technology Panel on Educational Technology) (1997). *Report to the President on the Use of Technology to Strengthen K-12 Education in the United States.*

Pelgrum, H. & Anderson, R. (Ed.) (1999). *ICT and the Emerging Paradigm for Life Long Learning.* Amsterdam: IEA.

Plomp, T., ten Brummelhuis, A. & Rapmund, R. (Eds.) (1996). *Teaching and Learning for the Future.* Den Haag: Committee on Multimedia in Teacher Training, Dutch Ministry of Education.

Singapore Ministry of Education (1997). *IT Masterplan for Education.* Singapore.

# From Teacher Education to Professional Development for E-learning in an E-society

Raymond Morel, Jean-Claude Domenjoz, Charles Lachat and Christine Rossi
*CPTIC (Centre Pédagogique des Technologies de l'Information et de la Communication), 2-4, rue Théodore-de-Béze, PO Box 3144, CH 1211 Geneva-3, Switzerland.*
*Raymond.Morel@tecfa.unige.ch, Jean-Claude.Domenjoz@edu.ge.ch, Charles.Lachat@edu.ge.ch and Christine.Rossi@edu.ge.ch*

**Abstract:** This paper concerns the development of a scenario aiming at the improvement of teacher education in Geneva in the field of media, image and ICT (MITIC) in a media- and pedagogy-oriented process instead of technology-driven action as is usually the case. Among a lot of observations, experiments and constraints, the key factors we address are the lack of well-educated teachers of teachers (level F3), willingness to enhance coherence in teacher education together with pedagogical research (innovative projects), the need to take into account the evolution of the demography of teachers in professional development and the necessity to promote an attitude to and an awareness of practices in collaborative and cooperative work. In this process we have built a prototype of a new concept of teacher (F3-MITIC), and we have cooperated in a national incentive policy and proposed an agenda for the remaining problems to be solved. We conclude the presentation of our contribution by the assessment of the fundamental necessity to put in action a real e-piloting including a set of strategies, as well as projects and tools which will have to be elaborated with the actors in the field, in the four following directions: sharing data, re-defining teachers' competencies, taking care of innovative projects and designing pedagogical models of e-learning.

## 1. INTRODUCTION

### 1.1 Change of paradigm: From teaching to learning

During the last decade, changes to the role of the teacher have been widely and frequently discussed. Some particularly instructive international studies have included the CERI-OECD study (2001) suggesting six scenarios for the school of the future, and UNESCO-IFIP Curriculum (2001) which stresses the strongly interdependent multicomponent approach (teacher education is a basic component) with implementation levels (emerging, applying, integrating, transforming), not forgetting the need to preserve local implementation conditions (languages, cultures, institutions, etc.)

To go further and produce concrete proposals to promote and put them into action, we took into consideration Jacques Tardiff's (1998) ideas and also the main results of a three-year EU project named FETICHE (Formation des Enseignants aux Technologies de l'Information et de la Communication: Changements et Evolution). At the national level we elaborated a prototype of an incubator of pedagogical projects to stimulate scenarios of integrating ICT (Plan d'Actions, 2002).

## 1.2 The need for coherence in teacher education

It is very important to identify and build a grid to maintain some coherence between skills, competences and professionnal development with respect to generic objectives and more general competencies (levels F1, F2, F3).

## 1.3 The bottleneck: From big announcements to reality in the field

National policies, e-Europe, e-Learning, declarations of targets and deadlines during the last 5 years forgot the reality in the field: instead of merging or converging initial teacher education, in-service teacher education and pedagogical research, what actually happens has often been poorly linked and far removed from the 'theory'. The result in some countries is an important bottleneck characterised by a lack of well-educated teachers of teachers who have a good understanding of institutional priorities and the change of paradigm.

## 1.4 The urgent need for more new teachers

The demographic evolution of teaching staff in the next five years shows that in many countries there is a need to educate an average of 40% of new teachers. Considering that, according to the most optimistic evaluations, the number of today's teachers presently mastering ICT amounts only to 20%, the huge gap stresses the urgency of bridging the chronic deficiency in educating the specialist teachers in particular.

# 2. THE F3-MITIC PROJECT AND THE TEACHER OF THE FUTURE

According to this picture of what to do for the teacher of tomorrow, the professional development (PD) programme for teachers was oriented towards a **model called F3-MITIC.**

We considered it necessary to expect from all teachers of teachers, irrespective of the didactics used or of teaching level, education competences in and through media, i.e. the capability of integrating MITIC in assisting the construction of knowledge.

## 2.1 F1, F2, F3 networked across the educational system

The following codes are used in the project to define 3 different levels of education:

**F1** = education received by students (independently of the level of education)

**F2** = initial and/or continuous teacher education received by teachers (independently of the levels of education)

**F3** = education received by teachers of teachers.

## 2.2 Some features of F3-MITIC

The programme is designed to focus on pedagogy, adult education, integration of ICT, collaborative learning, evaluation, basic and sustainable skills like producing document, exchanging of experiments, communicating, elaboration of scenarios, capitalising /mutualization of the production of the learners, piloting the PD through the learners i.e. the teachers of teachers, etc. The whole conception of this project is designed, as mentioned earlier, as pedagogy- rather than technology-driven. The spirit is close to Bent Andresen with his 'Design of Teacher E-Learning – the Scenario Model' (cf. IFIP WCC'2002 at Montreal August 2002).

# 3. THE PROTOTYPE OF F3-MITIC IN 2001-2002

A group of 25 existing teachers of teachers (practitioners of initial and/or in service teacher education) experimented with this model for one year (2001-2002) (Project FETICHE). The prototype F3-MITIC 2001-2002 offered very interesting observations in different directions, namely:

- implementation of the content

- environment for collaborative work
- new methods to introduce, to experiment or to apply the prototype
- modalities for piloting, measures for accompanying the plan of action
- organisational matter,
- different modalities for evaluation
- follow-up tools
- diffusion of the information.

70 scenarios were produced throughout the 10 modules. A draft analysis in the form of a typology of all the scenarios was achieved by a fellow researcher of the Faculty of Science Education, University of Geneva (http://wwwedu.ge.ch/cptic/f3mitic/0102/scenarios/analyse_f3mitic.pdf). A web site summarizes the whole activity (http://wwwedu.ge.ch/cptic/f3mitic/welcome.html).

## 4. A BRIEF DESCRIPTION OF THE PROJECT CALLED *F3-MITIC LEARNING PATH* FOR PROFESSIONAL DEVELOPMENT (PD) IN TEACHER EDUCATION IN GENEVA

F3-MITIC is a learning curve for teacher of teachers (F3) in media, image and ICT (MITIC) started by the Education Department of the Canton of Geneva.

The aim of the F3-MITIC process is to develop the motivation and competence of teaching professionals to provide courses to further teachers or to operate as resource-persons in teaching institutions.

The project is included in the general program of integrating pedagogical utilisation of MITIC in the teaching and learning processes at all education levels and is an attempt to answer the growing needs in education of teaching personnel in this field.

### 4.1 Learning objectives

The objectives of F3-MITIC are to ensure the education of teachers able to perform the specific education of teachers of teachers and of resource-persons for pedagogical integration of media, image and ICT (information and communication technologies) (MITIC) at the initial education level (IFMES) as well as inservice education. The F3-MITIC program is designed for teachers at the three education levels: primary, secondary (compulsory and post-compulsory) and professional.

## 4.2 Contents and organisation of this learning path

The F3-MITIC learning curve is distributed throughout the school year and brings together 25 teachers per cycle. In 2002-2003, 8 trainers from upper secondary education in Valais participated in the learning program. The program is composed of 10 modules of one to two days representing 100 course hours in class, completed by about 150 hours of distance collaborative work. Each module based on a theme provides the opportunity for the groups (two to three persons) to develop a pedagogical scenario of an innovative project using MITIC in teaching/learning and aims at developing strategies specific to adult education. From this perspective, reflexive analysis and the critique of the individual experience in each module is an integral part of this programme.

The F3-MITIC program which welcomes experienced teachers from media, image and/or ICT is not a place where new knowledge specific to each of these domains is presented but is rather a place for experimenting, exchanging practices and building up new competencies.

## 4.3 Programme

The programme is composed of the following 10 modules. It is completed in three half-days which enables the analysis of the pedagogical scenarios produced by the participants, three times a year (E-I, E-II, E-III).

## 4.4 Module list

1. Which new pedagogical competencies are required by the evolution of communication tools and practices?
2. Pedagogical and conceptual approaches to using MITIC in education.
3. Consolidation of the participants' technical and practical competences in MI, ICT (3A) and media based communication (3B).
4. Consolidation of the participants' pedagogical competencies in the areas of didactic use of fixed image or didactic use of information and communication systems.
5. Consolidation of the participants' pedagogical competences in the areas of didactic use of moving images or didactic use of modelling and simulation.
6. Didactic use of a multimedia document.
7. Realisation of a multimedia document.
8. Realisation of pedagogical Internet services.
9. Group communication using devices based on text, image and sound.

10. Ethics and social impacts of MITIC utilisation.

### 4.5 Information

Address of website: <http://wwwedu.ge.ch/cptic/f3mitic>.

Contact Jean-Claude Domenjoz, coordinator (jean-claude.domenjoz @edu.ge.ch).

## 5. TOWARDS A NATIONAL PROJECT (2002-2007)

During the present school year (2002-2003), the model F3-MITIC is being implemented at the national level through a 100 MCHF Project called 'PPP – ICT and Teacher Education' (5 years, 2002-2006, 2600 persons concerned ca. 2% of the teaching staff) (Communique De Presse, 2001).

The way to promote collaborative work through cantons (with different educational systems) is a key issue.

## 6. AN AGENDA FOR SOLVING THE REMAINING PROBLEMS

Such a plan obviously involves a series of problems to be considered and questions to be answered as soon as possible.

Some current issues:

- how to further reinforce the professional development phases of teacher education to encourage lifelong learning of the teaching staff ;
- for the teachers of teachers, how to implement continuing education plans to allow them to continue this evolution. How should they be certified? How to best use them after the F3-MITIC education ("rights and duties", "mixed" statutes – coexistence of statutes, working conditions, etc.)
- In the on-going generalisation the existence of a resource centre appears as a key factor to successfully complete the process. How to stimulate the establishment of such structures where they do not yet exist?
- How to stimulate the generation of innovative projects in the area of MITIC from the existing conditions in the field where partners are as numerous as spread-out, either at individual or institutional levels? (Plan d'Actions, 2002).

- Regarding competences developed by actors of F1, F2 and F3, how to ensure coherence which would favour learning with utilisations in phase with institutional objectives and priorities?

# 7. CONCLUSIONS

At federal as well as at cantonal levels a growing attention has now been given to the needs to **implement an e-piloting** going beyond simple ratios not reflecting the real situation. Therefore a plan of action "e-pilotage-CH" is being finalised by the Task Force "ICT et Teacher Education". The objective is to **develop a series** of strategies, products and tools in co-operation of actors active in the field, to allow them to **better manage the integration of MITIC** in teaching and learning in Switzerland thanks to the following activities:

- Data sharing
- Competence profile
- Management of innovative pedagogical projects
- Pedagogical models and e-Learning platforms.

Such a study program is certainly to be shared in the spirit of the meetings organised by IFIP (there is surely an opportunity to seize with the Focus Groups of the Working Conference).

# REFERENCES

Andresen, B. (2002). TelE-LEARNING: The Challenge for the Third Millenium. *Proceedings of the 17th World Computer Congress,* 25-29 August, Montreal, Quebec (Eds D. Passey & M. Kendall). Kluwer Academic Publishers.

L'École sur le Net (PPP-esn): Une Initiative de la Confédération, des Cantons et de l'Économie Privée. Retrieved from http://www.educa.ch/dyn/2992.htm

CERI-OECD (2001). *Quel Avenir pour nos Écoles*? Paris: OECD.

Plan d'Actions (2002). 'E-Pilotage-CH'. Task Force 'ICT et Teacher Education'. Working paper.

Project FETICHE (Formation des Enseignants aux Technologies de l'Information et de la Communication : Changements et Evolution). Retrieved from http:// www.grenoble.iufm.fr/fetiche

Tardiff, J. (Ed.) (1998). *Intégrer les Nouvelles Technologies de l'Information: Quel Cadre Pédagogique?* Paris: ESF.

UNESCO/IFIP (2001). *Curriculum Information and Communication Technology (ICT).* Retrieved from http://wwwedu.ge.ch/cptic/prospective/projets/unesco/en/welcome.html

# Technology Matters But Good Teachers Matter More

Geoff Romeo
*Faculty of Education, Monash University, geoff.romeo@education.monash.edu.au*

**Abstract:** This paper uses the strategic management technique of *scenario planning* to focus attention on plausible futures for the use of ICT in education and to stimulate strategic thinking about technology, teaching and learning. It begins by looking at some predictions about the use of technology in education and presents two scenarios as vignettes. Both scenarios are about Year 9 students and teachers. The first – *If I see another piece of multimedia I think I will puke* – describes a teaching learning environment where the technology is in control. The second – *e-ngage, e-mpower, e-nable* – describes a teaching and learning environment that is technology rich and the learner is in control.

## 1. EDUCATION AND TECHNOLOGY

Predictions about the future of education abound, especially visions concerning education and technology. Some of the predictions tend to focus on the technology. Pearson and Cochrane (1994), for example, believed that there would be widespread use of virtual reality for recreation and training, portable translation devices, virtual universities, subliminal learning, powerful expert systems, and broadband networked libraries. For Mooneyham (1993) the merging of entertainment and education enabled by technology, would be a matter of survival as people would not have time to pursue the two as mutually exclusive entities. Spender and Stewart (2002) believe that the future belongs to the e-teacher and the e-learner. There will be a shift to online teaching and learning and the notion of anywhere and at anytime learning will become a reality. Student-centered, project-based learning with peer and tutor support will be the norm and, increasingly, learning and earning will be inextricably linked. This will not mean the demise of the teacher but the role of the teacher will be redefined. E-teachers will no longer be the talking heads at the front of the class; they will be as adept with technology as they are with books and they will use new technologies to empower and engage learners. In the digital classroom, technology is infused with the learning process to create knowledge products, the one size fits all curriculum is banished, and digital repositories and learning objects are the new tools of the teaching profession.

Visions 2020 (U.S. Department of Commerce, 2002) informs us that Tele-robots will help students interact with experiments, that three dimensional virtual space that mimics the real space visually, aurally and tactually will be available (Bajscy, 2002), that large multimedia production and research centres will be used by students, that visual prosthesis systems so the blind can see will be used, that students will borrow digipacks – rugged mobile personal computer and communication consoles like they used to borrow library books (Chen & Arnold, 2002), that a *world to the desktop interface* – providing access to distant experts and archives, enabling collaborations, mentoring and virtual communities of practice will exist, as well as *interfaces for ubiquitous computing* – wireless devices that infuse virtual resources as we move through the real world, and *Alice in Wonderland interfaces* – which use avatars, computer based agents and digital artifact in virtual contexts for games and work in virtual reality (Dede, 2002), intelligent toys, game based learning, virtual mentors, internet in your ear, supersimulations and sensors, intelligent laboratory objects (Hinrichs & Gates, 2002), remote immersion systems – bringing interactive and stimulating classroom experiences to all student populations will also be accessible (Neumann & Kyriakakis, 2002).

Pausch (2002) is a little more curmudgeonly in his predictions about the future of schooling. He believes that virtual reality will finally arrive but we won't use it, that technology will allow children to access the world's experts on any given topic – but the experts won't have time to respond, that telepresence won't take over, children will still physically go to school – *touch and general proximity will still matter* - and that children won't learn to reason, make better judgments, become better citizens because of the technology - they will still need good adult role models (Pausch, 2002).

Other predictions about the future of education tend to focus not so much on the technology, but on the intersection between pedagogy and technology, and its effect on psychology, epistemology and teaching praxis. In Australia a constant theme underpinning the introduction of technology into classrooms has been the vision of using computers to help establish constructivist, humanistic, child centered approaches to teaching and learning based on the integration of the curriculum and inquiry learning (Romeo, 2000). Similarly in the US there has been a series of books, articles and reports predicting a teaching and learning future that exploits the technology to engage and empower learners – see for example Education and Technology: Future Visions (Office of Technology & Assessment, 1994).

A common theme underpinning this notion of an intersection between technology and pedagogy, and the future, especially for educationalists, is the notion of constructivism. The early use of technology in educational settings reflected a behaviourist view of teaching and learning. From a technology perspective, the behaviourist approach manifested itself in programmed learning such as that made available by Computer Assisted Learning (CAL), Computer Managed Learning (CML) and Computer Aided Instruction (CAI). Developments in technology, particularly those evident in multimedia, and increased understandings regarding the complexities involved in learning has led to the application of constructivist principles of learning to electronic environments (Hannafin & Land, 1997, p. 171).

A constructivist view of learning asserts that knowledge is not passively received by learners but actively built as they interpret new information in light of their existing understanding of concepts and phenomena. Philosophically, its roots lie with Plato, Socrates, Kant, and Dewey, all of whom suggested that knowledge does not lie outside the human sphere in a pre-existing form, instead that knowledge is more likely to arise from human experience of the world via the senses. These philosophical ideas were later expanded by Piaget, whose developmental theory of genetic epistemology identified cognitive equilibration as the psychological process by which human experience was converted to knowledge of the world (Hawkins, 1994; Ridgeway & Passey, 1991; VonGlaserfeld, 1991).

The constructivist view has recently been extended to include the idea of social constructivism (socio-cultural theory), which is generally attributed to Vygotsky's argument that the development or construction of knowledge is actually a socially mediated act. The acquisition of knowledge is viewed as a social process since it is through engagement, enabled by language with a more capable other, that a student will progress to the next level of understanding (Duffy & Cunningham, 1996, p. 175).

The theme of social constructivism is especially evident in technology teaching and learning futures espoused by writers such as Bosco, Kozma and Grant, Hunter and Goldberg, Cuban, Riel (Office of Technology & Assessment, 1994), and is strongly evident in many systemic initiatives such as the enGauge project. The enGauge project is concerned with the challenge of preparing students to live, learn and work successfully in today's knowledge based society and identifies six essential conditions – vision, practice, proficiency, equity, access and systems crucial to the effective use of technology for student learning. Under Practice, effective teachers actively engage their students in an ongoing process of enquiry and employ a broad selective range of technologies to add value and alignment across curriculum, instruction and assessment. Effective learning environments are technology rich, and conducive to meaningful student engagement (NCREL, 2002). In Australia the push for an education system underpinned by synergies between technology and the ideas of social constructivism is possibly even stronger and is reflected in the rhetoric of many of the curriculum documents produced by various state education departments (see for example Queensland's *New Basics Project* (Education Queensland, 2002) and Victoria's *Early Years Strategy* (DE&Tb, 2002) and *Middle Years* (DE&Ta, 2002) projects.

Does all of this speculation about technology and education help us to prepare for a future in which all we can be certain about is *change* and *uncertainty*? Or is it merely an amusing distraction? Business tends to be a little more analytical about the future and uses techniques such as *scenario planning* or *scenario analysis* to contemplate plausible futures. These techniques may not help us to accurately predict the future but they help us to focus on the issues and perhaps assist us in avoiding undesirable futures.

## 2. SCENARIO PLANNING

Scenario planning was first developed by Pierre Wack (head of corporate planning for Royal Dutch/Shell) in 1973 and further developed by Peter Schwartz (1996). Scenario planning is not an attempt to predict the future; it highlights perceptual limitations and allows trends, issues, and developments to be identified that may otherwise go unnoticed. There are a number of phases associated with scenario planning. The initial phase is the establishment of a focal point. The focal point is an issue on which it is important to develop insight. The next phase is to identify organizational mental models that exist. Next an environmental scan is conducted to determine what forces and trends are impacting on the focal point. From this, key themes are identified and placed on a matrix. The scenarios are then fleshed out and woven into a narrative (College of Marin, 2002).

The focal point selected for this paper is *how information and communication technologies (ICT) will impact on teaching and learning* and, as discussed, the organisational mental models that exist range from the use of ICT underpinned by socio-cultural theory to stunning technological developments that will make learning faster and easier. The forces and trends impacting include rapidly changing technology, curriculum reform, economic rationalism, accountability, and middle school reform. For the purposes of this paper I have chosen two themes. The first theme, not surprisingly, is the technology itself. In the future we may choose to saturate teaching and learning with technology or not. The second theme is teaching and learning theory. In the future we may choose the messy, expensive, rocky road of social constructivism or the highly structured, easily measured – let's do a multiple choice test – road of behaviourism and outcomes based education. The themes are placed on a continuum, intersected, and positioned on a matrix (see Figure 1). From the matrix scenarios are extracted. For the purposes of this paper I have extracted two scenarios and presented them as vignettes. In the first scenario I have drawn heavily on the work of Dede (2002). In the second scenario we meet Sue Shaw – good teacher.

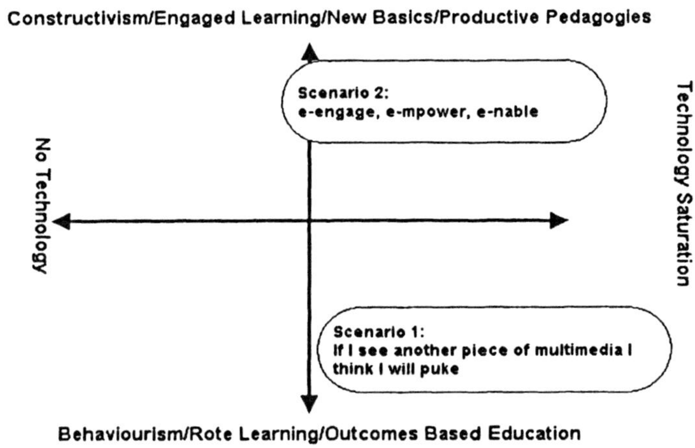


*Figure 1.* Scenario planning matrix

## 2.1 Scenario 1 – If I see another piece of multimedia I think I will puke

Jessica and Kimberley are in Year 9 at Plato Grammar School (PGS), an expensive private school in Melbourne's south eastern suburbs. Jessica's parents chose this school because of its exceptionally high Victorian Certificate of Education (VCE) scores, its traditional academic curriculum (this school has character building rigour!) and its superior information and communication technologies. The school boasts the best information and communication technologies in the country - ultra-fast workstations, high-speed digital connection to the Internet, video conferencing between campuses, and its crowning glory – *AchieveHigh2* – a machine based *intelligent* tutor system.

*AchieveHigh2*, manages content for all curriculum areas, assesses students, provides feedback to teachers and parents - including a clever system of intelligent web cams that allows parents to monitor students from homes and offices, personalizes instruction – even catering for multiple intelligences and remedial students, utilizes virtual tutors – agents to provide learners with critical friends to assist in the construction of knowledge (*that's what the brochure says*). *AchieveHigh2* cost squillions to develop and Plato Grammar School pays an exorbitant *per student* licensing fee to LernTek for updates, service packs and access to lightning fast servers located in the US. Version 2.1.4 is due out next year.

The licensing fees are passed on to the clients of course, but Plato Grammar is able to keep costs down and remain competitive because they have their own *content development* department. The *content department* has an international reputation for developing quality learning objects. Content and learning objects are now tradable commodities and content developed for *AchieveHigh2* by Plato Grammar is sold back to LernTek who then on-sell it to other schools. Plato Grammar also saves money by manipulating student-teacher ratios. *AchieveHigh2* is not only capable of monitoring student learning but it can also monitor and manage student behaviour. Virtual behaviour monitoring agents patrol the virtual and physical space making a simple trip to the bathroom a worrying ordeal for those who do not take the direct route. Now only one human teacher is needed for 150 pupils and five classrooms.

This morning, Jessica and Kimberley have arrived at school to be told that the output for Year 9 is to be increased by 5% because they have not been working hard enough. This decision would have been made by *AchieveHigh2* and based on student output over the last three weeks.

"This isn't fair," complains Jessica, "this stuff is so boring."

"Shh!" cautions Kimberley, "Ms Taylor will hear us or the microphones will pick up your whining and you will get me into trouble – again!"

A learning agent pops up on Jessica's monitor and asks her if she needs assistance as her workstation has been inactive for a few minutes.

"God I hate that Merlin thingy" complains Jessica, "and if I see another piece of multimedia I'll puke!"

Suddenly all the monitors go black and pandemonium erupts. *AchieveHigh2* has crashed - third time this week. For Jessica, Kimberley and the other Year 9 students it doesn't get much better than this, it will take about half an hour to reboot the system, time to chat – both girls reach for their mobile phones (Dede, 2002).

## 2.2 Scenario 2 – e-ngage, e-mpower, e-nable

Jessica and Kimberley have arrived early. They know Ms Shaw will be in her room and will allow them to come in and do some work. They want to work on their project. Jess and Kim are in Year 9 at Sunshine High School and their home teacher is Ms Shaw. Ms Shaw is also their English and Studies of Society and Environment (SOSE) teacher. The girls love Ms Shaw and they love coming to school. At Sunshine High they have some cool technology – super-fast computers, with super-fast network and Internet connections in every room, and students have easy access to digital cameras, handheld computers, laptop machines, scanners and other peripherals. The girls are very adept at pushing data around the Internet and the network and they also have their personal digital communicators and assistants (PDCA). In the old days people carried a palm pilot, a mobile phone *and* a laptop computer– Jess and Kim giggle at the thought and think how clumsy all of that must have been. These days high speed wireless networks make the handling of data and communications through a PDCA so seamless that even Jess's little brother can do it and he's an idiot.

"You buy a PCDA like you used to buy a mobile phone," Jess tells Kim. "At least that's what my Dad says, but what would he know?"

But the cool technology is not why Jess and Kim love coming to school. School is a social event - chatting to Ms Shaw, the canteen, watching the Year 12 boys play football at lunch time, the debating club, the house athletics, swimming, netball, writing a story for the school magazine, deciding what to do on the weekend, art classes, learning to speak Chinese, school excursions, the school social, the deb ball in year 11, wood working, community service.

"You know what is the coolest thing about this school?" Jess says to Kim.

"The Year 12 boys?" ventures Kim. "The new sixty centimetre plasma screens?"

"No, it's the ......" replies Jess.

"Don't tell me I want to guess," interrupts Kim. "I know. It's being able to use your PCDA in class."

"No, although that is cool, the coolest thing is that we get to have a say about what it is we want to learn and how we learn. You know how Ms Shaw does all that brainstorming with us how what we do in Maths, Science and other subjects is all connected to the topic we are studying and how we get a chance to select the topic and the sort of activities we want to do and all that stuff - that's cool," says Jess.

"What? You're out of your tree. Those sixty centimetre plasma screens in the classroom – now that's cool. The stuff you're talking about, the schooly, teacher, learny thingy can never be cool – them's the rules - or have the rules changed?" enquires Kim.

"Yes they have," says Jessica.

As the girls approach the room their PCDAs vibrate and they read the message. Ms Shaw has gone to the staff room to get a cup of tea she will be back in five minutes. The message was not specifically sent to the girls by Ms Shaw, she did not know they were coming, but the smart technology incorporated into the building allows messages like this to be received as people approach the door. This sort of technology is now available in many buildings throughout the city, last week the girls went to the new museum, as they passed exhibits they could access, download, send and store information via their PCDAs, as well as interact with the many exhibits. The girls also use their PCDAs to pay for movie tickets, public transport; they can even use them to buy a can of coke from a vending machine.

Ms Shaw returns, she greets the girls and they all enter the classroom. A student from the 1990s would find difficulty in calling this a classroom, some things are familiar but others are straight out of Star Trek. There are pods of several small flat LCD screens as well as two large plasma screens, projectors, cameras, printers, and all sorts of other devices. There are some very comfortable looking sofas, office type chairs, an area for formal instruction, tables arranged for small group work, whiteboards, and displays of students' work. A closer examination of the whiteboards and the notice boards and it is easy to determine that the students are investigating the topic *Australian Discovery and Exploration*. There are lots of concept maps, questions and ideas displayed all over the place. On one noticeboard several sub topics and focus questions have been written, and projects assigned.

Some other students enter the room and pleasantries are exchanged. Without direction from Sue screens flicker and digital images illuminate the room. Matthew and Kate want to show the others what they have been working on. They are investigating the expeditions of Matthew Flinders and Nicholas Baudin. Through their PCDAs and the wireless network they have downloaded their latest work onto the school network and have it displayed on one of the large plasma screens. Using some very clever programming they have created a very interactive piece of multimedia that helps to answer several questions that the class has about the rivalry between Flinders and Baudin and the significance of their expeditions. It starts by tracing the voyages of the explorers on a map of the world and as the ships reach certain points on the map the user is invited to explore what happened at these locations. Kim, Jessica and Sue watch fascinated. The pair has used primary historical documents available online at French and British museums to build their project. The paintings done by artists and scientists on the Baudin exhibition are stunning and the sea charts of the Australian coast made by

Baudin are exquisite. The love letters written by Flinders to the new bride he left behind for 10 years are interesting. Sue thinks about how she can use them to help the students understand the notions of *duty, honour, and glory for queen and country* and whether these things are still relevant today. It seems that Matthew has become very curious about the French and is talking about doing some research on some guy called Napoleon. Other teachers might reflect on the power of the technology and its impact on Matthew but Sue reflects on the power of *curiosity*. It drove Baudin, Flinders, generations of historians and scientists and academics and now it is driving Matthew. Curiosity may have killed the cat but the lust for *wanting to know* is probably one of the greatest gifts a teacher can nurture in her students. Sue thinks about how she can weave this thought into the students' learning.

Jessica and Kim have been investigating the First Fleet and are ready to show what they have done. Through the brainstorming done at the beginning of the topic they became very interested in what it was like to be a teenager on the First Fleet and a part of the First Settlement. They have decided to do this by presenting a series of two narratives – a female convict and a male convict. Their research has led then to primary documents available online, to several databases about the First Fleet, to an old Alan Ladd movie which they were able to download from the net and hundreds of web sites about the topic. They have decided that they will present the narratives to the class as a play. The play will be video taped for later reference. After the play the girls are going to get the class to pretend they have been transported and to write *Postcards from Port Jackson* back to their families in England. They have found some old quill pens for the activity. They love taking on the role of teacher when they present projects and have become very adept at choosing activities for the rest of the class that are challenging and engaging. Choosing not do a multimedia presentation has really put the pressure on Jessica and Kim. The writing of the narratives has to be spot on – crisp, accurate and entertaining. Sue is pleased with their choice as it gives her an opportunity to talk to the class about writing genres and writing for an audience. Kim and Jessica have the first narrative displayed on the screen. Kim gets a virtual agent to read the narrative and looks to the others for some feedback.

"That's horrible," states Matthew. "I would have just jumped overboard."

"Why don't you have some images on the plasma screens while you do the play?" suggests Kate.

Sue makes a few suggestions; the virtual agent makes some suggestions about spelling and grammar in the $18^{th}$ century. Jessica dictates the changes and the computer obliges. Jessica and Kim begin discussing the second narrative.

As the rest of the class start to arrive Sue takes a couple of minutes to reflect on the impact technology has made to the teaching and learning environment. If she chooses she can access a range of virtual learning objects on every topic and concept under the sun. She sometimes uses them to fill gaps in her own knowledge and sometimes to help her explain specific concepts to groups of children. She rarely uses them to assemble a *course* because she wants the students to have some control and ownership of the curriculum. Other teachers tell Sue that all the brainstorming, integration of subjects and a multidisciplinary approach to the investigation of topics is messy. She looks across at Jess, Kim, Matthew, Kate, and the others entering the room and thinks about the commitment these kids make to their own learning – yes it is messy but it is worth it. With the technology Sue can bring the outside world to the classroom and take the classroom to the outside world. Recent breakthroughs in wireless networks, data compression and bandwidth make synchronous video communication cheap and real. Later today the class will link to the British Museum to look at Captain Cook's journal and when John comes in later for a Maths class they will link to the maritime museum at Plymouth in the United Kingdom to analyse the mathematics of ship building in the 18$^{th}$ century.

For Sue and her students, the access to information, smart technology, bandwidth, PCDAs and other devices is stunning. When she first started teaching she never dreamed it would be like this and the breakthroughs they have made in the last 10 years have been astonishing. But the sobering thought is that students like Jess, Kim, Matthew and Kate are the privileged elite. For many in Australia the teaching and learning environment provided by this school is not accessible. For students in other parts of the world it is science fiction; the digital divide is wider than ever.

## 3. CONCLUSION

So what do the two scenarios tell about the trends, issues, and developments relating to the future of education and technology? I think the scenarios suggest that technology is changing the way we teach and the way we learn, but so is our increased understanding of how humans construct knowledge and achieve deep understanding. As the digital boundaries are pushed there is a temptation that the technology, and those developing the technology, will dictate how teaching and learning should happen in a digital world. There is danger in this hegemony for the likely outcome could well be scenario one, with the technology sector usurping a significant slice of the education budget and resulting in *a whole lot of puking going on!* However there is also danger in scenario two. The obvious danger is the widening of the digital divide but there is also danger in educators, through ignorance and arrogance, rejecting what the digital world has to offer.

The technology is important so is the recognition that teaching and learning is about curiosity, challenge, creativity, connectedness, excellence, engagement, and empowerment. Perhaps the most important thing of all to acknowledge is the desperate need for teachers like Sue Shaw with her ability to use the technology to help her establish powerful learning environments that are interesting, exciting, intellectually stimulating and underpinned by our understanding of the human condition. The technology matters, but good teachers matter more.

## REFERENCES

Bajscy, R. (2002). Technologies and learning. *Visions 2020*. Washington, DC: U.S. Department of Commerce, Technology Administration Office.

Chen, M. & Arnold, S. (2002). A day in the life of a young learner: A 2020 vision. *Visions 2020*. Washington, DC: U.S. Department of Commerce, Technology Administration Office of Public Affairs.

College of Marin (2002). *Scenario Planning, College of Marin 835 College Ave Kentfield California*. Retrieved October 17, 2002 from http://www.marin.cc.ca.us/scenario/what_exactly_is.htm.

DE&Ta (2002). *Middle Years, State of Victoria* (Department of Education & Training). Retrieved October 17, 2002 from http://www.sofweb.vic.edu.au/mys/

DE&Tb (2002). *Early Years strategy, State of Victoria* (Department of Education & Training). Retrieved October 17, 2002 from http://www.sofweb.vic.edu.au/eys/index.htm.

Dede, C. (2002). Vignettes about the future of learning technologies. *Visions 2020*. Washington, DC: U.S. Department of Commerce, Technology Administration Office of Public Affairs.

Duffy, T. & Cunningham, D. (1996). Constructivism: Implications for the design and delivery of instruction. In D. H. Jonassen (Ed.), *Handbook of Research For Educational Communications and Technology*. New York: Macmillan Library Reference USA.

Education Queensland (2002). *The New Basics Project*. The State of Queensland: Education Queensland.

Hannafin, M. & Land, S. (1997). The foundations and assumptions of technology-enhanced student-centred learning environments. *Instructional Science*, 25, 167-202.

Hawkins, D. (1994). Constructivism: Some history. In P. Fensham, R. Gunstone & R. White (Eds), *The Content of Science: A Constructivist Approach to its Teaching and Learning*. London: The Falmer Press.

Hinrichs, R. & Gates, B. (2002). A vision for lifelong learning - Year 2020. *Visions 2020*. Washington, DC: U.S. Department of Commerce, Technology Administration Office of Public Affairs.

Mooneyham, J. R. (1993). *The Rest of our Lives: What It'll Be Like*. Retrieved October 17, 2002 from http://www.jrmooneyham.com/rest.html

NCREL (2002). *Engauge, North Central Regional Educational Laboratory*. Retrieved October 17, 2002 from http://www.ncrel.org/engauge/

Neumann, U. & Kyriakakis, C. (2002). 2020 Classroom. *Visions 2020*. Washington, DC: U.S. Department of Commerce, Technology Administration Office of Public Affairs.

Office of Technology & Assessment (1994). *Education and Technology: Future Visions. Washington DC, U.S. Congress.* Retrieved October 17, 2002 from http://www.wws.princeton.edu/cgibin/byteserv.prl/~ota/disk1/1995/9522/9522.PDF

Pausch, R. (2002). A Curmudgeon's vision for technology in education. *Visions 2020.* Washington, DC: U.S. Department of Commerce, Technology Administration Office of Public Affairs.

Pearson, I. & Cochrane, P. (1994). 200 Futures for 2020, BT Laboratories. 2002.

Ridgeway, J. & Passey, D. (1991). A constructivist approach to educational computing. *Australian Educational Computing* 6(2), 4-9.

Romeo, G. I. (2000). *Computers, constructivism and engaged learning: Sue Shaw's story.* Australian Computers in Education Conference ACEC 2000. Melbourne: Computing in Education Group of Victoria & Briter Solutions.

Schwartz, P. & Australian Business Network. (1996). *The Art of the Long View: Paths to Strategic Insight for Yourself and Your Company.* St. Leonards, NSW: Australian Business Network.

Spender, D. & Stewart, F. (2002). Embracing e-learning in Australian Schools. Melbourne, Commonwealth Bank. Retrieved October 17, 2002 from http:// about.commbank.com.au/GAC_File_Metafile/0,1687,2003%255Fe%252Dlearning%255F report,00.pdf

U.S. Department of Commerce (2002). Visions 2020. Washington DC, U.S. Department of Commerce Technology Admnistration Office of Public Affairs. Retrieved October 17, 2002 from http://www.ta.doc.gov/reports/TechPolicy/2020Visions.pdf

VonGlaserfeld, E. (1991). Constructivism in education. In A. Lewy (Ed.), *The International Encyclopedia of Curriculum.* Oxford/New York: Pergamon Press.

# Reports of Focus Group Discussions:

# Group C – The Role of the Teacher

**Chair:** Margaret Cox, *King's College, London, mj.cox@kcl.ac.uk*
**Rapporteur:** *Steve Kennewell, University of Wales Swansea, s.e.kennewell@swan.ac.uk*
**Participants:** Janine Bowes (Australia), Roger Carlsen (USA), Ted Clark (Australia), Dianne Chambers (Australia), Harry Gankema (The Netherlands), Helene Godinet (France), Elizabeth Hartnell-Young (Australia), Tony Jones (Australia), Nancy Law (Hong Kong)

## 1. INTRODUCTION

Teachers' roles vary according to the educational system, the culture, the nature of the school and the age of their students. This diversity will be able to increase with the support of ICT.

The group's ideas similarly reflected a diversity of backgrounds and perspectives. We have identified some current trends in successful practice and combined these with our own values and visions for the future. Our ideas are not intended to be definitive in nature or exhaustive in their scope.

## 2. WHAT WILL BE THE CHARACTERISTICS OF TEACHING IN THE FUTURE?

If we are to consider the future role of the **teacher**, then it is clear that we need to set this in the context of the wider field of **teaching**, which may or may not involve the physical presence of a teacher. Through ICT, aspects of the role of teacher can be distributed in time, space and person leading to a transformation in the nature of teaching. The increased connectedness of individuals supports the formation of teams of people who contribute to a particular student's learning, and members of such teams can adopt different roles.

One fundamental difference in the future will be the availability of an **enabling** ICT infrastructure appropriate to the chosen pedagogy. The context of the learner in terms of age, location, circumstances and individual learning style will determine the most appropriate mix of learning strategy and mode. It is most important that the needs of learners determine the uses of ICT rather than ICT developments determining the educational agenda.

Three scenarios have been developed to illustrate the diversity and variety of approaches that are enabled by the availability of ICT. These scenarios are not intended to be mutually exclusive but rather illustrate how the educational process can be adapted to suit the needs of learners and optimise the learning experience, using ICT as an enabler. The context of the learner is crucial to the selection of pedagogy for a given circumstance. These scenarios are written for the role of the future secondary teacher.

## 2.1 Scenario 1 – face to face/in person

There is a building for protection from the elements, open continually. It consists of flexible spaces. Students are teenagers and anyone else who wants to belong (commit) to this community. The staff includes many types of professionals. The community is confident, has a sense of purpose and looks out to the world. Learner-teacher relationships are many-to-many and one-to-one: teaching roles can be split and regrouped, and the boundary between learners and teachers is crossed. Communication in the community and with others is synchronous and asynchronous; learning objects are physical and digital. Learners and teachers plan/discuss/negotiate the use of resources (people and things). Learning outcomes benefit the community and the individuals (assessment is changed).

The teachers care for each other as much as they care for other learners. Digital records of activity and outcomes are stored and published in a knowledge management system. They plan the use of resources and the appropriate application of technology. They connect with other professionals and are willing to share knowledge with colleagues, students, and the community. They have all developed their core competencies together with specialist expertise and work in a way that complements the abilities of their fellow team members and students.

They have knowledge of learning theories and are able to identify adequate learning processes for individuals and groups. They participate in teams that design the technology infrastructure. They have access to an electronic learning environment, including information outside the learning community, communication inside the building, and knowledge databases with open access at any time for every member of the community.

## 2.2 Scenario 2 – blended learning/hybrid learning

The context is extended educational time and space, with a mixture of synchronous and asynchronous groupings. This can be face to face and/or at a distance; integrating electronic alternatives; involving a team of educators with access to online resources and local and international partners via an ICT network.

Teachers are part of a dynamic team that designs and facilitates learning (face to face or at a distance) integrating ICT for individual students, selecting appropriate resources and learning strategies. Teachers take on many roles and are active participants in the learning space. They communicate with other educators, with the community and with learners, to design individual pathways for learners. They are open, dynamic and flexible and are able to adapt each day, each moment, and for each child, taking into consideration the diversity of learners (culture, language, background, interests) and the range of resources available on the network. They initiate and sustain communication and relationships with all stakeholders in the learning process (parents, learners, other teachers, media, experts, education authorities etc.). They empower students as independent learners and champion learning in the community. They act as the Hub: the focal point to structure and stimulate learning. They collaborate, share, and disseminate learning strategies, materials, techniques, resources, etc. with their colleagues, both local and distant.

## 2.3 Scenario 3 – distributed "teacher"

(In this scenario, names are intentionally used to highlight the distributed nature of the various roles whilst retaining the importance of someone [Sika] maintaining a holistic view of the individual learner.)

Sika's job is to maintain close network contact with 100 year 10 students studying a full curriculum in a cluster of four non-attendance schools. She knows each child's learning and social requirements intimately and deals with each child individually. She does not teach students content directly, but organizes learning programs for each student using a range of technologies and pedagogical software agents. She is occasionally called upon to organize a group online discussion. Today Sika is organizing an online rehearsal involving four groups of students. The production group has just completed their virtual placement and the teacher is confident that the show this year will be a success as both the staff from MediaEntertainment and the children have consistently reported with enthusiasm their progress in the weekly virtual Karaoke Show and Tell. However, she is a bit worried about Yuki whose pedagogical agent has reported her apparent loss of interest in the science project. Sika decides to contact Uba the Science coordinator via SMS to set up an extra tutorial for students working on similar projects. Before the rehearsal this afternoon, Sika has to meet with Shikiva and his parents who have just decided to join this distributed learning cluster because he has just been selected into the national swimming team. They need to discuss an appropriate program to take account of Shikiva's personal interest as well as his educational and social background.

# 3. CONCLUSIONS

The scenarios contain many common features, and highlight the key features of how the future teacher's role is supported by ICT. ICT adds complexity to the possibilities of teaching but it can also change the need for teacher control by supporting self directed learning and greater individualisation of programmes. Networks afford the sharing of ideas amongst teachers and growth in the sense of community, which provides a good model for students' learning.

Teachers need new competencies in ICT and in developing students' learning skills, but learners' access to a variety of learning sources – human and virtual – means that each individual teacher does not need all competencies. As learners have more choice about programmes, teachers need to gain their authority through evidence of pedagogical expertise. There will be a stage during which they need to challenge students' and parents' expectations of traditional teaching approaches.

They should balance the emphasis on pedagogy and on technology, making informed decisions on the resources to be deployed. They need to have time to fulfil their roles effectively, including managing the complexity in the task of teaching; this is an issue for leaders/decision makers to address.

Whilst there are changes in the roles of individuals involved in teaching, it could be argued that the characteristics of a good teacher of the future would encompass much of what we expect of a good teacher of the present day. In order to be successful, teachers or teaching teams in the future should consider and reflect on how ICT can modify, enhance or transform these traditional teacher roles. They may be required to:

- act as learning strategists who can identify pathways for individual learners;
- select appropriate resources, including sources of pedagogical expertise in subject specialisations;
- know how, when (and when not) to intervene;

- develop students' generic skills including learning how to be independent learners and contribute to their progressive understanding of subject content in the context of rich learning tasks;
- in relation to desired learning outcomes, design tasks, produce and select resources (including ICT where appropriate) and provide additional support, taking into account/according to learners' abilities and learning styles;
- motivate learners through demonstrating enthusiasm for learning and for the subject content involved;
- demonstrate and promote consistent values and attitudes;
- be open to innovation in pedagogy, take risks and continue to be life long learners;
- be closely connected within the team, and to learners, other colleagues and society.

# Reports of Focus Group Discussions:

# Group D – The Role of Teachers: Lifelong Learners in a Community of Practice

**Chair:** Wolfgang Weber, *State Institute for Schools, Soest, Germany, wolfgang.weber@mail.lsw.nrw.de*
**Rapporteur:** Trees Haaksma, *Christian Pedagogic Studycentre, Amersfoort, The Netherlands, t.haaksma@cps.nl*
**Participants:** Clayton Passoa (Brazil), Geoff Romeo (Australia), Sindre Røsvik (Norway), Toshinori Saito (Japan), Theda Thomas (Australia), Leena Vaino (Finland), Jose Valente (Brazil), Rosa Maria Bottino (Italy)

## 1. INTRODUCTION

We begin by thinking about the roles of the teacher. How can teachers support students to become lifelong learners in a *networking* society? To give an answer we have to answer different questions:

- What do the learners need, how do they learn, what do they want to learn, how can teachers achieve that?
- What must the teacher do, what tools does s/he need, what learning environment(s) can s/he offer/design?
- How do the answers to these questions influence the school's infrastructure and the school as an organization? What role can the teacher take in this process?

## 2. MISSION COMES FIRST

Our vision of education specifies the way we want our students to learn, what roles the teachers should have, how we use ICT and what organization of the school will make this work. All professionals involved in the school (not only the teachers, but the managers and supporters as well) should be aware of their mission. We as members of one of the working groups 'Roles of the teacher' made the following mission statement: "to support students to become lifelong learners in a *networking* society." Within this, we'll focus on the roles of the teacher.

First of all we have to define 'lifelong learning' and 'a networking society'.

Lifelong learning is defined as an attitude or mindset that you can learn at any time and at any place. A networking society refers not only to physical networks but also to the constant exchange, interaction and reflection of different institutions and people. Schools, teachers and learners should be viewed as an integral part of the networking society.

# 3. TEACHER ROLES

## 3.1 Supporting the learner

When the teacher has this role s/he should be able to create learning situations to enable learners to construct cognitive, affective and social knowledge.

In order to do this the teacher first of all must be a coach who knows the learner through formative evaluation of cognitive, social and affective knowledge. As a coach s/he also challenges the learner perhaps by confrontation or by putting up a mirror to create reflective situations, so both teacher and learner know where the learner stands.

With this knowledge the coach sets tasks with achievable goals. By doing this, the teacher motivates the students.

When the teacher uses this knowledge (i.e. the knowledge the learner has acquired from reflection) to find the right way (material or resources) to get the learner to the next step or a higher level, s/he acts as a facilitator. A facilitator also knows how and when each individual learner can attain the curriculum objectives.

The teacher in the role of conductor knows what has to be done to attain the curriculum objectives for the whole group/class. How and when to get there. S/he also knows how to manage the class(room).

Last but not least, the teacher is a resource. S/he knows where to get the relevant information and when to use her/his own knowledge to help the learner, or who or what else can help.

S/he also publishes the products of the learners' learning process for other learners to access and encourages the students to do so.

## 3.2 Supporting the learning environment

The learning environment has to be considered as a whole: the roles, the tools, the content, the tasks, the actors, their relationships, the context, et cetera. The teacher is the designer of the classroom arrangements. S/he brings in innovative elements, setting the tools and the activities the students have to engage in.

The teacher suggests from her/his background of media-, content- and pedagogical competences what elements of the learning environment could be helpful for the learning process.

In this sense s/he is a consultant and advisor for the improvement of the learning environment.

## 3.3 Supporting society

Teachers are accountable to society. Different societies might put varying pressures upon the teacher and this will affect the roles of the teacher.

Teachers need to make decisions about their role and how they implement social issues within their learning community.

Specific roles within the 'societal' role are discussed below.

### 3.3.1 Duty of care role

Teachers have a duty of care to their students in the absence of the parents. This may include acting like a social worker and a parent. Crucial to this would be a communication role with the parents. This communication can be facilitated by ICT.

### 3.3.2 Ethical role

Ethics can be perceived differently by different people. The teacher has a role to play both in behaving ethically themselves and promoting ethical behavior in the students. This ethical stance will be influenced by the culture within which the school is situated. Good citizenship both online and in society are necessary in this role.

### 3.3.3 Cultural role

Teachers make decisions about how to present cultural aspects of their curriculum. ICT may be used by the teacher to raise awareness of their own and others' culture.

In some cultures the teacher has a role in facilitating the parental role in the education process.

### 3.3.4 Certification role

Society expects the teacher to produce students of a specified standard. These expectations may be through benchmarks, external examinations and/or certification.

### 3.3.5 Organizational role

The teacher is a cooperator, a change agent and an integrator. Overall s/he is a lifelong learner.

### 3.3.6 Cooperator

S/he is aware of the mission given by society, s/he is able to discuss it, and to make it concrete by developing a platform of common values with her/his colleagues. In this way s/he acknowledges the vision of the school to be communicated within the organization and outside to the stakeholders.

### 3.3.7 Change agent

The change- agent is a leader. S/he is future oriented, is a meaningful part of her/his team and has the skills to be a team player. Seeing the importance of making the school a learning organization, the teacher needs to contribute to change, always ready to share ideas to construct collective knowledge. Of course s/he also fulfils her/his responsibilities within the organization.

### 3.3.8 Integrator

The integrator makes different things on different levels fit within the organization, with the student at the centre of the developments. People and ideas are adopted in a functional/rational way.

It is essential that teachers are organized in teams. Roles are distributed within the team according to talent and competencies. Even though teachers within teams are responsible of different aspects of the teacher roles, they all need to take care of 'all' roles, if needed.

# 4. CONCLUSIONS AND RECOMMENDATIONS

## 4.1 Conclusions

The role of supporting students to become lifelong learners in a networking society is multi-faceted and complex. It is not fair or reasonable to expect all the roles defined to be in one person. 'Teacher' in a networking society needs to be a team. The expectation is that teachers must be professionals who are members of a community of practice. The community should be an eclectic mix of professionals with different expertise within and outside the school. Within this framework ICT is used to enhance and expand the team and to help individuals to grow personally and professionally.

## 4.2 Recommendations

1. When organizing a teachers' team it should be realized that this has consequences for the school as an organization. It should not be a hierarchy, but a learning organization that knows how to use Human Resource Management and how to deal with teachers who are also learners.
2. The teacher as a lifelong learner must have full access to ICT and be given enough time to develop as a professional.

# Section 4

# Teaching and Learning Environments of the Future

# Mathematical Teaching and Learning Environment Mediated by ICT

Giampaolo Chiappini, Bettina Pedemonte and Elisabetta Robotti
*Istituto per le Tecnologie Didattiche – Consiglio Nazionale delle Ricerche, chiappini@ima.ge.cnr.it*

**Abstract:** This paper presents a theoretical model we draw on when designing and developing ICT-based systems for mathematics teaching and learning which falls within the cultural-historical framework inspired by the work of Vygotsky. The main objective of this work is to demonstrate that technological tools can assume a crucial role in supporting teaching and learning processes if they allow teachers to reconfigure mathematical objects with the aim to create activity settings where students can interact with mathematical knowledge integrating a perceptive-motor approach to mathematical knowledge with a symbolic-reconstructive one. Re-configuring a mathematical object, which is abstract and formal, means transforming it in order to make it more concrete with the aim of using it in the student's Zone of Proximal Development, where learning can occur and teaching can be defined. In the paper two examples of application of the model will be furnished, making reference to the work of design and implementation we are developing within a European project called aITALES.

## 1. INTRODUCTION

Over recent years there has been increasingly widespread debate over the mediation role that ICT-based systems can play within mathematics education. For some time research in this field has focused either on mathematics teaching on the one hand or on mathematics learning on the other.

The experience of CAI (Computer Aided Instruction) focused on the contents to be learned and on transmission methods, assigning the computer the role of mediator in the transmission and presentation of mathematical contents and concepts.

Later, criticism of the transmission approach together with the development of more advanced technologies shifted the focus towards more constructivist applications of computer technology in didactic practice. The idea of the learner-centred approach was developed: students were seen as being active players in the construction of their mathematical knowledge.

Computer assisted learning (CAL), which is still a significant element in present-day education, has focused on the construction of highly interactive systems based on microworlds. These systems incorporate a domain of mathematical knowledge that the students can explore through interaction with the primitives present in the system interface. These systems are no longer created for transmitting content, but rather for supporting student learning processes; learning is seen as the outcome of student-software interaction (Abelson & diSessa, 1981; Papert, 1980).

The cultural-historical frameworks inspired by the work of Vygotsky highlighted the necessity within all educational activities to intertwine the teaching and learning processes (Bartolini Bussi, 1994). The link between these two processes is to be found in what Vygotsky defines as the Zone of Proximal Development (ZPD) (Vygotsky, 1978). The cultural-historical framework is centred on educational activity in its entirety. Elements of crucial importance are the use of tools and the role of the teacher: the tools are seen as mediator of the individual's actions and of the communication that takes place between participants in the activity; the teacher is seen as a co-participant in the activity who gives assistance to the students' performance.

Our work in designing mathematics teaching/learning systems falls squarely within this framework of reference, which on the one hand appears extremely promising for educational applications but on the other raises a series of research issues and questions:

- What criteria should be used in the design of mathematics learning systems to ensure that they can be used to support teaching and at the same time to mediate learning activities?
- What criteria should be used for selecting the resources for incorporation in the system, which is to foster the teaching and learning of a particular knowledge domain?
- What types of cognitive and epistemological references should be taken on board when implementing the chosen maths resources so that interface characteristics are appropriate for the students' knowledge level and for the development of significant mathematics learning?

This paper will seek to address some of these questions and will describe some of the reference works we draw on when designing and implementing systems for mathematics teaching and learning. To these ends, we will discuss our activity in the European project called ITALES (Innovative Teaching and Learning Environments for Schools IST-2000-26356); our involvement entails the design and development of ARI-LAB-2 (Bottino & Chiappini, 2001), a system for mathematics teaching and learning in primary and secondary school. This system is a teaching and learning environment for primary and secondary school. In order to explain and justify the criteria and the references we draw on when designing maths systems, we will concentrate in particular on two microworlds we are developing for inclusion in ARI-LAB-2: these microworlds are currently undergoing implementation.

## 2. GENERAL CRITERIA FOR DESIGNING OF ICT BASED SYSTEMS SUPPORTING TEACHING AND LEARNING PROCESSES IN MATHEMATICS

Research in the psychology of learning has shown that, fundamentally, there are two modes of knowledge building: the perceptive-motor approach and the symbolic-reconstructive approach. The former is not limited to the initial phases of cognitive development, but is also involved in the most advanced learning processes, which includes mathematics (consider the role played by graphic representations in mathematics or that of mathematical machines for the development of specific ideas). The perceptive-motor approach involves action and perception, and produces learning based on doing, touching, moving and seeing. The second mode of knowledge acquisition is the symbolic-reconstructive approach, which is active from the very beginning of the child's cognitive development. This works with symbols (linguistic, mathematical, logical) and involves the mental reconstruction of 'objects', meanings and their mental representations. It is a more sophisticated way of knowing, one that requires awareness of procedures together with appropriation of the symbols used and of their meanings.

It is important to note that both of these approaches to knowledge acquisition are mediated by tools of a different nature, and that these carry out their mediational functions in profoundly different ways (Vygotsky, 1978). Vygotsky distinguishes between two types of mediation tool for each human activity: technical tools and psychological tools. The former mediate the interaction of the individual with the outside world, and are directed towards the control of nature. The use of such tools brings about a transformation in objects: that is, it produces external effects on the object that can be controlled at the perceptive-motor level. Psychological tools, by contrast, are directed toward the mastery or control of one's own processes of behaviour. They are directed internally and do not produce any transformation in the object. Vygotsky, moreover, notes that the development of the higher psychological functions involved in all processes of comprehension and of meaning construction is the result of an integration of technical and psychological tools in the activity.

The acquisition and application of technical tools, controlled by means of the perceptive-motor approach, extends the individual's sphere of influence and allows the development of new experience, while the acquisition and application of new psychological tools, controlled by means of the symbolic-reconstructive approach, raises the levels of influence and awareness of the processes and phenomena which characterise human activity (Engström, 1997).

The acquisition and application of these two different types of tools occur in the student's Zone of Proximal Development (ZPD), defined by Vygotsky as "the distance between the actual developmental level as determined by independent problem solving and the level of potential development as determined through problem solving under adult guidance or in collaboration with more capable peers" (Vygotsky, 1978, p. 86).

A student's ZPD is characterized by a strict connection between teaching and learning process. Effective teaching can be defined as being within a student's ZPD.

Tharp and Gallimore give a very useful and operative definition of teaching: it consists in assisting performance through a student's ZPD. Teaching occurs when the performance of a student engaged in a task is achieved with assistance.

Tharp and Gallimore point out that assistance is best provided through instructional conversation, a dialogue between teacher and learner in which the teacher listens carefully in order to grasp the students' communicative intent, and tailors the dialogue to foster their emerging understanding (Tharp & Gallimore, 1999).

According to Tharp and Gallimore there are different ways of offering assistance; the forms of assistance for student learning need to be accomplished by creating activity settings that maximise opportunities for co-participation and instructional conversation with the teacher and with peers.

One criterion for activity settings is that they need to permit maximum assistance in the performance of the task at hand. These settings must engage students in goal-oriented activity in which the teacher may participate as an assistant or co-participant as the need arises.

Within this framework we believe that appropriate tools can assume a crucial role in the structuring of activity settings in which assisted performance can be maximised; we believe also that assisted performance can be maximized if the mathematical teaching objects, which are abstract and formal objects, can be reconfigured in appropriate way in order to create activity settings where it is possible:

- to exploit a perceptive-motor approach to mathematical knowledge both during the problem solving activity and the relate instructional conversation
- to favour a strict integration between the perceptive-motor approach and the symbolic-reconstructive one during the development of the didactical activity.

Our work on designing and implementing systems for mathematics teaching and learning is based on the idea that ICT can play an important role in the reconfiguration of the mathematical objects of teaching according to the above mentioned aims.

In the following sections we will try to analyse some problems which we have taken into account in order to reconfigure mathematical objects of teaching in the domain of the rational numbers.

## 3. THE CONTEXT OF APPLICATION: THE CASE OF RATIONAL NUMBERS

In standard practice the teaching of rational numbers in lower secondary school is primarily based on the development of algorithmic and calculus skills.

Numerous investigations into mathematics teaching have highlighted that the knowledge gained by students is often lacking in stability. At best, satisfactory technical training is achieved, as well as correct use of calculation rules. In standard practice there is a marked split between the treatment of fractions on the one hand and meaning on the other. It is hard to get students to develop concepts about the properties that typify rational numbers and that distinguish them from, say, natural numbers. It is difficult to get students to develop ideas regarding concepts like the class of equivalence, of order or of density in Q.

It thus seems that teachers experience difficulty in providing a structure for the thoughts and actions that lead to the development of sound ideas about these concepts, and this makes it difficult for students to cope with tasks that entail non-standard use of these properties.

In addition, we note that in standard teaching practice great importance is given to the symbolic-reconstructive approach; for example, graphic representation is employed only for building the concept of the fraction as an operator. This type of teaching approach appears unsuitable for getting students to construct appropriate meaning in this knowledge domain.

To overcome these difficulties, we have designed two microworlds, the Fractions Microworld and the Manipulator Microworld. The former can be employed for shaping an activity setting that encourages exploration of the properties of rational numbers, conjecturing about those properties, and then empirical validation.

The Manipulator Microworld can be used for shaping an activity setting that fosters the capacity to manipulate symbolically numerical expressions in Q so as to demonstrate the properties of rational numbers that have emerged during work with the Fractions Microworld.

Figure 1 outlines a visual model, based on Thale's theorem, that will be embedded in the Fractions Microworld in order to allow students to explore the properties of rational numbers. The model is comprised of two half-lines that have the same origin: the half-line r of numbers and the half-line t for performing divisions and carry-overs of selected lengths along r.

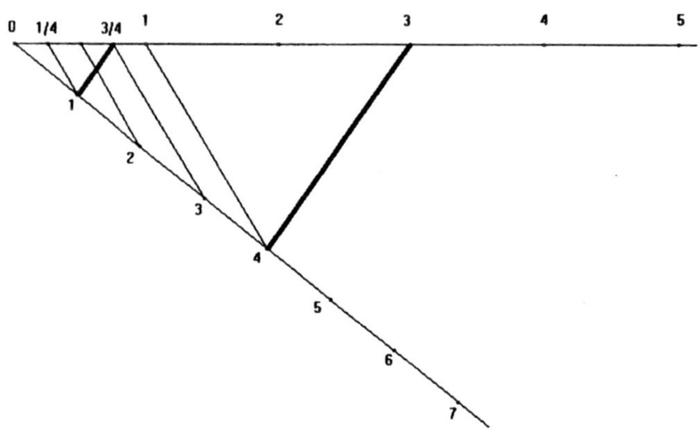


*Figure 1.* Visual model of the fraction microworld

Interactions with this visual model in the microworld allow the students to construct a mental image of concepts such as the class of equivalence, of order or of density in Q. This is done by performing divisions of selected lengths along r, by using specific commands (for example zooming in on points along the line), by reading and interpreting the graphic effects produced when using the resources at hand.

The visual feedback of the Fraction Microworld has been studied in order to promote the construction of concepts related to rational numbers, exploiting geometrical properties that can be controlled by means of a perceptive-motor approach.

The microworld also makes it possible to develop schemes for performing rational number operations based on division, and on carry-over, the sum and the difference of lengths selected along the half-line r of numbers.

We remark also that in this microworld the perceptive-motor activity produces effects on the symbolic fraction notation. In this way meanings constructed through the perceptive-motor activity can contribute to assign a sense to the use of fraction notation.

Figure 2 shows the set of commands available in the Manipulator Microworld for performing symbolic manipulations of numerical expressions in Q.

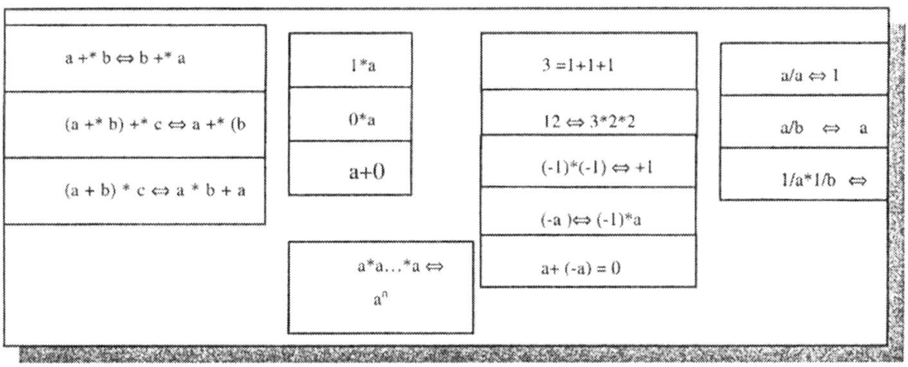


*Figure 2.* Command list in the interface of manipulator microworld

This set of commands has been designed for the building of an activity setting in which manipulation of numerical expressions in Q is seen not as application of calculus rules but as a demonstration of the equivalence of two forms of numerical expression. This demonstration can be worked out by means of axioms reified in the interface of the system that allow the user to visualize and to make explicit mathematical entities and the relations that occur in the symbolic manipulation.

In addition it should be noted that this microworld was designed to be used together with the Fractions Microworld so as to demonstrate conjectures about the properties of rational numbers that emerge during work with the Fractions Microworld (e.g. for demonstrating that 1/3 is equivalent to 1-2/3, that 2/3+3/5 is equivalent to (2x5+3x2)/(3x5)).

We note that the prototype models of these two microworlds underwent two years of trials and testing in the classroom, where students used paper and pen, ruler and compass, under the guidance of highly motivated and expert teachers. The trial results highlighted the specific needs of students in problem solving, and those of teachers in providing assistance. When the two microworlds were used, totally new possibilities were opened up through the potential for visualisation, interaction and computation offered by the technology.

## 4. CRITERIA FOR THE RE-CONFIGURATION OF THE MATHEMATICAL TEACHING OBJECTS

In the previous section we saw that the mathematical teaching objects are not only accessible by means of a symbolic-reconstructive approach, but also starting from a perceptive-motor approach. They are objects that can be re-configured by means of the appropriate use of specific technologies. Re-configuring a mathematical teaching object, which is abstract and formal, means transforming it in order to make it more concrete so as to use it in the student's ZPD, where learning and teaching can occur.

The mathematical teaching object begins to come alive through the incorporation of specific 'mathematical resources' for the activity embedded within a technological tool.

Through the process of incorporation of a mathematical resource in a system an important cultural transformation is accomplished. A resource that, up to that moment, could exist only on a purely mental plane because it was accessible only through a symbolic approach, is reified and is made available in a tool with which the subject can interact, being able to observe the effects produced by the system. Let us see some examples.

The Fraction Microworld embodies the possibility of using operational schemes based on divisions of selected lengths (which can be controlled by a perceptive-motor approach) in order to relate different fractions, which are equivalent to each other, on the same point in the number line. In this way students can approach rational number concepts such as the class of equivalence of fractions by means of a perceptive-motor approach.

The Manipulator Microworld embodies the elementary properties of the arithmetical operations. These properties are incorporated in the Manipulator Microworld through the use of specific commands that can be used to demonstrate the equivalence of two numerical expressions in Q.

When students use these commands they exploit the experience of other people who in the past have tried to resolve problems similar to those with which the student is involved. This experience is reflected in the commands available in the interface of the system.

Through this process of incorporation, the system user is provided with the operational means for tackling and solving classes of problems related to the knowledge domain that the system addresses.

We observe that the mathematical resources embedded in a system reify mental processes involved in interaction with aspects of the system's mathematical culture of reference. Incorporation therefore creates the conditions whereby a formal, abstract knowledge domain can become an operative, concrete field of experience for both students and teachers (Boero, Dapueto, Ferrari, Garuti, Parenti & Scali, 1995).

The framework thus far described implies that the designer of a mathematics learning system needs to tackle and solve problems that are critical to the system's educational purpose. These can be summed up in the following questions: When addressing a particular knowledge domain, which resources should be incorporated and why? How should those resources be incorporated?

We note that the answer to the first question determines the particular epistemology of mathematical knowledge that may emerge through the activity, and thus the particular type of mathematical experience that the student can develop with the system's mediation. Choosing a geometrical model based on Thale's theorem in order to approach rational numbers steers the students towards the development of a didactical practice focused on the exploration of properties of numbers, rather than the teaching of rules and algorithms of calculus.

Presenting the manipulation of numerical expressions for demonstrating equivalence between them strongly influences the kind of classroom activity the teacher can adopt and, consequently, the type of mathematical experience that students engage in with the system's mediation (Cerulli & Mariotti, 2002).

As to the second question, we note that a mathematical resource is the expression of a system of rules that defines the socially shared process through which the resource produces an acceptable mathematical result.

At the very least, the incorporated resource expresses a single rule but it usually corresponds to a set of rules. We note that if the system has been designed to pursue efficiency and economy of thought, then the resource will probably be associated with a complex, interconnected set of rules. In such cases it may prove difficult to work back from the outcome reached and arrive at the set of rules underpinning the resource; hence, the system is opaque from the user's point of view. However, it is often educationally useful to incorporate resources in such a way as to achieve greater transparency, so that the user can recognise the rule involved on the basis of the outcome of interaction. This has been the aim behind the design of the two microworlds described in this work.

The Fraction Microworld makes available elementary resources of division, carry-over, sum and difference of lengths. They produce effects that can be easily understood by students using their spatial experience.

Moreover, through interaction with the system, the meaning constructed using these resources can contribute to the use of fraction notation.

The Manipulator Microworld, as distinct from other comparable systems, provides the students with resources for working out elementary transformations, each of which corresponds to only one axiom. We think that this choice is particularly appropriate for students who are approaching algebraic manipulation. As a matter of fact the application of the 'commutative property' resource on a part of the expression produces an effect on the form of the expression which can be grasped at the visual level. This allows students to recognize the rule underlying the use of this axiom.

The analysis reported suggests different criteria for evaluating the efficiency brought to mathematics teaching/learning by the incorporation of resources within a system.

We believe that an effective re-configuration of the mathematical teaching objects can be realized if resources embedded in the system:

- are able to suggest to the students possible courses of action to take when solving the task at hand and/or encourage the emergence of objectives to that end;
- make it possible to validate the strategy employed in task solution and/or offer support for strategy planning that can be controlled at the perceptive-motor level;
- produce graphical and spatial effects useful for developing a mental image related to the mathematical teaching objects of reference for the system;
- produce effects on the symbolic notation that can be put into relation with graphical and spatial effects obtained through the use of resources that can be controlled at a perceptive-motor level;
- produce effects according to mathematical rules which the student can recognize and control through interaction with the system interface;
- produce effects that can, in subsequent instructional conversation between teacher and students, be interpreted as mathematical phenomena through the metaphorical use of what the interface has exhibited *dynamically* and *concretely* in the interaction.

These criteria allow us to consider possible scenarios for the use of the microworld while still in the design phase.

We think that these microworlds can contribute to structuring an activity setting that allows students to solve meaningful tasks in the domain of rational numbers and permit teachers to assist students' performance in their ZPD.

Our work does not seek to propose a generalisation from the specific domain of knowledge considered, but rather to subject our particular experience to a systematic and critical analysis that stimulates thinking about similar issues in other domains of mathematical knowledge.

# 5. CONCLUSION

To conclude, we believe it is important to tackle an important research issue regarding the relationship between the tool and the construction of meaning, which is a subject of international debate (Jones, 1998).

The cultural-historical framework considers a tool as the result of cultural evolution, produced for specific aims and consequently incorporating an idea. That does not imply that the tool itself is the source of meaning or that, at the didactic level, meaning emerges from the interaction between the student and the tool. Rather, meaning resides in the purposes for which tools are used, in the strategies that gradually take shape in the course of purposely designed activity undertaken with those tools.

We think that the meaning resides not in the tools but in the aims for which the tool is used; in the plans that are developed for using it. These plans, expressed in socially shared language, gradually realised in the course of the activity with the tool, constitute the meaning, in that they reflect the course of the activity mediated by the tool and orientated toward an aim.

Accordingly, the key element in the construction of meaning is the type of activity setting that the teacher creates and manages, so as to maximise opportunities for technology-mediated co-participation and instructional conversation between teacher and student and among the students themselves mediated by technologies.

In this paper we have addressed a vital aspect of the construction of an activity setting, namely the reconfiguration of teaching objects via suitable technologies. However, there is another aspect to be considered, and that is the 'reconfiguration' of teachers, so that they are able to make full use of the potential offered by the tools available in the learning process. This is a matter of crucial importance; unless it is solved, computer technology (no matter how important and advanced) will fail to bring about any innovation whatsoever in teaching practice.

# REFERENCES

Abelson, H. & diSessa, A. (1981). *Turtle Geometry: The Computer as a Medium for Exploring Mathematics*. Cambridge: MIT Press.

Bartolini Bussi, M. G. (1994). Theoretical and empirical approaches to classroom interaction. In R. Biehler, R. W. Scholz, R. Strasser & B. Winkelmann (Eds), *Didactics of Mathematics as a Scientific Discipline*. Dordrecht: Kluwer.

Bottino, R. M. & Chiappini G. (2002). Advanced technology and learning environments: Their relationships within the arithmetic problem-solving domain. In L. D. English (Ed.), *Handbook of International Research in Mathematics Education* (pp. 757-786). London: Lawrence Erlbaum & Associates.

Boero, P., Dapueto, C., Ferrari, E., Garuti, R., Parenti L., & Scali E. (1995). Aspect of the mathematics-culture relationship. *Proceedings of PME XIX Recife* (Vol. 1, pp. 151-166). Brazil: Universidade Federal de Pernambuco.

Cerulli, M. & Mariotti M. A. (2002). L'algebrista: Un micromonde pour l'enseignement et l'apprentissage de l'algèbre sciences et techniques éducatives. In J. F. Nicaud, E. Delozanne & B. Grugeon (Eds), *Logiciels pour l'Apprentissage de l'Algèbre Nicaud* (Vol. 9, No. 1-2, pp. 149-170).

Engström, Y. (1987). *Learning by Expanding.* Helsinki, Finland: Orienta-Consultit.

Jones, P. (1998). *Tools, Symbols and Ideality in Ilyenkov ISCRAT (International Society for Cultural Research and Activity Theory).* Aarhus: Denmark.

Papert, S. (1980). *Mindstorms.* Brighton, Sussex: Harvester Press.

Tharp, R. & Gallimore R. (1989). *Rousing Minds to Life. Teaching, Learning and Schooling in Social Context.* Cambridge, MA: Cambridge University Press.

Vygotsky, L. S. (1978). *Mind in Society: The Development of Higher Psychological Processes.* Cambridge, MA: Harvard University Press.

# Distant Actors on a Digital Campus, or Sharing and Crumbling Pedagogical Responsibility

Hélène Godinet
*Maître de Conférences par ISPEF (Institut des Sciences et Pratiques d'Education et de Formation), Université Lumière Lyon 2, 16 quai C. Bernard, 69365 LYON 7, France, helene.godinet@univ-lyon2.fr*

## 1. INTRODUCTION

It is now common to say that the Internet opens up the classroom, that learning has to turn into e-learning with regard to the networked society and the knowledge society. Obviously, learning and teaching tasks are more and more complex. In order to make this complexity explicit, we have observed networkers on a virtual campus.

We focused especially on various competencies that learners and teachers are supposed to have or to acquire when they are collaboratively and interactively networking on a web-based learning platform.

It seems that on a digital campus, the teacher's role is being diluted into various and separated tasks, which require growing expertise. These tasks (for example creating on-line learning materials, defining flexible curricula, on-line tutoring, etc.) are so specialised that one person is not able to do everything. This raises the question: if each task is carried out by an expert or a team of experts, then who is in charge of the learner? Who assumes the pedagogical responsibility?

## 2. BROWSING AN EXAMPLE: FORSE, A DIGITAL CAMPUS FOR EDUCATIONAL SCIENCES

This Campus, called FORSE (FORmation Ressources en Sciences de l'Education: http://www.sciencedu.org/), is part of the 'campus numérique français' project (http://www.educnet.education.fr/superieur/campus.htm). It was created to respond to specific needs: students who are far from the university because of their personal or professional life; trainers and teachers who decide to complete their knowledge or certify their professional experience. Campus FORSE offers to around 1000 students the opportunity to obtain a diploma (graduate level), by learning at home, over two or four semesters. Students are French speakers, from more than 15 countries. They are certified by European Credits (ECTS).

European teams, experts on each topic, create multimedia resources. Authors are not obliged to be involved in the virtual campus or to network on the learning platform, even if they are teachers in the University. Most of them write their course, sell it to the consortium and do not feel concerned by the way the learning material is used, whether or not it is efficient, whether it makes sense with regard to other modules.

Some teachers and/or researchers agreed to be 'on-line tutors'; they received no specific training. They learn on-line tutoring by doing and sharing with others. They interact with virtual workgroups, using mails, forums and various collaborative tools.

Each level is organized as blended learning: students have to spend some time in the University; at home they receive printed documents and CDROMs; they have to use a learning platform, offering working spaces and on-line resources.

This virtual community involves various actors: learners, teachers, tutors, coordinators, evaluators, administrators, designers and so on.

Reports on this experiment were written by our Master's degree students in educational sciences; they collected various data, that is, questionnaires filled in by students using the platform, interviews with tutors and coordinators, and about 2000 e-mails sent over two years.

## 3. RESEARCH RESULTS

### 3.1 Networking competencies

Firstly, our analysis shows that collaborative networking requires specific competencies. If the technical ability to integrate the web-based training system is easy to acquire (more and more users are computer literate), what about the communicative ability? It is not taught at school. Students today still find it difficult to listen to and discuss with teachers and peers. Even if they are encouraged to work in groups, they are learning individually because assessment and diplomas are mostly individual. We are far from the concept of 'collective intelligence.'

Communicating at a distance through ICT is quite new for almost all users. We know how much time it takes to 'speak' using a keyboard, to verbalize feelings and problems by writing sentences instead of interacting face to face; how artificial it is to meet a distant partner on a screen; how frustrating it can be to ask for an explanation by mail and get the answer two or three days later. Do we need to add that communicating within a web-based training system is time consuming? When a tutor interacts with students around the world, what about night and day, working time and holidays?

## 3.2 Learning competencies

Secondly, our analysis shows that being 'interactors' in an ICT learning environment, working within a collaborative learning space cannot simply be ordered. It has to be described in 'meta-capabilities', and not simply by using concepts such as *autonomy* and *motivation*. We can list some of them:

- self-studying capability:
  - information retrieving,
  - ability to understand multimedia documents,
  - ability to reconstruct information so that it becomes integrated knowledge,
  - self management of time
- ability to verbalize (discursive competency):
  - to express and share feelings,
  - to ask and answer questions,
  - to discuss with others, listening, understanding and accepting various points of view
- ability to produce and share documents, as part of collective knowledge:
  - self assessment,
  - ability to provide a critical feedback,
  - providing help

In fact, students (even if they are adults, teachers, trainers etc.) are never quite autonomous. They ask for more individual feedback. In answering questionnaires, most of them suggested more time spent at the university as a good way to feel part of a learning community. Only a few of them agreed to put their personal work onto the collaborative space. They often sent mails to the tutor, rarely to their peers, and never to the courses' authors.

We know that we are in a period of transition; that these communicative competencies could be developed in our networked society. We know that introducing ICT in learning cannot consist only of 'new packaging for old products'. It also raises questions about the teacher's role.

## 3.3 Teaching competencies

Finally, according to other experiments on networking that we have previously observed, we will try to explain that, in our opinion, the teacher's role is changing, probably because the educational space is changing.

Furthermore, as the 'master-disciple' duo is far away, as the preceptor's status silently disappeared at the beginning of the 20th century, can we imagine that the teacher's status as the responsible guide of an identified learning group might disappear? Can we imagine that he or she would simply join a team of experts, in charge of specific tasks such as the following:

- expert in a domain of knowledge;
- producing and updating on-line resources, including new media (pictures, videos, sound, simulation), cooperating with programmers and designers;
- imagining new teaching methods (not only giving specific content, but also thinking how it could make sense related to other methods or as part of a learning project);
- cooperating with tutors to understand if and how the learning material is useful or not;
- imagining and experimenting with new ways of assessment and certification;
- defining new curricula, knowing that students can learn in different institutes, in a consumer-like way;
- running virtual workshops and newsgroups;
- tutoring;
- managing, marketing, and so on?

This non-exhaustive list shows how complex it is to define the teacher as a professional networker, an expert in specific areas, able to interact and share with various partners, face to face and/or at a distance.

Some of these tasks can be instrumentalized (elaborating curricula, managing the students, managing financial aspects etc.). For example, some ODL prototypes already use virtual tutoring (see for example Exploragraph - http://www.esi.umontreal.ca/~dufresne/Publications/HypermediasDufresne.pdf).

However, we know that it's stupid to imagine that educational robots and agents will replace human guidance. Some questions are so inextricable that only a dialogue with a human tutor can help the student to go further.

Many research reports confirm that human mediation is necessary in the learning process. The concept of school is defined not only by buildings and classrooms; learning and e-learning has something to do with human interaction.

## 4. A QUESTION RATHER THAN A CONCLUSION

It seems important to stress that the growing number of users, scattered across a world-wide, web-based learning space, might dilute pedagogical responsibility.

We are conscious that agreeing to open up the classroom, to integrate networking, offers opportunities to learn without identified teachers. On the other hand we know that the learner needs to meet others, that cognitive conflict is necessary to construct one's understanding and identity. Are we convinced that the teacher is the 'hub' that structures important links, elaborates meaningful tracks and maps between knowledge, the learner and society?

This digital campus can be considered as a case study. We have chosen to observe it as a picture of what the University might be, offering opportunities to learn inside and outside, face-to-face and at a distance, alone or guided. This kind of blended learning might well answer the growing need for life long learning.

## REFERENCES

Castells, M. (2001). *The Internet Galaxy. Reflections on the Internet, Business, and Society.* Oxford University Press.

Dufresne, A. (2001). Modèles et outils pour définir le soutien dans les environnements hypermédias d'apprentissage. In *Hypermedias et Apprentissages*. 5ème colloque. INRP.

Godinet, H. & Klein, A. (2000). The teacher as a mediator in a networked society. In *Communications and Networking in Education.* Kluwer Academic Publishers.

Godinet, H. (2001). Hypermedias, réseaux, université virtuelle: l'innovation technologique vecteur de l'innovation pédagogique? Conference Proceedings, Lyon. *JRES 4$^{ème}$ Journées Réseaux.* Retrieved from http://rri.uhp-nancy.fr/documentation/jres2001/

Levy, P. (1994). *L'Intelligence Collective.* Paris, La Découverte.

OECD (2001). *Learning to Change: ICT in Schools.* Retrieved from http://www.oecd.org/

Paquette, G., de la Teja, I. & Dufresne, A. (2000). *Explora: An Open Virtual Campus.* Montreal: Ed-MEdia'2000.

# ICT and the Quality of Teaching: Some Hungarian Results of the OECD ICT Project

Andrea Kárpáti
*UNESCO Centre for ICT in Education, Faculty of Sciences, Eötvös University, Budapest, Hungary, karpatian@axelero.hu*

**Abstract:** The educational research institute of OECD, CERI, commissioned an extensive study to investigate if and how ICT resulted in changes in the quality of learning. Between 1999 and 2002, a network of National Research Experts was set up who co-ordinate research in their countries and discuss the centrally developed tests, questionnaires and study outlines that were intended to capture similarities and differences of educational ICT policy in the countries concerned.

The primary goal of the studies reported here was to understand how ICT can relate to educational innovation. The present paper discusses results related to teacher competence, performance and motivation in the use of ICT in the 'model schools' of Hungary that proved to be especially effective in ICT use.

Diffusion process. Who were the early/late adopters of both the innovation and ICT? What incentives existed for adoption? Which organisational structures or processes were particularly important facilitators of change or barriers to it?

Role of leadership. Who directed the innovation? Did the role or manner of leadership change over the adoption period?

Importance of staff training: methods of achieving staff competence in using ICT and integrating it into the curriculum.

## 1. INTRODUCTION

Information and communication technologies-related educational investments are among the highest for all European countries. In the first phase of investment, between 1996-98, in Hungary, as everywhere else in Europe, most government funds were allocated to hardware and Internet connectivity. All around the world schools were supplied with tens of thousands of computers, and Internet connections were provided before substantial research on their functions and use had been conducted. The second phase, therefore, focused on content: development of educational software, quality assurance and promotion/evaluation of public-private partnership (OECD, 2001). The educational research institute of OECD, CERI, commissioned an extensive study to investigate if and how ICT resulted in changes in the quality of learning. The research project entitled 'ICT and the Quality of Learning' involved 23 member and allied countries.

The three sub-themes of the project were: Topic 1, 'Software Quality Issues', a series of national surveys that provided information on educational software development, quality assurance and monitoring of school use; Topic 2, 'Public-Private Partnership', which yielded an international collection of case studies of co-operation between industry and education, discussing and documenting a variety of internationally relevant, good models of encouraging, developing and maintaining such partnerships; and Topic 3, 'Experimental Studies', the Hungarian results of which will be discussed in detail in this paper, which investigated two main areas. National research teams conducted ethnographic surveys on the functioning of schools that incorporated ICT in education, internal and external communication and management. The other area was the study of ICT competencies in the framework of a 'quasi-experimental study' to test the development of computer skills, learning to learn skills and ICT-related attitudes of 17-year-old students who were taught with the help of new technology within the school year of 2000-2001 (Venezky & Davis, 2001).

As part of Experimental Studies, there were school-based case studies that evaluated the functioning of schools incorporating ICT in their education, internal and external communication and management. Altogether 91 cases were documented in 23 countries to verify five pairs of hypotheses through 3-6 school studies per country The anthropological/qualitative approach included structured interviews, observation of teaching and extracurricular activities, and analysis of students' ICT-related work. Schools were revisited after 6, 12 and 18 months to see how educational change due to the introduction of ICT culture had occurred. The primary goal of the research reported here was to understand how ICT can relate to educational innovation. When making huge investments in computers and educational software, Hungarian educational policy makers were convinced, just like almost every other participant in the OECD study, that reforms would naturally follow. After the first phase of the computerisation campaign, 1990-98, statements about the effects of ICT became more modest, emphasising the importance of good practice and the leading roles of about 15% of secondary and 3-4% of primary schools that excelled in ICT policy and practice. As the OECD research project focused on cutting-edge institutions, we hoped to obtain results to be used in the second, more difficult phase of ICT-related reforms.

Data collection was carried out employing both qualitative and quantitative methods: interviews with teachers, administrators, students, parents, and technology specialists, on site observations of school life – production of video films and photographs of spaces equipped with computers and related activities, analysis of digital products of students and teachers, survey of teacher ICT practices in class and in back office hours, analysis of public e-mail logs and interviews with knowledgeable people outside of the school: inspectors, principals of feeder and feed-to schools, business partners, community members, individual sponsors etc.

The Hungarian sample of ICT pioneers comprised two primary and four secondary schools, selected on the basis of successful involvement in at least two major national educational computing projects and providing evidence of regular ICT use in teaching and learning as well as communication and management. School 1 was an alternative secondary school of economics in Budapest – the first private secondary educational institution established after World War II in the country, in 1988. As a flexible and innovation-oriented institution, it readily embraced the educational potential of the computer and tailored its functions and software options to the needs of a business-oriented institution cherishing humanistic values. With individual study programmes for every student, mixed-age student groups and a publishing house for textbooks written by the staff, this school was a paradigm example of ongoing reform. In contrast, School 2, another educational frontrunner – the first bilingual (English and Hungarian language) secondary grammar school in Budapest – safeguarded traditional values and study forms. A large and well-funded institution housed in a prize-winning, modern school building, it showed how tradition and innovation can be harmonised through ICT. School 3 was totally different from both: a modestly equipped primary school about 30 kilometres north of Budapest, in a village of small landowners that excelled in one respect 'only' – highly trained staff, totally devoted to ICT. This school acted as a catalyst for computer culture in the whole settlement where parents could learn about ICT only from their children. School 4, another primary school from a well-to-do town in southern Hungary, boasted a relatively good infrastructure and constant parental support in computer matters. School 5, a secondary vocational and grammar school in a middle-sized, unemployment-stricken town an hour's drive from the capital, was selected because of its excellent work in establishing a knowledge centre in its library and offering training in the most up-to-date ICT-related vocations. School 6, another secondary vocational school, was situated in one of the most affluent county seats and enjoyed the support of an interested and knowledgeable local government and parent community. Cutting-edge technology, a wide range of foreign connections and good management all contributed to making this school an ideal candidate for the study of best practice.

From the five investigated in the research project (discussed in detail in Venezky & Kárpáti, in press), the following two problems will be summarised in the paper, based on Hungarian data: the diffusion process of ICT culture, and the role of school leadership in using ICT for more effective teaching, learning and communication. Both are related to the role of the teacher in the successful integration of ICT technologies. In a country with modest resources and traditionally good mathematicians and computer scientists, the human capital is the most important asset any reform can rely on. Our results show that Hungarian teachers are in fact the key players in the ICT in education game.

## 2. DIFFUSION PROCESS OF ICT IN EDUCATION

In 2002 about 2.1 million Hungarians – 25% of the adult population – possess a computer. The number of Internet subscribers has quadrupled within the last two years. In a country of about 10 million inhabitants this is still not satisfactory but represents a 40% increase as of 2001. 85% of Hungarian Internet users have access at school or work. The largest age group (an estimated 50% of the total) among regular computer users, as in other countries, is the young: students and professionals between 18-29 years of age. The digital divide in Hungary is age-related, similarly to the gap separating the yuppie generation from their parents. Only 6% of those above 60 years of age were sufficiently courageous to try out and use computer technology. (Considering the percentage of teachers employed near and above pension age – 62 years for women and 65 years for men – about 30% of teachers belong to this 'ICT – no, thanks' subculture.) Another divide is of a geographical nature: a little less than 50% of Internet surfers live in the capital, Budapest and a further 30% are the inhabitants of a county seat or big country town. These data place Hungary in the middle of European computer user rates.

In Hungarian public education, Information Technology as a discipline dates back to the 1970s. From the 1980s, a shift is observable from a technology-centred towards a teaching/learning-centred approach (Kárpáti, in press; Turcsányi-Szabó & Ambruszter, in press). Today, it is a compulsory discipline for grades 6-8 (student ages 12-14) in the primary and 6-grade secondary school and grade 9 (age 15) in the 4-grade secondary school. The content of ICT studies has shifted from subject-specific studies towards a cross-curricular approach – teachers of all disciplines are trained and encouraged to teach ICT skills related to their area of studies. At present, training of intelligent users seems to be at the focus of curricula (Körösné Mikis, 2002).

When we examined diffusion patterns of ICT culture in the OECD study, we wanted to find out if the diffusion pattern by Rogers (1995) was applicable in countries with a wide variety of cultures and financial means. The starting point for Rogers is to view schools as social systems composed of individuals with varying degrees of openness to technological innovations. He divides potential adopters into five categories, based upon socio-economic status, communication behaviours, and personality values. This diffusion pattern includes a small group of Innovators (the first 2.5% to adopt), a larger group of Early Adopters (the next 13.5% to adopt), an even larger group of Early Majority (the next 34%), with the rest distributed among the remainder groups of Late Adopters and Laggards. In the OECD study, national researcher teams did not provide such quantitative definitions, only general trends described in the model were verified. Traditional diffusion patterns held in almost every school in the OECD sample – Hungary included.

In School 1, the early adopters included junior staff members who came fresh from college with reasonably up-to-date ICT skills. As transparency of operations and democratic forms of communication between leader and staff, teachers and students were facilitated by computer culture, its importance for flexible learning management in this school with individual study paths was soon declared as a necessity. Late adopters were few: mostly teachers of arts who feared their discipline would suffer if the 'human touch' was even partially replaced by touching buttons. In School 2, bilingual educators soon realised the Internet was an invaluable asset for authentic language learning. Here, Early Adopters included English teachers quickly followed by science and the fine arts educators. The latter, an elderly lady who learnt computer-assisted design at the age of 65, became a national role model for media oriented art teachers. However, most older teachers decided to wait. Laggards were those who thought pension age was too close to bother about learning new, seemingly complicated skills.

Schools 3 and 4, the two primary institutions showed that the ideal age for successful teaching in a computer-supported environment was between 35 and 45. Contrary to our expectations, best educational users – those who were most competent in the use of ICT for teaching and self-guided studies – turned out to be middle-aged professionals who were experienced in the practice of teaching and knew how to harmonise new methods with traditional ones. Young teachers were often afraid of entering 'the road less travelled' and were too preoccupied with the chores of teaching and the intricate process of fitting into a school staff (cf. Fehér, 2000). Similar findings were reported in another European study on school culture that monitored average institutions. (For Hungarian results, see Kárpáti, 2001.)

In Schools 3 and 5, the head teacher dictated the pace of changes – more about this in the following section on the role of leadership. The staff followed the lead more or less enthusiastically because the mission statements of both schools, and all financial and other management decisions that followed, clearly indicated that you either adopt ICT in your teaching practice or leave. There was an immense pressure from parents who demanded education in marketable jobs for their children that made Schools 5 and 6 among the first in the country to adopt ICT-supported vocational training programmes.

Interestingly, gender was not an issue. As the majority of primary and more than half of secondary school teachers are women, ICT pioneers had an equal number of male and female teachers in the Early Majority category – although among Early Adopters, the number of male teachers was higher. Being an ICT teacher is also a suitable and attractive profession for women – perhaps because male ICT specialists will rarely choose the teaching profession as they have other, more lucrative job offers that major family providers (in Hungary, these are the men) cannot refuse. In Schools 3, 4, 5 and 6, we met competent female systems operators who most often served as ICT teachers as well, and who could in turn serve as role models for girls, having in fact made them interested in computer culture.

Incentives for adoption included free courses in educational computing – to learn a fashionable skill turned out to be very motivating. 'Computers for teachers' campaigns by the educational government offered cheap PCs for home use for those who demonstrated ICT skills in teaching. The most important facilitators of change were systems operators – in fact, their role turned out to be crucial. Three of our schools – 1, 2, and 6 – employed a full-time support person. The others managed to have only part time help but intended to exchange this arrangement for at least one full time position.

In the late seventies, teacher training programmes and in-service training courses were introduced in large numbers to satisfy the accelerating need for ICT educators. Already at this phase, an important objective was formulated but, unfortunately, not realised until about two decades later: to train teachers of different disciplines in basic programming and/or educational software use to enable them to use computers in their preparation and daily teaching practice. Thus, teachers of disciplines other than ICT had to rely on their own initiative at the start – a fact that made diffusion slower than expected. Today, a wide range of in-service training programmes facilitates computer-supported learning and, as a result, the spread of new tools and methods has accelerated. In all of our selected, frontrunner schools, at least 60% of staff has a certificate in educational computing. In School 3, the smallest and poorest of all, 100% of staff has obtained a diploma in ICT education and thus managed to overcome deficiencies of infrastructure and become one of the best performers among primary schools in this area. Diffusion, we found, is more closely related to teacher training and motivation than to available material resources and equipment – a result that gives hope to less affluent countries showing the predominant role of human potential in ICT-related educational reforms.

The location of schools turned out to be another important factor influencing use patterns and teacher roles in educational computing. Most primary teachers living in villages expressed their discontent with ICT training, tools and infrastructure - they seem to be more critical than their counterparts in towns and cities with similar equipment. Apparently, the Internet as a source of information and communication has a geographical value in education. It means entirely different things for a teacher living in close proximity to libraries, museums, universities and community centres than for those who have to make up for the lack of all these through skilfully using the Net. Access to traditional teaching resources and in-service training is also difficult for this group of educators so they are ready to use ICT to make their own up-to-date teaching aids using a scanner and desktop publisher to construct learning materials from the text and image databanks on the web.

However while its diffusion pattern is similar to those of previous educational innovations, (overhead projector, educational television, pen and pencil tests, project-based teaching, portfolio assessment), computer technology still functions differently as it is extremely flexible and thus targets all areas of teaching and learning, management and assessment.

## 3. ROLE OF LEADERSHIP

The most intensive phase of hardware development in Hungary occurred between 1995 and 1997, when the World Bank and PHARE launched their big ICT projects in the country (cf. Turcsányi-Szabó & Ambruszter, in press). Between 1997-1999, however, the Ministry of Education initiated a massive computerisation movement. 3 billion Hungarian forints (HUF) (approx. 500,000 USD) was allocated, to connect all secondary schools (about 700 in number), 30% of primary schools (400 in all), and one educational institute per county (22 in all), to the Internet. By the end of

1999, this ambitious plan was accomplished. The role of school leadership in applying for grants and facilitating the work of ICT-oriented teachers has been crucial from the start. As most resources were and still are allocated on an application basis, head teachers are key elements of innovation.

At present, Hungarian schools are moderately equipped – and, as our results show, the dedication of management and the level of infrastructure are closely related. A good example of this is School 2, that had been in the front line of all innovation and research efforts related to ICT and made an optimal use of computer culture in all areas of school life. It had an entrance registration system with chip cards, an intranet was the basic source of communication for the large staff, the Internet was regularly used for teaching. There were also high quality teacher pages and alumni even kept coming back to design and run the student pages and news network.

But what if the head teacher prefers other areas of innovation? In School 5, one of the flagships of computerisation at the time of our survey, there was a change in leadership that resulted in a preference for other educational areas. The school still enjoys a relatively up-to-date infrastructure but staff dedication and innovative projects are on the decrease. From cutting edge to average in ICT – it took only two years for this school to completely change orientation. Decrease in performance was even quicker in School 3. After our survey, the local educational authority decided not to prolong the contract of the head teacher who turned out to have been instrumental in ICT-supported reforms. The school excelled in practically every learning criterion and attracted groups of visitors interested in village ICT culture from all over the country. Thus, the forced change in leadership could not have indicated discontent with results, but a wish of local authorities to change directions of development. The head teacher left together with about 15 loyal staff members (70%) and today the school has practically abandoned all features that qualified them as outstanding in ICT. As a consequence, village children have lost a chance to obtain free training in key labour market skills.

When leadership does not prefer ICT, interested teachers must turn to peer support (Leask & Younie, 1999). The Hungarian Schoolnet was established in 1998 to provide educational and technical help for connected schools. Members of our Schoolnet receive free, 24-hour Internet connection (mostly ISDN), a computer laboratory with up to 20 PCs and a server, a software and printed manual package called Internet Starter's Kit. The Schoolnet Office employs a large group of part-time subject specialists who create a weekly updated, authentic content-rich and therefore increasingly popular web site: http://www.sulinet.hu. It is a problem that the Hungarian Schoolnet is mainly for secondary schools, so most of their materials are not directly useful for primary school teachers. In Schools 3 and 4, therefore, teachers must engage in adaptation or even in the development of software – a time-consuming innovation that would have been impossible without firm leadership support (Halász, 1998, 1999).

School leadership in Hungary is at present not in the position to totally disregard ICT-related innovation. Obligatory data provision is Internet-based and so are information resources vital for the day-to-day functioning of educational institutions. Through central measures, the Hungarian government managed to make the use of ICT practically compulsory for all schools in the country – at least for management purposes. The Central Educational Information Database (KIFIR) supplies information on educational institutions in the country and is an essential resource for teachers who are obliged to offer study and career counselling to students and parents. The KIRSTAT system is our Central Educational Statistics Database that requires the submission of digital data regularly from all schools. Head teachers in our survey first found these requirements difficult to meet but soon reported that computerised data processing made their work a lot easier. Similar findings were disclosed from other national studies (e.g. Csákó, 1989, 1999; OEAS-Europe Survey, 2000).

The role of leadership in ICT-related innovations was generally considered highly important in the OECD survey. The integration of ICT into instruction and learning was found to depend mostly upon staff competence with head teachers playing an instrumental role. As they decide on the allocation of finances and co-ordinate most grant applications, providing means for ICT-generated reform is clearly in their hands. Teachers are trained to choose and use ICT applications suitable for their discipline in every country and thus may facilitate and, through their demands for new tools and teaching aids, encourage the work of leadership. We found that the best and most innovative teachers are likely to be good ICT users as well. Influential figures in their schools, they often act as a body of consultants for their head teacher and thus support the innovation process that naturally follows the introduction of ICT. Similar relationships were also reported in other international studies (Passey & Samways, 1997).

# 4. CONCLUSION

Both leadership and good teachers, however, have to be convinced that expensive infrastructure that requires constant maintenance will actually result in better teaching and more effective learning. In-service training courses conducted at well-equipped college campuses or laboratories of training firms were found less effective as teachers were returning to their schools and being faced with problems of a different, inferior infrastructure, and so could not employ freshly gained knowledge. Therefore the Hungarian research team invited participating schools to join on-site, school-based training courses and teaching experiments during the OECD ICT project: Learning communities for teachers and university staff members. This proved to be highly effective in facilitating improvement and gained positive recognition from school leadership. Teaching experiments for six disciplines, which lasted for two years, were expanded to involve 90 schools. A series of manuals, videotapes, demo CDs, test software as well as pre- and in-service training modules for teacher training programmes was elaborated. These are now being used as propaganda materials for convincing hesitant head teachers about the benefits of ICT for education.

In Hungary the OECD/CERI research project, entitled 'ICT and the Quality of Learning' has been slightly altered in direction to emphasise the importance of dissemination of good practice in computer-generated reforms. The title of this paper indicates this endeavour and formulates our most important result: though ICT can be used for traditional, frontal delivery of knowledge, it opens new perspectives for modern educational paradigms and has an inherent motivating capacity for teachers and students alike. In this paper, the pattern of diffusion and the role of leadership in the diffusion process was outlined – in papers that follow, the importance of technology, teacher education and student competence will be evaluated and contrasting view about the effects of ICT-related reforms discussed (Venezky & Kárpáti, in press).

## REFERENCES

Csákó, M. (1989). *Computers, Schooling and the School (Számítógép, Oktatásügy, Iskola).* Unpublished research report (in Hungarian). Budapest: Institute for Social Studies (Társadalomtudományi Intézet).

Csákó, M. (1999). *Teacher Attitudes towards ICT at School - with Special Regard on the Internet.* (*Pedagógus Attit_dök az Iskolai Informatikával szemben - különös tekintettel az Internetre.*) Unpublished research report. Budapest: Institute for Social Studies (Társadalomtudományi Intézet).

Fehér, P. (2000). *The Road Less Travelled: ICT Culture of Hungarian Village Schools.* Presentation at the Ninth EARLI Conference, Friburg, Switzerland. Retrieved from http://www.mek.iif.hu/porta/szint/tarsad/pedagog/infoktat/road

Halász, G. (Ed.) (1998, 1999). *Report on Hungarian Public Education.* Budapest: National Institute for Public Education.

Kárpáti, A. (2000). ICT in Hungarian education: Who/What is inside the Trojan horse of education? *International Journal of Educational Theory, Research and Practice*, *2*, 23-30.

Kárpáti, A. (2002). ICT Culture in Hungarian schools – Results of the OECD study from a central European perspective. In *Proceedings of the IFIP SEC III Conference*, Dortmund, University of Dortmund (CD-ROM publication).

Kárpáti, A. (2001). *Report of the Hungarian case studies of the EMILE Project* (full English online version available at the project web site: www.emile.eu.org).

Kárpáti, A. (in press). ICT in Hungarian public education – An overview. *Journal of Educational Multimedia and Hypermedia.*

Körösné Mikis, M. (Ed.) (2002). *ICT Across the Curriculum* (Informatikai kereszttanterv). Budapest: Ministry of Education (Oktatási Minisztérium). In Hungarian.

Leask, M. & Younie, S. (1999). Characteristics of effective on-line communities for teachers: Issues emerging from research.' In *Proceedings of IIIrd Open Classroom Conference* (pp. 192-197). Balatonfüred: EDEN (European Distance Education Network).

OECD (2001). *Schooling for Tomorrow – Learning to Change: ICT in Schools.* Paris: OECD.

OSEAS-Europe Survey: Education of Hungary (2000). Retrieved from http://www.ksh.hu/pls/ksh/docs/index_eng.html

Passey, D. & Samways, B. (Ed.) (1997). *Information Technology: Supporting Change Through teacher Education.* London: Chapman and Hall, IFIP.

Rogers, E. M. (1995). *Diffusion of Innovations.* New York: Free Press.

Turcsányi-Szabó, M. & Ambruszter, G. (in press). The past, present and future of ICT in education – the Hungarian image. *International Journal of Continuing Engineering Education and Life-Long Learning.*

Venezky, R. & Davis, C. (2001). *Quo Vademus? The Transformation of Schooling in a Networked World. Draft Executive Summary of the OECD Project, 'ICT and the Quality of Learning'*. Paris: OECD.

Venezky, R. & Kárpáti, A. (Eds) (in press). *Case Studies on ICT and Educational Change – Issues from the OECD Project ICT and the Quality of Learning.* A special Issue of *ECI (Education, Communication and Information)*.

# Developing Research Models for ICT-Based Pedagogy

Steve Kennewell
*Department of Education, University of Wales Swansea, Hendrefoelan, Swansea SA2 7NB, UK, s.e.kennewell@swan.ac.uk*

The need for evidence concerning ICT's positive effects on learning has been recognised since the early instances of computer aided learning (Rushby, 1979), yet over the past 25 years the results of our quest for such evidence have been less than overwhelming. Yet it seems that increasing numbers of educators are convinced of ICT's potential and, despite our inability to demonstrate clear gains from merely providing ever more technology for schools and colleges, governments have continued to fund a rapid expansion in ICT resources for education (for example, BECTA, 1998). This investment has been maintained because of a political conviction that ICT is beneficial for all aspects of life in the 21$^{st}$ century, and that education should be able to exploit the features of ICT (TTA, 1998) in the same way that business does. There are now indications, however, that this investment may not continue unless politicians can be reassured that learners are benefiting to an extent which is commensurate with the level of provision. A significant body of qualitative/interpretative research over recent years has yielded valuable insights into the underlying processes of learning with ICT, but such studies do not directly compare the impact of different factors. It is unlikely that isolated case studies of successful teaching, or detailed interpretive analyses of learning processes, will provide convincing evidence for the political audience.

If we are to establish a credible case for resourcing ICT in education, there is a need for measures of the gains in learning over other methods. There are two main ways in which quantitative methods have been used to analyse learning gains:

1. quasi-experimental models, in which the gains in knowledge for groups of students using ICT have been compared with gains for groups

learning the same subject matter using a standard approach (Tellez, 1993);

2. post-hoc models, in which students' knowledge over a range of subject matter has been statistically correlated with the amount of ICT which they had available in their institutions (for example BECTA, 2001; Watson, 1993).

These suffer from major disadvantages, however. The main difficulty for each approach is that of measuring the gains in knowledge, since the knowledge gained through the use of ICT may be of a different nature from that gained by other methods and is not effectively assessed using standard tools. In addition, each model poses problems for those seeking to apply the results; in the case of the quasi-experimental model, the pedagogical conditions of the intervention study may not easily be reproduced in other classrooms, whilst the use of a post-hoc model may show only small effects since, even in well-resourced schools, ICT is used for a small minority of the time - less time, in fact, than students use ICT outside school.

I suggest that it will be fruitful to develop a Progressive Improvement (PI) model for analysis of pedagogical interactions with ICT. This will draw on the strengths of the Instructional Development model (Willis, 1993) and Action Research (Somekh & Davies, 1991) for enquiry into the development of ICT-based pedagogy. Rather than make purely quantitative comparisons between with/without ICT, or qualitative interpretations of interactions involving ICT, we should combine an interpretative study of the interaction of factors in pedagogical situations with limited measurements of changes in students' abilities. Our aim in applying such approaches is to learn where in the curriculum ICT is best used, and how it is most effectively integrated into different pedagogical environments, styles and strategies. The qualitative observations help us to examine the way in which features of the teacher, the student and the resources interact during pedagogical situations; the measurement of learning enables us to evaluate the effect of different combinations of these features. A PI model recognises that there is no absolute best way of using ICT in teaching and learning particular aspects of the curriculum; whether and how best to use ICT depends on many other features of the context.

One possible design for a PI model involves the analysis of affordances and constraints (Kennewell, 2001). Affordances are the attributes of the setting that provide potential for action; constraints are the conditions and relationships amongst attributes that provide structure and guidance for the course of actions. These features cannot be considered absolute in nature, however; affordances and constraints must be considered in relation to the abilities of the students in the activity they support. When students are working on a task designed to bring about learning, their progress towards the task goal depends on:

- the potential for appropriate action provided by the affordances of the setting;
- the structure for appropriate action provided by the constraints of the setting;
- their abilities in the subject they are learning and in other skills such as literacy (and ICT if it is involved in the activity).

The role of the teacher is to orchestrate the affordances and constraints in the setting in order to maintain a gap between existing abilities and those needed to achieve the task outcome; a *learning gap* that is appropriate to the development of intended abilities. If students find the task easy, little learning will result and the affordances and constraints need to be reduced. Similarly, if they find the task too hard, other features can be added or the current ones adapted in order to provide more appropriate support. This orchestration involves adding, removing and changing features of the setting as the students become attuned to the features, and then focusing their attention on the features during subsequent reflective activity in order to develop conceptual schemes and improve the students' subsequent performance.

Where the teacher has a direct role in the orchestration of the setting, this may be planned in advance (proactive) or may be contingent on the continuous stream of events in the classroom (reactive) (Kennewell, 2001). Where ICT is used, the orchestration may be completely delegated (in the case of an Integrated Learning System) or shared (in the case of a Virtual Learning Environment).

Simple forms of the model can be used by teachers - as individuals or in action research groups - to evaluate and develop their own practice. Teachers are already using measurements of pupils' attainment to demonstrate improvements in learning. What a PI model does is help them plan specific developments in their teaching of topics using ICT, and to evaluate the effects of these changes by focused observation of how the features of ICT provide potential and structure for both action and reflection.

ICT in education is here to stay. In advanced technological societies, too much has already been invested to abandon the quest for improvements in learning through the use of ICT. Rather than establishing that the use of ICT is intrinsically better than other methods of teaching, we should focus on demonstrating progressively improved use of ICT and establishing how best resources should be allocated and teachers educated in order to replicate success. This will be achieved, not by large-scale projects requiring significant levels of funding, but rather by large numbers of individual teachers researching their own practice. Their findings will be disseminated through the networking of practitioners using a system that affords classroom-based enquiry, the sharing of ideas, and reflection on practice and learning. This idea is currently being piloted in Wales, where the General Teaching Council is funding Continuing Professional Development for teachers in a variety of innovative forms, including teacher research bursaries and professional networks. These initiatives show great potential for generating and disseminating evidence concerning how ICT can help bring about improvements in the learning of specific subject matter.

## REFERENCES

BECTA (1998). *Networking Schools, Connecting People.* Coventry: BECTA.

BECTA (2001). *Primary Schools – ICT and Standards.* Coventry: BECTA.

GTCW (2002). *Professional Development Pilot Projects.* Cardiff: General Teaching Council for Wales.

Kennewell, S. (2001). Using affordances and constraints to evaluate the use of ICT in teaching and learning. *Journal of IT and Teacher Education, 10,* 101–116.

Rushby, N. (1979). *Introduction to Educational Computing.* London: Croom Helm.

Somekh, B. & Davies, R. (1991). Towards a pedagogy for information technology. *Curriculum Journal, 2,* 153–170.

Tellez, K. (1993). Experimental and quasi-experimental research in technology and teacher education. In H. Waxman & G. Bright (Eds), *Approaches to Research in Technology and Teacher Education.* Charlottesville VA: AACE.

TTA (1998). *The Use of ICT in Subject Teaching: Expected Outcomes for Teachers.* London: Teacher Training Agency and the Departments of Education.

Watson, D. (Ed.) (1993). *The Impact Report: An Evaluation of the Impact of Information Technology on Children's Achievements in Primary and Secondary Schools.* London: Kings College.

Willis, J. (1993). A research and development agenda. In H. Waxman & G. Bright (Eds), *Approaches to Research in Technology and Teacher Education.* Charlottesville, VA: AACE.

# Technology Access: Resources Wasted in Computer Laboratories

Kristian Kiili
*Tampere University of Technology, Pori unit, Korkeakoulunkatu 10, Tampere, Finland, kristian.kiili@tut.fi*

**Abstract**: The technological infrastructure of Finnish schools varies a lot. In some schools there are computers for almost every pupil in the classroom. On the other hand there are also schools with only a few computers in the whole school. The purpose of this paper is to study how teachers from different schools and school levels utilize technological resources in their teaching. The hypothesis is that good technological infrastructure does not guarantee the use of technological devices in teaching. The data was gathered with an electronic questionnaire in Fall 2002, in order to investigate whether pupils used computers more when the computers were placed in the classroom. Likewise teachers' use of computers for demonstration increased when the computers were placed in the classroom. The number of computers in separate computer rooms did not increase the usage. Thus the most important thing to be considered when planning schools' computer infrastructure is the location of computers.

## 1. INTRODUCTION

According to the national strategy of the Ministry of Education in Finland, the task of the school is to give every pupil the basic skills of knowledge acquisition, communication and maintenance needed in information society and further studies (Alajääski, 2000). To reach this goal and guarantee high-quality technology education there must be a certain technological infrastructure in schools. Even if schools have a good technological infrastructure, education does not always fulfil the requirements of the Ministry of Education. There can be several reasons for low use of technological devices in schools. One reason could be teachers' level of mastery of technology that varies a lot. Teachers may have prejudices against technology and their skills in technology may be poor. Nonetheless there are also technologically skilful teachers who do not utilize their skills in teaching. The question is, why? Maybe these teachers do not see the value of technology in education or the technology in schools is difficult to access. The number of computers is not the only way to consider the infrastructure of schools.

## 2. METHOD

Survey research was conducted in Finland in Fall 2002. The 80 schools that took part in the survey were chosen in terms of judgement sampling. The electronic questionnaire was sent to 800 primary and high school teachers via e-mail. There were 12 questions in the questionnaire dealing with teachers' computing skills, work experience, ways of using computers in their profession, opinions about using computers in schools and schools' infrastructure. Before distribution the questionnaire was tested by two teachers and some modifications were made to it.

According to Kerlinger (1988), mail questionnaires have serious drawbacks unless they are used with other techniques. Return percentages are usually low and given responses cannot be checked. These same drawbacks are valid also in e-mail questionnaires. In this study the response rate was as low as 9.7% (N=78), although it took only five minutes to fill in the questionnaire. Because of the low response rate and small sample, valid statistical generalisations cannot be made. Although the sample is geographically comprehensive, it is not representative. The data gathering technique used, electronic questionnaire distributed via e-mail, is not appropriate for this study. It might be that the teachers who replied to the questionnaire are more familiar with computers than an average teacher in Finland because of the way the questionnaires were distributed. To gather more valid data the questionnaire should be distributed in paper format via mail to teachers. That would offer those teachers who cannot or will not use e-mail the possibility of answering. Some interviews should also be carried out.

Finally four groups were formed from teachers on the basis of the class level that they had been teaching.

- Lower primary school teachers (9–10 year old pupils, n=14)
- Middle primary school teachers (11–12 year old pupils, n=22)
- Upper primary school teachers (13–14 year old pupils, n=18)
- High school teachers (15–16 year old pupils, n=24)

The data was analysed by descriptive tests and by calculating correlation matrices between variables formed from gathered data.

## 3. RESULTS

First participants' computing skills were measured by defining which applications they could use. Teachers marked from the questionnaire those applications items that they could use satisfactorily. Naturally this is only a superficial description of teachers' skills. All teachers were familiar with word processing and e-mail. 97% of teachers could use the Internet. Approximately half of the teachers could use some spreadsheets, graphics programs and presentation programs. Only 26% were familiar with learning environments and 10% had used multimedia programs like Flash. On the basis of these results it seems that almost every teacher had good basic skills to organize computer-aided teaching.

According to teachers' estimates, pupils used computers in schools for approximately 67 minutes per week on average. Figure 1 shows that pupils of higher school levels used computers more than pupils of lower school levels. Lower primary school pupils used computers for about 35 minutes per week. High school pupils use computers for about 90 minutes. When the correlation between school levels and the time that pupils used computers in school was calculated, a significant relationship was found (p=0.0012). There was no significant relationship found between the amount of teachers' work experience and the time that pupils used computers in school (p=0.1976).

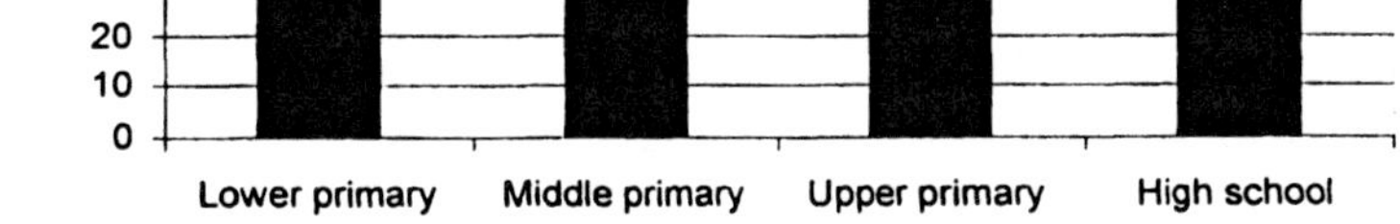


*Figure 1.* Pupils' average use of computers per week according to teachers' estimates

Pupils used computers more when computers were placed in classrooms than in separate computer laboratories. When the correlation between the time that pupils used computers and the number of computers in the classroom was calculated, a significant relationship was found (p=0.00145). Surprisingly the number of computers in computer rooms did not increase the use of computers. When the correlation between the time that pupils used computers and the number of computers in computer rooms was calculated, no significant relationship was found (p=0.706). It seems that the location of computers is a more important factor than the number of computers in the school when evaluating the time pupils use computers. On the basis of these results computers should be placed into classrooms not in separate computer laboratories.

One way to use computers in teaching is demonstration. In this paper demonstration includes a wide range of ways to use computers in teaching, varying from simple PowerPoint slide shows to complex animations used to clarify abstract concepts. Figure 2 shows that teachers of higher school levels used computers for demonstration during lessons more than teachers of lower school levels.

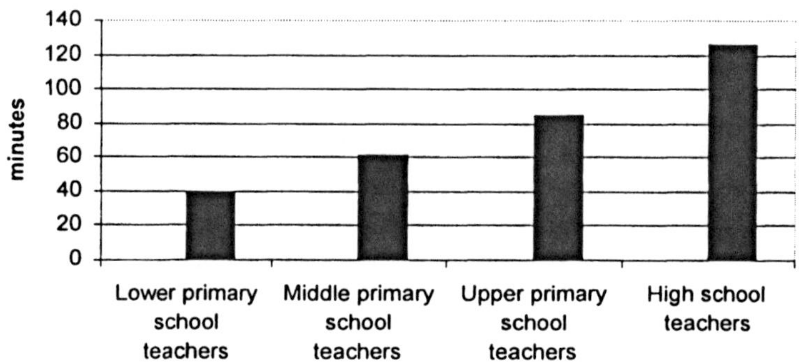


*Figure 2.* Teachers' average use of computers for illustration during lessons per week

High school teachers used computers for demonstration 126 minutes per week on average. The least use of computers for demonstration was by lower primary school teachers, only 39 minutes per week on average. When the correlation between teachers' use of computers for demonstration and school levels was calculated, a significant relationship was found ($p=0.00202$). In addition when correlation between teachers' use of computers for demonstration and the number of computers in the classroom was calculated, a very significant relationship was found ($p=0.0000004$). On the other hand there was no significant relationship found between teachers' use of computers for demonstration and the number of computers in computer laboratories ($p=0.3929$). It seems that computers in computer laboratories are not fully used. This also supports the idea that computers should be placed into classrooms.

Teachers use computers for approximately two hours per week to prepare lessons. Teachers of higher school levels use computers in preparing lessons more than teachers of lower levels ($p=0.0086$). When the correlation between work experience and preparation time was calculated an almost significant relationship was found ($p=0.0481$). Inexperienced teachers used computers in preparing lessons less than experienced teachers.

## 4. DISCUSSION

It seems that the location of computers is a very important factor in the accessibility of technology in schools. Pupils and teachers used computers in schools more when computers were placed in classrooms rather than in separate computer laboratories. One reason for lesser use of computer rooms might be the extra work that they cause to teachers. Teachers have to book the rooms a long time before the lessons and adjust their teaching to the availability of the laboratories. If there are only one or two laboratories in a school, situations can arise when several teachers would like to use the computers at the same time. When this kind of conflict happens often it may decrease the use of the laboratories. Another bad aspect of laboratories is that teachers usually use them for one hour at time. When computers are placed in the classrooms they can be used on impulse. Shorter periods of use are possible, and the use can be better integrated into other subjects. At least one computer should be in every classroom so that the teacher can use it for demonstration during lessons. School decision makers should sit down and reconsider the organization of school infrastructure.

## REFERENCES

Alajääski, J. (2000). *The Development of Mastery of Computer Teaching-related Topics and the Impact of Computer Teaching in an IT-based Teaching Environment as Assessed by the Teachers in the Teacher Training School in Rauma.* Tampere: Tampere University of Technology Publications 287.

Kerlinger, F. N. (1988). *Foundation of Behavioral Research.* New York: Holt Rinehart & Winston.

# Teacher in the Mobile World

Jari Multisilta, Harri Keiho and Harri Ketamo
*Tampere University of Technology, Pori Pohjoisranta 11C, PO Box 300, FIN-28101 Pori, Finland, jari.multisilta@pori.tut.fi, harri.keiho@pori.tut.fi, harri.ketamo@pori.tut.fi*

**Abstract:** In this paper, we discuss wireless technologies and their role in educational applications and in teachers' everyday work. Today we already have powerful handheld devices that have wireless internet connection. History has shown that new technologies are often applied to merely do the same tasks as previous technologies. Handheld devices could provide teachers with new opportunities, but not by simply transforming current WWW content to handheld devices. What would be the best way to apply these technologies? In this paper we present the results from the study of Finnish youth as users of mobile phones. Based on this study we can say that Finnish youth are ready to adopt new mobile technologies for everyday use. In addition we discuss three current mainstream technologies, namely Wireless Application Protocol (WAP), Java MIDlet and PocketPC as examples of new mobile technologies and implementation platforms. In particular we try to focus on how teachers could apply these technologies in their teaching.

## 1. INTRODUCTION

Effective knowledge creation as well as support for life-long learning are among the biggest challenges in today's education and training. Mobility can be one approach to supporting life-long learning effectively in the context of place-independent information. Today, the typical distance learning environment includes a desktop computer and a modem-based Internet connection. This kind of setting does not offer full time-and-place independence. It can be achieved, however, by using wireless handheld devices such as mobile phones or handheld computers. The equipment available today makes it possible to create educational applications for demonstration purposes. For example, Ketamo (2002) has designed and experimented with geometry games for the Compaq Ipaq handheld computer.

However it is clear that mobile environments cannot offer all the services available, for example, in today's web-based learning environments. In Table 1 we characterise different distance learning environments and compare their features.

*Table 1.* Different distance learning environments and their features

| Environment | Example setup | Pros/Cons |
|---|---|---|
| Desktop environment | Desktop computer<br>• modem<br>• xDSL<br>• cable connection | • Fast access<br>• Low cost<br>• Large screens<br>• "Normal" User Interface |
| Laptop environment | Laptop computer<br>• Modem<br>• GSM phone<br>• Wireless LAN (WLAN) | • Place independent<br>• Slow connection<br>• Restricted operating time<br>• Limited network access in WLAN |
| Simple handheld | Smartphone<br>• WAP phone<br>• Java enabled phone | • Compact<br>• Limited applications<br>• Limited programming<br>• Limited processing power<br>• Limited screen size<br>• Restricted operating time<br>• Expensive data transfer rate<br>• Unstable |
| Advanced handheld | PDA, integrated PDA<br>• Compaq iPAQ + GSM<br>• Nokia Communicator 9210 | • Large scale of apps<br>• Advanced programming<br>• Acceptable screen size<br>• Expensive data transfer rate<br>• Restricted operating time |

When designing educational material for the different environments listed above it would help if the author could use only one set of designing and publishing tools. This is not the case today. In Table 2 there is a comparison of different implementation tools that are available for each environment. If the teachers want to design material for mobile phones they have to use either the WML language or XHTML. XHTML can also be viewed in an ordinary desktop system (WWW browser), but there is not much XHTML based material available yet. A good possibility for the future will be small Java applications for mobile phones (called MIDlets).

In the next sections we discuss simple handheld and advanced handheld environments and present some examples of using them in education. Children could use (and are using) their mobile phones in every day school work especially in those countries where mobile phone penetration is high. Finland is one of the countries with high mobile phone penetration.

*Table 2.* Comparison of the implementation tools

| Application environment | Available tools |
|---|---|
| Web browser | • html pages<br>• xhtml & xml applications<br>• server side scripting<br>• limited user side scripting |
| WAP browser | • xml and wml pages<br>• wml scripting<br>• server side scripting |
| OS related software development | • EPOC SDK<br>• Microsoft CE SDK<br>• PALM OS SDK<br>• Java implementation (pJava) |
| Java enabled phones | • MIDlets (kJava) |

## 2. SIMPLE HANDHELD LEARNING ENVIRONMENTS

An example of a simple handheld learning environment is a mobile phone with a WAP browser. Small applications can be programmed for simple handheld learning environments using, for example, WML or preferably XHTML. However, the user interface is very limited in simple handheld learning environments.

Wireless Application Environment (WAE) and Wireless Application Protocol (WAP) provide industry-wide standards and specifications for developing applications and services that operate over wireless communication networks (Mann, 2000; Niskanen, 2000; Wireless Application Protocol Forum Ltd, 1999a, 1999b). WAP is a major attempt to achieve universal Internet-based information access on wireless devices. WAP is now transforming towards XHTML based content.

Wireless Markup Language specification describes the markup language, WML, which include semantics, Document Type Definition (DTD), and encoding extensions. WML and XHTML are markup languages based on Extensible Markup Language (XML). XHTML support is available also in today's Web-browsers so some information can be viewed with a mobile phone or PC if it is in XHTML format.

WAP applications can be developed with special toolkits, for example the Nokia WAP Development Toolkit,[1] the Ericsson WAP development

[1] Nokia WAP Development Toolkit (http://www.nokia.com/wap/).

kit[2] or the UP.PHONE development environment.[3] These toolkits include smart editors, phone simulators and a help system.

The screen size in a WAP phone is typically very small and existing WWW applications have to be converted to smaller screens and a simpler user interface.

## 3. ADVANCED HANDHELD LEARNING ENVIRONMENTS

An advanced handheld learning environment consists of a PDA computer and a wireless network connection. At best, these are integrated to a compact equipment such as Nokia Communicator 9210. The types of PDA equipment available today use several operating systems, namely Microsoft Pocket PC (Microsoft CE), EPOC or Palm OS. The features of these operating systems are compared for example in Tasker (2000). Typically the PDAs provide programmability not available in simple handheld learning environments.

Using EPOC operating system with the JAVA programming language is the easiest but still not an easy way to create a handheld learning environment with interactive features for advanced handheld devices. It is possible to make interactive learning environment applications by using pure EPOC programming, but at the moment EPOC SDKs are a little bit too complicated and inflexible. It is also possible to create distance learning applications by using the C++ programming language with the EPOC operating system. This kind of programming is powerful and has versatile features but is a quite complicated way to create an application. Using pure C++ language with the EPOC operating system makes the programmer often think that it is useless to re-invent the wheel. Programming advanced handheld devices using the EPOC operating system with C++ and Java has much potential, but it is necessary to develop better programming environments and tools.

## 4. THE REQUIREMENTS OF A GOOD LEARNING ENVIRONMENT IN A PDA

On the basis of learning theories, the following properties are required from a good computer based learning environment: 1) The environment has to support the constructivist view of learning and thus it has to engage the

[2] Ericsson WAP Development Kit (http://www.ericsson.com/WAP/).

[3] UP.PHONE Development Environment (http://www.phone.com/products/upsdk.html).

learner in active work. 2) The environment has to support social interaction in order to maintain co-operative or problem-based learning tasks. 3) Delivering information, tasks, objectives and feedback should be possible in the environment. 4) The environment should be open and able to be extended. It should be possible to bring other teaching materials, documents and tasks to the environment (Bereiter & Scardamalia, 1993; Hopper, 1998; McGee & Howard, 1998; Multisilta, 1999; Ruokamo & Pohjolainen, 1998).

The advantages of PDAs can be seen especially in problem-based learning support. A portable mobile learning environment makes possible many different forms of communication with which the children can discuss learning problems or tasks even without seeing each other. The communication may be delivered for instance as traditional phone calls, image calls, literal text messages, on-line chat boards or off-line message boards. All these forms can be utilised between two or more partners. It is also possible to arrange a personal working area for each learner where the others can send messages and the learner can respond to them in whichever way he/she prefers. In this way, it is possible for the learner to have the opportunity of asking for advice from a teacher without the other participants even knowing it. This kind of 'facelessness' has been reported to have led to enhancement at least in university students' discussion (Marttunen, 1997). Traditional teacher-centered instruction is also possible in the mobile learning environment of this study, but it is assumed that the learning will be self-directed to encourage social knowledge construction between students (Ketamo, Alajääski & Multisilta, 2000).

Though PDAs have certain benefits in educational usage, they still have obstacles in regard to software. The software of the PDAs has to be customized in order to utilise it for effective communication. Complete software packages can not be found yet. This can be seen, for example, in the video conferencing applications that are advertised. These applications are more or less library classes, which have to be embedded in some executable application. In the WWW environments, PDAs support only limited scripting. This creates many conflicts when trying to convert recent WWW applications to PDAs. This can be seen at the moment in iPAQ, where the 'window.open' system does not work at all and it is one of the most recent methods of controlling frames or windows in the WWW browser. This makes the use of frames difficult. Also, the screen size in a PDA is limited. In order to use existing web based learning environments, such as WebCT, the layout of the pages needs to be converted to support smaller screens. When these kinds of obstacles are solved, the usability of the PDAs will rise.

# 5. FINNISH YOUTH AS USERS OF MOBILE PHONES

In this section we describe the results of the recent study of the habits of using mobile phone among Finnish youth. The study has been repeated three times in the Satakunta region in the years 2000-2002 and it gives valuable information for the teachers and parents about how mobile phones are used among children. The questionnaire was implemented as a web form and the form address was emailed to all schools in the Satakunta region. The students in different age groups were asked to go to the web and fill in the questionnaire. The answers were recorded to the server automatically (using cgi-scripts). The size of the sample is over 2300 students in total, n = 1055 (year 2002), 657 (2001) and 717 (2000).

The percentage of children who own their own mobile phone can be seen in Figure 1. The number has increased rapidly during the last two years. It can be seen that the percentage is significantly high for 13 years old and above. During the last year (2001-2002) the percentage was increasing only in the group of the youngest children.

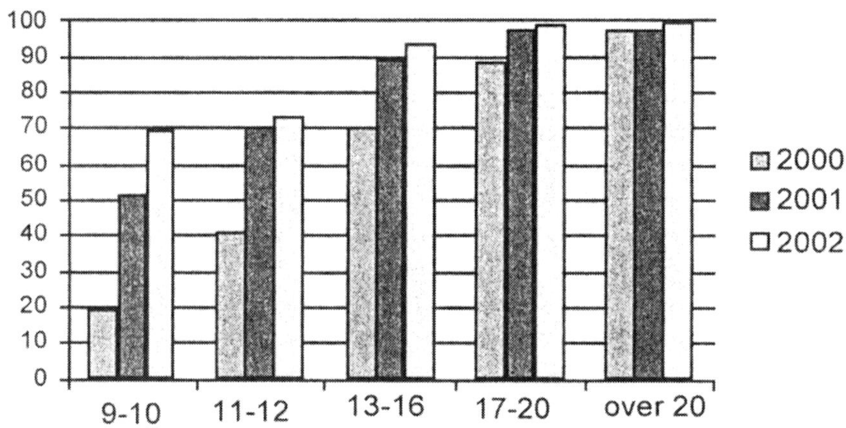


*Figure 1.* The percentage of children who own a mobile phone in different age groups (vertical axis shows percentages; horizontal axis shows age groups)

Figure 2 shows the number of calls children said they make with their mobile phones in a month. The figures are quite high. We do not expect that children actually do make as many real calls. It is widely known that children sometimes make a call that is not intended to be answered. For example, a child could call to her school friend and let the phone ring once. This means "goodnight". Two rings could mean "call me". This is predicated on the fact that the caller number is saved to the phone's memory.

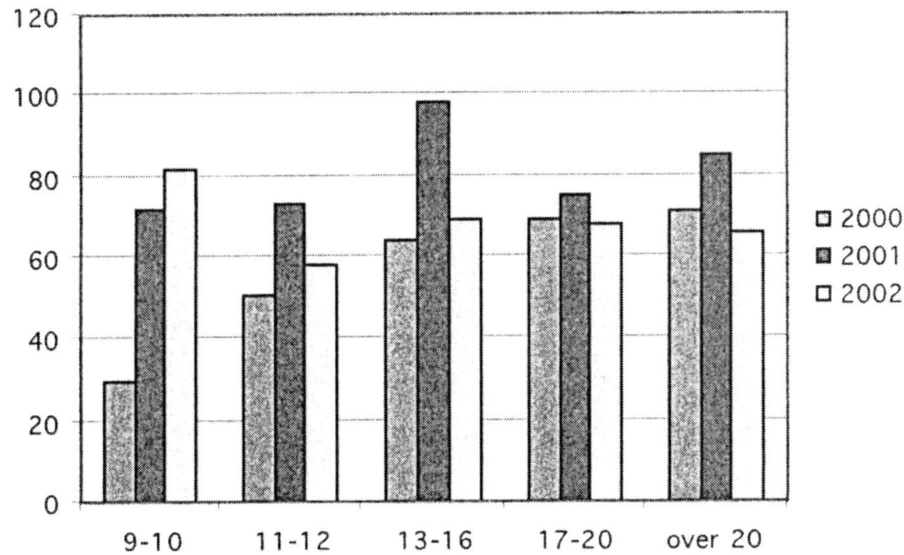


*Figure 2.* The number of calls made in a month by different age groups (vertical axis shows number of calls; horizontal axis shows age groups)

The children sent quite a number of short text messages (SMS) in a month (see Figure 3). However, the number of SMSs has decreased from year 2001 when the number of sent SMSs was much higher. The new Multimedia Messaging Services (MMS) have just been launched in Europe. It will be interesting to see if young people will adopt these services as they did with SMS.

The phones the children own are typically at most one year old (see Figure 4). This means that children have the newest models available on the market. With these new phones the children are ready to use the latest applications (based on MMS or Java technology).

The most important facts when buying a new phone are technical features, price and the brand (Fig. 5). In this study we did not ask what brands the children use - in Finland, however, Nokia has the biggest market share and they do have phones with features attracting young people. It is interesting that children want to buy their phones themselves – the phones do not come from 'second-hand' stores or as presents.

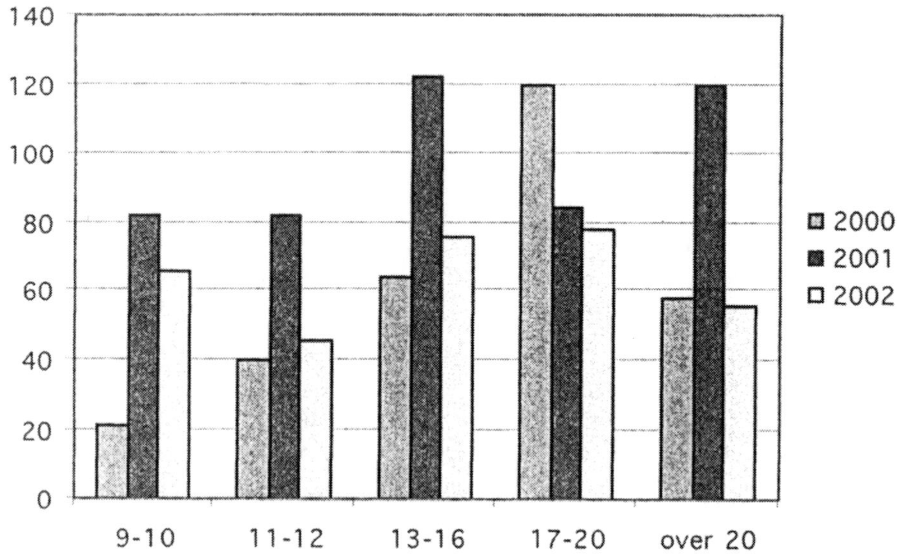


*Figure 3.* The number of sent text messages (SMS) per month (vertical axis shows number of text messages sent; horizontal axis shows the age groups)

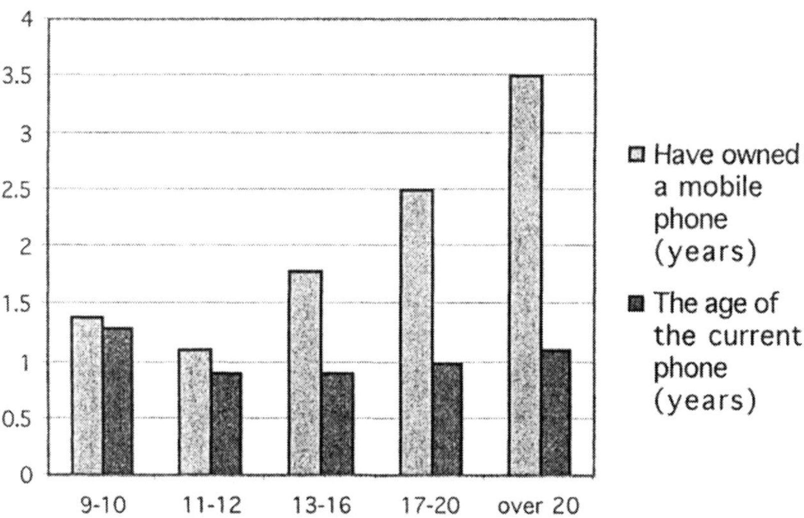


*Figure 4.* How long the mobile phoned have been owned (vertical axis shows the number of years; horizontal axis shows age groups

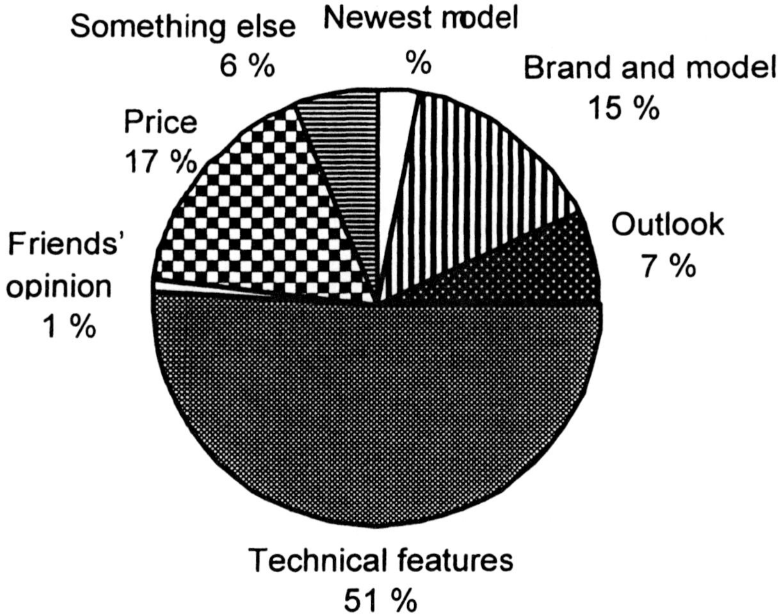


*Figure 5.* The most important criteria when buying a mobile phone

# 6. CONCLUSIONS

At its best, learning with the Internet makes learning even more effective than the traditional teaching methods used in the normal classroom. What is needed is some imagination from the teachers, programmers and other developers of the technology - and pedagogical views that ensure that the learning via the Internet is effective and motivating for both students and teachers. However, there is one important thing to bear in mind: for a teacher and students the computer is always just a tool; the main focus is and will be on the content of the course and the learning processes of the students. We should also take particular care that students and learners in networked learning environments develop their social skills.

In this paper we have discussed the role of wireless handheld devices in educational applications from the point of view of the production of content. In general there are two different types of handheld learning environment, namely simple and advanced. Simple handheld learning environments include WAP phones. Advanced handheld learning environments are, for example, PDA equipment. The advantages of PDAs can be seen especially in problem-based learning support. A portable mobile learning environment makes possible many different forms of communication with which the children can discuss learning problems or tasks even without seeing each other. Though PDAs have certain benefits for educational usage, there are still obstacles in regard to software. The software of the PDAs has to be customized in order to utilise them for effective communication. Complete software packages can not be found yet. Based on our study of Finnish youth, children in Finland are ready to apply these wireless technologies. What is needed is pedagogically meaningful applications for mobile devices.

## 7. REFERENCES

Bereiter, C. & Scardamalia, M. (1993). *Surpassing Ourselves. An Inquiry into the Nature and Implications of Expertise.* Chicago, IL: Open Court.

Hopper, M. (1998). Assessment in www-based learning systems: Opportunities and challenges. *Journal of Universal Computer Science, 4.* Retrieved from http://www.iicm.edu/jucs_4_4/assasment_in_www_based/paper.html].

Keiho H., Lahti J. & Multisilta J. (2000). Teaching WAP technology as a part of a multimedia course. *Proceedings of the ED-MEDIA 2000*, Montréal, Quebec, Canada

Keiho, H., Lahti, J. & Multisilta, J. (2000). Teaching WAP technology as a part of multimedia course. *Proceedings of 16th IFIP World Computer Congress 2000*, Beijing, China.

Ketamo, H. (2002). *User and Platform Adaptation in Web-based Learning Environments.* PhD thesis, Tampere University of Technology Publications 381, Tampere, Finland.

Ketamo, H., Alajääski, J. & Multisilta, J. (2000) eLearning - The Next Generation: A Vision about Mobile Technologies in Elementary Education. Paper submitted to WCCE: The 7th World Conference on Computers in Education, Copenhagen, Denmark.

Mann, S. (2000). *Programming Applications with Wireless Application Protocol. The Complete Developers Guide.* New York, USA: John Wiley & Sons.

Marttunen, M. (1997). Electronical mail as a pedagogical delivery system: An analysis of the learning of argumentation. *Research in Higher Education, 38*(3), 345-363.

McGee, S. & Howard, B. (1998). Evaluating educational multimedia in the context of use. *Journal of Universal Computer Science, 4.* Retrieved from http://www.iicm.edu/jucs_4_3/evaluating_educational_multimedia_in/paper.html].

Multisilta, J. (Ed.) (1999). Open learning environments – Old wine in new wineskins? In *Proceedings of AI-ED, What Do we Know of Open Learning Environments?* France: LeMans.

Niskanen P. (2000). *Inside WAP.* Helsinki, Finland: IT Press.

Ruokamo, H. & Pohjolainen, S. (1998). Pedagogical principles for evaluation of hypermedia-based learning environments in mathematics *Journal of Universal Computer Science, 4.* Retrieved from http://www.iicm.edu/jucs_4_3/pedagogical_principles_for_evaluation/paper.html

Tasker, Martin et al (2000) *Professional Symbian Programming.* Birmingham, UK: Wrox Press Ltd.

WAP Forum (2000). Retrieved January 24, 2000 from http://www.wapforum.org/

Wireless Application Protocol Forum Ltd (1999a). *Official Wireless Application Protocol. The Complete Standard with Searchable CD-ROM.* New York: John Wiley & Sons.

Wireless Application Protocol Forum Ltd (1999b). DTD. Retrieved January 31, 2000 from http://www.wapforum.org/DTD/wml.xml

# Using Portable Computer Technologies to Support Learning Environments

Paul Newhouse
*School of Education, Edith Cowan University Mount Lawley, Western Australia, p.newhouse@cowan.edu.au*

**Abstract:** This paper addresses questions concerning the use of portable computer devices in schools by proposing a framework within which to address the questions, presenting an example, and synthesising the findings of research. The benefits and barriers to implementing portable technologies are discussed leading to some recommendations.

## 1. INTRODUCTION

Since the first computers became available to educators many have provided rationales for their use to support learning. As the technology has become more powerful, at lower cost, these arguments have become more insistent and linked to discussions of 'reforming' schooling (e.g. Clouse & Nelson, 2000). This paper does not debate whether computers should be used but, rather, considers the use of portable computing systems.

Understandings of the link between schools, learning and computers are critical to a discussion of the use of computers in schools. This paper will assume that educators should adopt technologies that address educational problems and/or improve productivity. The rationale for the use of a technology to support learning should arise from a sense of dissatisfaction with the educational opportunities offered to learners and a striving to do better (Schank & Cleary, 1995).

There is gathering momentum for the use of computers to support learning environments in schools that better reflect constructivist principles (e.g. Clouse & Nelson, 2000). There is a convergence of support for constructivism, clearly explained in the report by the Committee on

Developments in the Science of Learning (2000). A critical component is the concept of proximal learning with computer technologies adding to the range of resources that may be used to provide support for student learning (DeCorte, 1990). Technology may support those learning environments that are known to be ideal but have not been implemented widely. The Committee (2000) addressed the issue of what should be considered in developing learning environments and defined "four interrelated attributes of learning environments that need cultivation" (p. 23): *learner-centred*; *knowledge-centred*; *assessment-centred*; and *community-centred*. They suggested that these provided challenges for education systems, some of which may be met with ICT solutions. Five ways to use ICT to establish and sustain effective learning environments were suggested. These, along with similar theses, provide frameworks to guide the implementation of computer support for constructivist learning environments.

## 2. A SECONDARY SCHOOL EXAMPLE

For three months in 2002 the author conducted research in a Society and Environment class for 13 year olds, where a class-set of Toshiba notebook computers with wireless networking was available for use during class time. The author worked with the teachers to implement a new problem-focussed, project-based programme. The programme was based upon the idea that the students would work in groups of four on a project that would aim to solve a problem and be open ended, practical, collaborative and involve the creation of new knowledge. The student groups were to produce a number of assessable items including maps and a physical model, to present in a multimedia presentation. The only task that had to involve the use of the computers was a Powerpoint slideshow although they were encouraged to use the computers for any of the other tasks and to support group processes. The project aimed to develop and use mapping skills and knowledge and culminate in a multimedia presentation. It was described in a document provided to the students as,

> The School is developing a Strategic Plan for the year 2050. The school needs to be able to predict what it needs to offer its clients now so that they can put plans in place. The School favours developing another campus in the Perth Hills as well as maintaining the current campus. The School are asking for tenders to redevelop the school.

Initial background data indicated that almost all of the 24 students were well positioned to benefit from computer-supported learning experiences at school and at home. They appeared to have the necessary skills and positive attitudes. However, there was a need to address some gaps in their knowledge and skills and the teacher-dependency of many students.

The physical configuration of the classroom was modified a number of times to accommodate whole-class, group-work and individual access to the computers. Computers were usually used at the desks although often if the batteries were flat the computers were used at the long benches at the side of the classroom so that power points could be used. In the 21 lessons that were observed the computers were used for about 50% of the available class time, which is quite a high use of a resource. The short lesson time (mainly 45 minutes) contributed to a relatively large proportion of time spent in transition (15%). Overall the students spent about half the time working individually or in groups, an indication that the environment was not teacher-centred. On a field trip to a national park in the hills overlooking Perth eight students (2 groups) collected a variety of pre-determined data on one of three sites that had been marked out with help from a handheld GPS system.

Almost all students indicated that they enjoyed the project and perceived the computers as being most useful for creating slideshow presentations, drawing logos and to a lesser extent collecting information and instructions from the intranet. Many did not consider the computers useful for drawing the maps. In the interviews it became clear that one important reason was that they wanted to use a mouse rather than the AccuPoint Device. However, generally problems in using the computers were minimal.

A number of recommendations were made to the teacher and school administration to improve the implementation of the project, most being procedural. In terms of the use of the computers, the students needed an easy method of file transfer between school and home, and needed to be encouraged to use the intranet information and CorelDraw for the map drawing. Having their own portable devices with some locally stored information would have addressed a number of the concerns.

Was the teacher in the research project able to use the notebook computers to support a more constructivist based learning environment, and did the portability of the technology help? An analysis was conducted of the changes instigated by the teacher, and the outcomes of these changes, by mapping them against the four learning environment attributes provided by the Committee on Developments in the Science of Learning (2000). This showed a move to a more constructivist environment. An analysis of the ways in which ICT was used to support the learning environment was also conducted.

Why did the teacher choose particular applications of ICT and would other teachers choose similar applications? Why don't more teachers implement such programmes and why was this teacher doing so only in 2002?

## 3. TEACHER CHOICE OF COMPUTER SUPPORT

Since the early 1990s the author has conducted research into the impact of computer use on learning environments in schools and the factors influencing implementation of computer support for learning. As a result a model has evolved to explain the relationships involved (Newhouse, 1998). (A schematic representation of the link between the main constructs can be viewed at http://edresearch.ed.ac.cowan.edu.au/paul/model.htm.)

The model starts with a consideration of the learning environment and the actions of the teacher within the environment since almost always the teacher determines whether computers will be used in a learning activity, even where the students have their own computers (Newhouse, 1998). The extent to which teachers facilitate computer support for learning is determined by a balance of psychological *forces* (indicating a resultant action) tempered by the presence of *obstacles* associated with the learning environment.

Of the forces experienced by teachers, there are some that *encourage* and others that *discourage* them from facilitation of computer use with the resultant force determining the extent (both quantitatively and qualitatively). This extent, or *Level of Facilitation* (LoF) is represented by an 'energy level' plateau with an initial 'hump' (developed from Vernooy-Gerritsen's (1994) model) representing the need to overcome obstacles. These forces are primarily perceptions in the mind of the teacher that ultimately influence actions, and may be based on external entities, or internal beliefs, or a combination.

Obstacles are external to the teacher being those things that could be removed immediately by the actions of another person or the teacher. Both negative forces and obstacles represent barriers to increased facilitation of computer support. The difference is that to change a force requires a change in the teacher, while removing an obstacle does not. However, the nature of obstacles and their removal are directly related to the teacher so that an obstacle may be diminished by long-term changes in the teacher but may also be counteracted immediately by the actions of other people.

The affect of the resultant force on the LoF of computer support for learning is mediated through the teacher's *Type of Response* (ToR) to the opportunities. However, the LoF is also dependent on the affect of obstacles associated with the learning environment. Because the technology is an interactive element of the environment the LoF has an impact on the learning environment completing a feedback loop. This explains why successful facilitation leads to increasing levels of facilitation. This model may be applied to choosing a portable computing solution.

# 4. CHOOSING A PORTABLE COMPUTING SOLUTION

The ideal solution for many educators (e.g. Hill, Reeves & Heidemeier, 2000; Rowe, 1993) is for ubiquitous access to an adequate level of computer processing and software relevant to student learning needs. The question is whether this is best provided through the use of portable computer systems, reliance on network access, or a combination as described by Collis (1989). Currently in most Australian schools ubiquitous access means either the use of a computer laboratory or portable devices (the sharing of classroom-based work-stations may allow pseudo-ubiquitous access). Many (e.g. Rowe, 1993) argue against the computer laboratory scenario because it tends to promote techno-centricity. Alternatively portable computer systems may be used wherever the students are, supporting individual or group work in what could be termed computer-saturated environments.

There are many ways in which it could be considered that portable computing supports ubiquitous access, from portable hardware to portable software and data. Students need access to their data files with appropriate software and hardware. One solution (e.g. notebook) is to carry some of the hardware (including a processor), software and data files. Another is to carry data files on a disk and access software and hardware in each place students are required to work. Alternatively, students could access their files and software configurations on a server with access through networked devices. Where portable computer devices are used there is further choice in terms of functionality and size from the traditional notebooks, to handheld PDAs (Personal Digital Assistants), Palmtops, and Tablet PCs.

## 4.1 Portability removes obstacles and generates positive forces

For all Australian schools it is no longer ridiculous to suggest that every student have a portable computer device. Becker (2001) has shown that the cost is comparable with implementing desktop solutions. The question is whether the portability of the systems provides benefits beyond that of alternative solutions such as thin or thick client systems?

There are a number of key benefits of portable computing for schools that researchers (e.g. Gardner, Morrison, Jarman, Reilly & McNally, 1994b; Hill et al., 2000; Rowe, 1993) tend to quote, including: ubiquitous and flexible access, a greater level of invisibility, reduction of techno-centric focus, and better support for constructivist environments leading to better support for student learning. Where the computers are student-owned further benefits are perceived, such as: customization of computer systems, increased student responsibility for the management of data, and assumption of student access to the computer at home.

Increasingly research findings are supporting, with some exceptions, these perceived benefits. Most studies have found that students like using portable computers (Walker, Rockman & Chessler, 2000) with Gardner et al. (1994b) going further to conclude that because students are less likely to perceive that they were going to computing this more readily permits the integration of computer use with any learning task. However, students respond to and use computers in different ways (Rowe, 1993).

Some research has found positive, although inconsistent, effects on student achievement (Walker et al., 2000). A large early study found little improvement in cognitive outcomes that it was argued was because the computers were used to support process-oriented attainment targets rather than the measured content-oriented targets (Gardner, Morrison, Jarman, Reilly & McNally, 1994a). A number of studies (e.g. Crawford & Vahey, 2002, p. 40; Newhouse, 1998; Walker et al., 2000) have found that the increased ubiquity and flexibility has led to more use and a greater range of use of the technology.

There is tremendous variation in teachers' responses to the availability of portable computing. Some teachers find the availability liberating and supportive in the way Sandholtz, Ringstaff and Dwyer (1992) describe, "in the beginning of the project teachers sometimes thought only of how the technology increased their workload, before long many teachers doubted they could ever return to a traditional classroom" (p. 480). Gardner et al. (1994b) reported that some teachers interacted more with students and felt that "the portables had provided them with opportunities for innovative teaching approaches" (p. 31).

A number of studies have found that by teachers facilitating the use of portable computing devices they are encouraged to use more constructivist pedagogical practices probably because of the focus on student action resulting from control of the computers (Loader, 1993; Metis Associates, 1999; Walker et al., 2000). In terms of the model the availability of portable computers may provide some powerful forces (e.g. availability and flexibility) to encourage teachers to facilitate the use of computers with students, while overcoming some obstacles (e.g. adequate access). Even so there will still be some opposing forces and additional obstacles to overcome.

## 4.2 Addressing barriers to portability

Apart from the cost of the hardware, researchers have identified some barriers (either obstacles or opposing forces) to realising the potential of portable computing. There are technical barriers concerning weight, battery life, durability and networking and non-technical barriers concerning teacher skills and experience, school organization, curriculum and pedagogy, and the perceptions, attitudes and beliefs of teachers. Most of the latter barriers do not relate specifically to the use of portable computers.

There are now solutions to most, if not all, of the early technical barriers although one recent study reported some of these as critical obstacles (Hill, Reeves, Grant & Wang, 2001). In particular, battery life is longer, notebooks are lighter and more durable, and the advantages of IEEE 802.11 radio wireless networking are clear when students take only minutes to open a computer and connect to the Internet (Newhouse, 2001). More recently, a variety of alternative devices, such as PDAs and Tablets, overcome these barriers. Despite this there will still be barriers in some school settings due to using new technologies in physical environments designed for older technologies (Hill et al., 2001).

Apart from the early concerns with the weight of laptops there are broader ergonomic concerns specific to portable computers such as the awkwardness of carrying the computers, some I/O devices (e.g. AccuPoint), and the tendency for use in a variety of environments leading to poor body posture. Harris and Straker (2000) raised this latter concern but suggested that "many of the consequences of their [laptop] use do have solutions" (p. 346) mainly associated with the management of the students and technology.

Shortcomings in the skills and computer-related knowledge of teachers have been well documented (Sandholtz et al., 1992) although more recent research (e.g. Becker, Ravitz & Wong, 1999; Newhouse, 1998) has highlighted the critical nature of teacher understanding and experience, rather than operational skills. A lack of teacher operational skill is not as critical where student-owned portable computers are used because the students are competent at operating their computers. However, students become readily dissatisfied with inefficient or inadequate integration of computer use with the curriculum. Unfortunately, most teachers have inadequate experience with using computers to support student learning, irrespective of enthusiasm and computer literacy, and significant teaching experience (Becker et al., 1999; Newhouse, 1997). This obstacle can be diminished by providing teachers with both technical and curriculum support.

Serious barriers to facilitation of computer support are connected with educational policies and practices, and the organisation of schools. For example, many secondary schools have short lesson times with segregated specialist teachers providing a disintegrated curriculum not sharing resources and expertise which create unnecessary obstacles (Gardner et al., 1994b; Newhouse, 1998; Sandholtz et al., 1992). These are obstacles that can be addressed with appropriate system and school policy decisions as evident in a number of Australian 'laptop schools' (Loader, 1993).

The link between curriculum, pedagogies and use of computers is encapsulated in the aim to embed computer support as a critical component of the learning environment by integrating with the curriculum and pedagogical practice. Unfortunately computer use has often been an interesting but readily discarded accessory (Becker, 1994). Disappointingly, a recent study reported that even with laptops, the use of the technology support was still "outside the curriculum" (Hill et al., 2001, p. 61) with the only real impact being increased access to online information and an increase in presentations.

Irrespective of the obstacles there are some teachers who facilitate the use of computers more readily than others. Teachers whose practices are more instructivist in nature will be less likely to consider computers as useful cognitive tools for students (Newhouse, 1998). Hannafin and Savenye (1993) suggest that teachers may resist changes in learning theory. The need for changes in an internal force based on beliefs is a long-term process and meanwhile the technology may be discarded once obstacles are encountered.

## 4.3 Selecting appropriate systems

Which type of portable computing devices, from the wide array available, should be chosen to suit the needs of learners? There are four interrelated issues that tend to guide the selection for a school: the degree of standardisation required by the school; the degree of user control encouraged by the teacher; the degree of hardware and software portability practicable within the school; the ownership of the hardware and software.

The first two issues pitch ICT maintenance convenience against the link between learning and the technology. Those responsible for maintenance tend to want standardisation while educators guided by constructivist theories want to maximise learner control, and match the variety of learners and learning tasks. Thus the balance should be towards more user control and connectable systems rather than identical systems. An interesting manifestation of this balance has been the debate on the merits of 'thin client' technology based on increasing productivity (Good, 2001). However, productivity gains for standardised centralised systems can't be generalized (Friedlander, 2000). The other issues of degree of portability and ownership tend to be related to the first two in that those who advocate standardised, centrally controlled systems tend to support using non-portable centrally owned systems while those advocating maximising learner control tend to want more portable systems with a level of personal ownership.

There is now a wide array of options for providing computer processing support to students varying in size, capacity, speed, and connectivity. Which components of a system need to be carried and which should be left in the classroom or on the server? For example, as a minimum students could just carry a disk with them to plug into processing devices. Or the disk could include some components of operating and applications software, as is the case with the OQO system (OQO Corporation, 2002). Choices are likely to depend on the age and capabilities of the student with some research finding that class sets of school-owned notebooks being a good model for younger students (Newhouse, 2001), with personal ownership models being more suited to older students (Newhouse, 1998). Perhaps in the early years each student could have access to devices such as Tablet PCs kept at school and graduate to notebooks at about the age of 12 years. For the early teenage years most children could own a notebook or smaller device carried to and from school, perhaps graduating to a PDA. Schools would probably have to provide some extra processing and peripheral devices.

Portable devices are eventually individually owned, as with calculators. Should the computers be owned by the students or by the school? This raises three concerns: cost, security, and identity. Although becoming less of a factor, portable devices cost more than equivalents. As devices become the responsibility of the user there may be less concern for their physical security but the implications for the logical security of a school's network and the potential for system incompatibilities are concerns (Kessell, 2001). Research has not found these to be major problems, with the reduced corporate responsibility for physical security offsetting the increase in cost of school network maintenance (Newhouse, 1998). The important sense of personal identity is more readily sustained with personally owned computers (Rowe, 1993). However, this increases the difficulty in the provision of operational support to students who must be more independent. Monitoring inappropriate behaviour is more difficult but, as Crawford and Vahey (2002) found, personal ownership can lead to useful unplanned learning experiences.

## 5. CONCLUSION

It is relatively safe to suggest that students in the future will have some form of portable computer device. The impact on schooling is difficult to predict. If children do need better schooling and computer support will assist in providing this, then portable computer technologies implemented with the appropriate support will realise the potential so long envisaged. This may require changes to school organization, curriculum, and pedagogy, and will take considerable effort by teachers and depend on their expertise, experience and beliefs.

## REFERENCES

Becker, H. J. (1994). How exemplary computer-using teachers differ from other teachers: Implications for realizing the potential of computers in schools. *Journal of Research on Computing in Education, 26*(3), 291-321.

Becker, H. J., Ravitz, J. L., & Wong, Y. T. (1999). *Teacher and Teacher-Directed Student Use of Computers and Software.* (Teaching, Learning, and Computing: 1998 National Survey. 3). Irvine, California: Center for Research on Information Technology and Organizations, University of California, Irvine.

Becker, J. P. (2001). The wireless revolution. *NEA Today, 19*(6), 8-10.

Clouse, R. W. & Nelson, H. E. (2000). School reform, constructed learning, and educational technology. *Journal of Educational Technology Systems, 28*(4), 289-303.

Committee on Developments in the Science of Learning (Ed.) (2000). *How People Learn: Brain, Mind, Experience, and School.* Washington, D.C.: National Academy Press.

Crawford, V. & Vahey, P. (2002). *Palm Education Pioneers Program March 2002 Evaluation Report*: SRI International.

DeCorte, E. (1990). Learning with new information technologies in schools: Perspectives from the psychology of learning and instruction. *Journal of Computer Assisted Learning, 6*, 69-87.

Friedlander, D. (2000). *Thin-Client Cost of Ownership: The Numbers Don't Add Up* (Idea Byte). Cambridge, MA 02142, USA: Giga Information Group.

Gardner, J., Morrison, H., Jarman, R., Reilly, C., & McNally, H. (1994a). Learning with portable computers. *Computers in Education, 22*(1/2), 161-171.

Gardner, J., Morrison, H., Jarman, R., Reilly, C., & McNally, H. (1994b). *Personal Portable Computers and the Curriculum* (Practitioner Minipaper 13). Glasgow: Scottish Council for Research in Education.

Good, D. G. (2001). *Investing in K-12 Technology Equipment: Strategies for State Policymakers* (Reports - Evaluative). Denver, CO: Education Commission of the States.

Hannafin, R. D. & Savenye, S. (1993). Technology in the classroom: The teacher's new role and resistance to it. *Educational Technology, 33*(6), 26-31.

Harris, C. & Straker, L. (2000). Survey of physical ergonomics issues associated with school children's use of laptop computers. *International Journal of Industrial Ergonomics, 26*, 337 - 347.

Hill, J., Reeves, T. C., Grant, M., & Wang, S. (2001). *The Impact of Portable Technologies on Teaching and Learning: Year Two Report.* University of Georgia: Athens Academy.

Hill, J., Reeves, T. C., & Heidemeier, H. (2000). *Ubiquitous Computing for Teaching, Learning, and Communicating: Trends, Issues & Recommendations.* Athens, Georgia: Department of Instructional Technology, College of Education, The University of Georgia.

Kessell, S. R. (2001). *Evaluation of the Personal Laptop Program at Penrhos College [1998-2000]: Final Report.* Perth, Western Australia: Curtin University of Technology.

Loader, D. (1993). Reconstructing an Australian school. *The Computing Teacher, 20*(7), 12-15.

Metis Associates (1999). *Program Evaluation: The New York City Board of Education Community School District Six Laptop Project.* New York: Metis Associates.

Newhouse, C. P. (1997). The impact of portable computers on classroom learning environments. *Australian Educational Computing, 13*(1), 5-11.

Newhouse, C. P. (1998). *Teachers' responses and classroom learning environments associated with student access to portable computers.* Unpublished PhD, Curtin University of Technology, Perth, Western Australia.

Newhouse, C. P. (2001). Wireless portable technology unlocks the potential for computers to support learning in primary schools. *Australian Educational Computing, 16*(2), 6-13.

OQO Corporation. (2002). *OQO Ultrapersonal* [online]. OQO Corporation. Available: http://www.oqo.com/ [2002, 3/7/2002].

Rowe, H. A. H. (1993). *Learning with personal computers.* Hawthorn: Australian Council for Educational Research.

Sandholtz, J. H., Ringstaff, C., & Dwyer, D. C. (1992). Teaching in high-tech environments: Classroom management revisited. *Journal of Educational Computing Research, 8*(4), 479-505.

Schank, R. C. & Cleary, C. (1995). *Engines for Education.* Hillsdale, NJ: Lawrence Erlbaum Associates.

Vernooy-Gerritsen, M. (1994). Schools with SPIRIT, a new approach to implementation. Brisbane: Australian Computers in Education Conference: APITITE'94.

Walker, L., Rockman, S., & Chessler, M. (2000). *A More Complex Picture: Laptop Use and Impact in the Context of Changing Home and School Access* (The third in a series of research studies on Microsoft's Anytime Anywhere Learning Program. 3). San Francisco, CA: Rockman et al.

# E-Learning, ICT, and Learning Portals for Schools

Ferran Ruiz Tarragó
*Government of Catalonia - Department of Education, Spain, fruiz@pie.xtec.es*

**Abstract:** E-learning and learning portals are two closely associated concepts coined mainly outside education. An increasingly powerful industry offers software platforms, digital contents and learning services to commercial companies and academic institutions. Given their goals, design, and content orientation there is concern that e-learning environments are poorly suited to serve school education in many respects: catering for the specific needs of young learners; accommodation of suitability and flexibility features for teachers; compatibility with the schools' experience of learning with and through ICT; and issues of privacy, control and academic freedom. To contribute to overcome such difficulties some specific features and criteria for school learning portals are proposed. Before that the paper revises the origins and rationale of e-learning and briefly considers its impact on university education. It also considers the consolidation of e-learning services through learning portals, and the broad aims and implications of ICT in schools.

## 1. E-LEARNING IN BUSINESS AND UNIVERSITIES

### 1.1 Learning and training needs of corporations

The companies and institutions of the information society have to innovate continuously in order to develop and succeed in competitive world markets and in international arenas. Besides equipment and infrastructure, innovation requires substantial and continued investments of an intangible nature, notably in the fields of human resources development, redefinition of labor and hierarchical relationships inside companies, development of information structures and knowledge management. Employees have to learn new concepts and skills, and have to adapt themselves continuously to new assignments, project teams and working environments. This has a strong impact on the training policies of enterprises and corporations. Human resources departments need to offer flexible training methods, increase the range of opportunities to facilitate new learning, and provide suitable contents and support at the right moment.

'E-learning' has recently come out as the solution for this huge problem. Across the globe business personnel are using the web to access learning materials and to communicate with colleagues and training tutors at any moment and from any geographical location. Such people are 'e-learners' and 'e-learning' – a term that refers both to technology and methodology- provides them availability and flexibility that traditional learning and training methods do not offer. It is generally admitted by the business sector that e-learning provides substantial advantages in company training, and that it is more effective than conventional methods at a lower cost, partly because e-learning courses and online training do not require travel and interfere less with working time.

## 1.2 The business of e-learning and its components

Many companies provide e-learning services and products to other business, corporations and institutions. Hardware, software, telecoms, publishing and service companies see education and training as a potentially huge market: e-learning is considered a hot business topic on which many economic expectations are placed. According to a study by International Data Communications (IDC), worldwide spending on e-learning will surpass $23 billion USD by 2004.[1] A number of international conferences and 'e-learning festivals' are being held, often supported by powerful high-tech corporations and consulting companies. "E-learning is the next major killer application," proclaimed Cisco CEO John Chambers at Comdex in Las Vegas (Moore & Jones, 2001). The underlying assumption of business people in such forums seems to be that e-learning will deliver workers 'just in time' online knowledge and training at the desktop, which is decisive for increasing productivity and profits.

Education is "an industry that, from a stock market standpoint, didn't exist in any meaningful way five or six years ago" (The ABCs of Education Stocks, 2001). It is mainly composed of textbook publishers, corporate-training companies, and educational software, content providers and service companies ranging from reliable and valuable leading bluechips to innovative and fragile startups. The economic slowdown actually improves the outlook of this industry because "as unemployment rises, more employees seek to upgrade their skills to sharpen their job prospects" (The ABCs of Education Stocks, 2001).

[1] http://www.ffg.com/resource/why-e-learning.asp, September 28, 2002.

E-learning business is a complex economic sector of which content is the key element: without content to be delivered electronically to customers there is no e-learning business. The intellectual knowledge to be offered to users has to be created either from scratch or adapted from existing materials, implemented in the most suitable multimedia format combining texts, graphics, tables, animation, audio, video and simulations, and it has to be localised or customized for specific countries or sectors or clients, using local languages while taking into account cultural issues.

Software is the second main component of e-learning. The online interactions between learners and content materials, the interactions among learners themselves and between students, teachers and tutors, and the access to a variety of administrative and support features are realised through specific software platforms, often referred to as virtual learning environments. Such platforms enable users to submit and retrieve information via a browser, and allow for the activity of tutors and administrators of the system as well. They are leased or sold as 'e-learning solutions' and many companies are engaged in their design, development, and support.

Besides content and software platforms the e-learning industry has other components that can't be considered here but seem worth mentioning because their implications for education and specifically for schools. To name only a few: issues of cost (pay-per-course, pay-per-user, etc.), pricing and taxation for national and international users; issues of copyright, electronic rights and intellectual property, and permission to manipulate the materials; issues of control, privacy and secure use; aspects of content maintenance, standards, bandwidth for correct delivery and user support; and finally the explicit or hidden relationships with the infrastructure side: servers, hosts and operating systems.

## 1.3 E-learning in companies

Every company adopting e-learning is likely to develop an e-learning strategy, the main elements of which relate to content and to management. The decision of whether to buy off-the-shelf courseware appropriate to the company's needs or to undertake custom course development is crucial. The former implies matching company needs with suppliers' products, licensing and support, and the latter launches the company into a generally complex process of instructional and interaction design, creation or adaptation of materials, technical implementation, and evaluation and feed-back.

The management of e-learning is frequently linked with the information and administrative systems of the firm using a learning management system or LMS, that is, enterprise-wide software integrated within the human resources system to track employee records, web-based training and classroom delivered courses, as well as online course enrollments (Guest & Juday, 2001). The LMS registers users, monitors online interactions of various kinds, records data from learners, manages the library of courses, handles contents from multiple publishers, and provides reports to the management. Although it usually doesn't include authoring capabilities, it can allow for the development of materials and courses (Kaplen-Leiserson, 2002).

It is worth noting that integrated e-learning environments may allow for the complete surveillance of the employees' learning behaviour: interests and attitudes, performance and levels of attainment, frequency of use, personal profiles, etc.

## 1.4 E-learning and universities

The everyday activity of the students in a fast-growing number of universities revolves around computer networks and e-learning. Course descriptions, lecture notes, course content and supplementary materials, assignments, schedules, etc. are available online. E-mail, chat rooms and web surfing are part of the students' everyday life.

The use of information technology in the delivery and practice of higher education is already mandatory in many universities and this could become the general scenario in a mid-term future. As asserted the Vice Chancellor of the University of Melbourne: "e-learning could become the environment in which the majority of human beings are educated beyond the secondary level" (Symonds, 2001). In the developing world the delivery of college education to enormous cohorts of students could be well beyond the reach of conventional education institutions, giving maybe the strongest impetus to e-learning in the academic world.

The pressure of the e-learning business mentality on higher education is gaining momentum and conventional universities seem to consider it as a powerful tool to extend their areas of activity and influence. As Business Week points out, "the dot-com bubble may have burst in the world of commerce, but the promise of harnessing the Internet for paradigm-changing growth - and even profits - still thrives in the halls of academia" (Symonds, 2001). This is so because, despite the economic downturn, e-learning is emerging as one of the Internet's most useful applications. E-learning allows universities to broaden the scope of their limited market by selling digitized courses taken from the knowledge of their faculties. In postgraduate studies and further education the economic slump even drives more part-time adult students into e-learning courses provided by universities in as far as they are forced to re-qualify and acquire new degrees.

The rapid spreading of e-learning in universities is cause for concern in at least two areas. One of them concerns participation and control. As Noble (1998) points out, "the high-tech transformation of higher education is being initiated and implemented from the top down, either without student and faculty involvement in the decision-making or despite it". The generalization of the use of information technology for teaching and learning based on whole-campus learning management systems reinforces the control of university administrators and undermines the autonomy and academic freedom of the faculty. "Once faculty and courses go online, administrators gain much greater direct control over faculty performance and course content than ever before and the potential for administrative scrutiny, supervision, regimentation, discipline and even censorship increase dramatically", puts Noble (1998) bluntly.

The second area of concern is related to the intellectual rights of the authors of content. Online education is to some extent turning university professors into content creators. They are asked to develop materials for digital courses which are designed and implemented in learning portals by technicians or companies and are often paid a flat fee. Authors are compelled to surrender their intellectual rights to the university, which owns and manages them as intellectual capital. In this way the institution capitalizes on the intellectual activity of its most valuable workers. The pre-packaged courses are commodities that can be freely traded. They can be imparted by other professors or by less qualified personnel at a fraction of the cost of the salary of a university professor. The e-learner becomes a consumer of educational products.

These are crucial issues that deserve close scrutiny and debate, and which to some extent can translate into school education.

## 2. ONLINE LEARNING PORTALS

The use of consolidated websites that offer individuals and organizations access to learning services, content and training resources from single or multiple sources, is a defining element of e-learning, both in universities and in the business world. Such 'online learning portals' or 'learning portals' are virtual education and training centers in which the user can get online courses chosen from a structured catalog, may be allowed to personalize his/her learning path, and can receive individualized coaching. Content may be created specifically by the institution or company that runs the learning portal or may come from a variety of providers.

A number of today's online learning portals could be considered as instruments for the delivery of programmed instruction. They provide interactive instructional content through sophisticated multimedia presentation techniques. Powerful database systems with huge storage and retrieval capabilities, coupled with efficient and pervasive programming techniques at server and browser levels can manage interactions tailored to the user, based on the analysis and feed-back on student results. Possibly such systems are on the way to fulfilling the wildest dreams of early computer-assisted instruction or computer-managed learning proponents, in terms of performance, scope and completeness. Their social acceptance is increasing by the combined impetus of a powerful industry and huge training needs.

Fortunately, online learning portals also set the scene for a variety of forms of personal communication and interaction through today's fast low-cost communication systems. This allows for substantial improvements over earlier machine-driven CAI approaches.

Most of the learning portals function as for-profit businesses, even in universities, but a fraction of them are based on advertising revenues or are non-profit services funded institutionally. This is often so in the case of learning portals specific for school education that are created and maintained by governments and education authorities, with or without private support. Given their specific objectives, their design should contain features appropriate to the goals of schooling, to the characteristics of young learners, and to the professional activity of teachers.

# 3. ICT IN SCHOOLS

## 3.1 The broad aims and implications of ICT in schools

In its origins e-learning is not an academic term. At the top of the Internet hype of the late 90's 'e' was added as a prefix to many areas of activity. E-government, e-commerce, e-procurement, e-learning are some of the terms that popped up without a clear definition, gaining wide acceptance following the popular hold of 'e-mail'. (One may wonder whether 'e' means 'efficient'.) Such terminology is still in common use after the short-lived 'dot com' era. The term e-learning has become well accepted in the business sector and governments use it widely. Maybe it's here to stay but up to now has not been popular in the world of primary and secondary education. Teachers with native languages other than English may be prone to ignore it and its equivalents in their language.

Beyond terminology issues, schools have been getting to grips with exploring, using and even integrating ICT in education at a growing scale and pace since at least the mid-80s. Many individual teachers, school departments and even whole schools are applying basic and specific ICT tools and applications across a range of subjects, fostering the participation of students in collaborative projects, and using interactive multimedia curriculum content, often delivered by the Internet.

Big investment and training plans have been and are being deployed at national and local levels. Corresponding with the rising levels of infrastructure, school education is defining, experimenting and assessing ways of accommodating ICT tools and contents in different school situations and within many pedagogical perspectives, and a fair amount of momentum and experience has been gained so far. An illustrative Australian report (Commonwealth Department of Education, Training and Youth Affairs, 2001) states that schools use ICT to enhance teaching and learning in two ways: 1) using technologies to support the development of skills - uses often referred to as 'learning with technology'; and 2) using ICT to support constructivist approaches to learning - uses central to approaches referred to as 'learning through technology'. The complexity of school-deep innovation through ICT is parallel to those of companies because it requires substantial amounts of team-work, revision of beliefs and practices, training, reorganization, management skills, and leadership.

Also according to the same report the range of outcomes the schools consider important are "much broader than those specified in current curriculum frameworks and systemic testing and assessment programmes". Schools seek "to enhance the level of student engagement in their learning by focusing on the needs of individual students, rather than establishing a learning environment that is focused principally on the curriculum" (Commonwealth Department of Education, Training and Youth Affairs, 2001, p. 85). So automated content delivery for self-instruction is not the core issue as it is in businesses. Researchers have also reported that social competencies of students are enhanced through collaborative modes of learning.

Computer-based cognitive tools and learning environments are often used to enable and facilitate critical thinking and higher-order learning. Although transmitting knowledge to students by means of ICT can play a role, even a significant one, the technologies should be given to learners "as tools for analyzing the world, accessing information, interpreting and organizing their personal knowledge, and representing what they know to others" (Jonassen & Reeves, 1996). It is worth noticing that within this paradigm the learner is free and at the same time teacher control is not in question, this being compatible with the fact that many students use computers and the Internet a lot on their own initiative, even outperforming teachers.

## 3.2 Issues of structure and resources

The adoption of e-learning systems and methods in companies is usually driven by their management, which guarantees or facilitates coordination and the supply of information, resources, commitment and leadership. Considerable expense may be devoted to this end. Schools and high schools, as well as universities, do not fit easily into this scheme, for a number of reasons, some of which are structural.

Schools are "professional bureaucracies" (Mintzberg, 1979). The professional character of the activity means that power of decision-making is not exclusively concentrated among the top management of the organization, while diversity of specialization within the profession involves an even distribution of power. Despite the regulations for standardization and the organizational rules, professionals exert a considerable degree of control over their own work - they can't work otherwise. Professionals make decisions about their own actions, and when necessary adopt strategies of evasion and non-intervention. These features give shape to a complex organizational framework that of necessity must maintain a considerable stability if it is to provide a public service which is of great importance and in considerable demand. ICT and e-learning can only thrive if they are compatible with such structural factors derived from the typology of educational organizations and the service they provide (Ruiz Tarragó, 1994). A strong interplay of bottom up and top down approaches is then indispensable.

On the resources side let us only mention that individual schools in general find it difficult to devote time, money and intellectual energy to plan for ICT and students' e-learning. They are short of personnel to plan and implement them, and they are not able to pay extra bills for external consulting and services, so innovation in this field is really difficult. In this context, the supply of suitable and specific e-learning services for schools may be of great help.

# 4. LEARNING PORTALS FOR SCHOOLS

## 4.1 The young e-learner

We have commented on the key role that content plays in e-learning in companies. Such content is to be used by adult professionals and employees. They are generally assumed to have ample capabilities of independent study and of setting long-term goals. But young learners do not share such characteristics. It can be confidently stated that school students don't need nor feel the need to track courses in an online catalog, that their learning doesn't depend on doing automated courses, nor is their learning activity in schooling years going to take place independently, away from teachers, companions and parents. Although self-testing by means of a computer may be helpful, it is nevertheless of limited importance. School students are certainly not in the business of just-in-time learning for retraining and skills improvement.

The long-term vision, autonomy and commitment of the young learner cannot be guaranteed, and even high school students do not share some of the maturity characteristics that are expected in university students. Moreover, the coaching and human guidance of the teacher cannot be automated. Even in the case that the output of day-to-day school teaching resulting from the intellectual labor of teachers could be packaged and marketed as a commodity, it would have limited practical value because the young learner needs to be continuously stimulated, monitored and supported by physically present teachers. No savings seem to be possible if human care, quality and public service are to be maintained. Some differences between universities and schools in this respect may perhaps exist.

Given all those specific characteristics maybe it would be useful to use a formulation of e-learning specific to school education. It should place students and teachers first and well above content, teachers should recognize it as close to their professional role and related to their experience of ICT. It should also convey academic freedom and professional discretion, understood as the power of the teacher to lead or accompany the student according to his or her own judgment, overriding when needed any technical system.

The school e-learner would thus be any pupil who, with the guidance and support of the teacher, in a variety of learning approaches and situations, and having different levels of autonomy, uses ICT and the Internet to some extent: to work with suitable productivity tools or specialized environments; to access, retrieve and process digital content for study and learning purposes; and to communicate or to interact with teachers, tutors, other learners or experts.

This concept may prove compatible with the broad issues and implications of ICT in schools because it emphasizes the roles of the learner and the teacher. Correspondingly learning portals for school education should accommodate fully the needs of the young learner as well as those of the teacher.

## 4.2 Specific features of a learning portal for schools

Based on the ideas above, we introduce a few characteristics that could be useful to consider when designing a learning portal for school education. Such features, which are being implemented on the learning portal for students, www.edu365.com, of the Department of Education of Catalonia, aim at defining a common working environment for teachers and students.

*Teacher repository.* The learning environment should provide every teacher with facilities to create, manage, index and retrieve his or her own private digital repository of teaching instruments: lesson plans, exercises, notes, documents, readings, assignments, formulae, tests and exams, computer programs, URLs, databases, multimedia files, etc, irrespective of their format, volume and completedness. Maintaining such a private repository is not to be confused with courseware authoring, activity that should by no means be mandatory. The teacher neither is nor should be a digital content designer – although he/she could eventually become one if he or she wants to – nor be obliged to make use of pre-established content.

*Students' grouping.* Dynamic grouping of students should be made very easy in order to facilitate the assignment of specific tasks and collaborative projects and to cope with diverse students' needs. Groups could be made with pupils from within the classroom, from other classrooms of the school, or even with students from other schools, with teachers' prior agreement.

*Design and assignment of activities.* The environment should allow teachers to design curriculum activities for pupils with just a few keystrokes or mouse clicks, using materials chosen from their personal repository or selecting them from any other source, including pre-packaged e-learning courseware. It should allow for the assigning of activities to individual pupils or groups of students and for receiving their input whenever appropriate. It ought not to impose frequency of use nor imply that the activities of the students have to be computer-based. E-learning in schools doesn't mean and shouldn't imply always working online. The system should provide to all its users facilities for online and offline, synchronous and asynchronous activities.

*Learning agenda.* The system should facilitate for both teachers and students the cooperative management of individual agendas, allowing the students to keep track of their assignments, classroom events (exams, group activities, etc.) and homework. Whenever appropriate it should be a communication tool to inform families about their children's regular assignments, learning and school events.

*Personal desktop.* The learning portal should provide every user with a personal digital desktop furnishing communication and groupwork facilities, productivity tools for working with information, personal working space and a storage area on the server for the management of personal files and web pages. Either online or offline, the browser should be the only computer software needed to use the desktop.

*Personal interface.* It should cater for age and school levels, personal interests and profiles of any user of the learning portal.

## 4.3 Users' privacy

This is a key issue that should be taken into account in learning portals for schools. By design they have to ensure that activities and interactions of teachers and students are private: they belong to them and to nobody else. No-one should see the students' contributions against the wishes of their teachers. Exchanges should not be known by other teachers not involved with the student nor by the school administrators, unless authorized by the teacher in charge of the student. Administrative monitoring of the teachers' use of the e-learning system by school boards, principals or department heads should not be permitted, except for formal inspection procedures developed according to pre-established and public criteria.

The use of electronic systems for communication between teachers and parents regarding homework assignments, students' performance, etc. that may be the subject of a school policy, is to be distinctly separate from the electronic interaction between student and teacher, which should not be made public without previous agreement.

The digital productions of the students such as projects, designs, writings, messages and files belong to them, are their intellectual property. Therefore nobody should be allowed to seize students' work irrespective of its intrinsic value. Similarly, any content created by teachers is their property, and academic authorities should not be allowed to oblige teachers to transfer or make public the instruments, interactions and results of their job, except when this is legally permissible.

For widespread and long-term use of the system, teachers and students have to be confident of its reliability and its intimacy, so that nobody except the intended recipient can see their actions, ideas and feelings.

# 5. CONCLUSION

We end the paper by quoting an internal report of the *European Schoolnet*:

> The voice of education is not always heard. Education users do not articulate their needs: tools and services developed for consumers, business and universities need considerable modification before they are

suitable for young learners. (Equipped, trained ... and now what? Trends and issues in elearning in European school systems, 2002)

ICT in schools is much broader than e-learning, and young e-learners are different from adults. Content and services for schools should be driven by the demands of teachers and students, not by the needs of industry. Teachers' discretion and freedom should not be restricted by technical factors but, under teachers' control, such technical capacities may be most relevant to learning. This paper aims to foster the debate over such issues.

## REFERENCES

Commonwealth Department of Education, Training and Youth Affairs (2001). *School Innovation: Pathway to the Knowledge Society*. Canberra: Commonwealth of Australia.

Equipped, trained ... and now what? Trends and issues in elearning in European school systems. (2002). *European Schoolnet*, 3 September.

Guest, S. & Juday, J. (2001). Guidelines for Buying E-learning Services. *Learning Circuits*, November. Online magazine of American Society for Training & Development (ASTD). Retrieved from http://www.learningcircuits.org/2001/nov2001/guest.html

Jonassen, D. & Reeves, T. C. (1996). Learning with technology: Using computers as cognitive tools. In D. Jonassen (Ed.), *Handbook of Research for Educational Communications and Technology* (pp. 693-719). New York: Simon & Schuster Macmillan.

Kaplan-Leiserson, E. (2002). E-learning Glossary, *Learning Circuits*. Online magazine of American Society for Training & Development (ASTD). Retrieved from http://www.learningcircuits.org/glossary.html

Mintzberg, H. (1979). *The Structuring of Organizations*. Englewood Cliffs, NJ: Prentice-Hall.

Moore, C. & Jones, M. (2001). *Comdex: E-learning takes stage as next killer app*. Retrieved 15 November 2001, from http://www.infoworld.com/articles/hn/xml/01/11/15/011115hnelearnmantra.xml

Noble, D. F. (1998). Digital Diploma Mills: The Automation of Higher Education. Retrieved from http://www.firstmonday.dk/issues/issue3_1/noble/

Ruiz Tarragó, F. (1994). The integration of new technological environments in education. *Educational Media International, 31*(1), March.

Symonds, W. (2001). Giving It the Old Online Try. *Business Week Online*, 3 December. Retrieved from http://www.businessweek.com/magazine/content/01_49/b3760072.htm

The ABCs of Education Stocks (2001). *Business Week Online*, September 24. Retrieved from http://www.businessweek.com/magazine/content/01_39/b3750057.htm

# Slash 21: A New School and a New Way of Learning

Henk van Dieten
*Marianum School, Stichting Carmelcollege, Drienerparkweg 16, Hengelo, Netherlands, hdieten@marianum.nl*

## 1. A NEW SCHOOL AND A NEW WAY OF LEARNING

Slash 21 or /21 is the name for a whole new kind of school in the Netherlands, a school as a quest for knowledge, where students learn how to study individually as well as together with age peers. That means problem solving, finding solutions quickly and seeing connections between subjects from different disciplines, hence being able to work more easily and more effectively.

To realise this goal, /21 sees the computer as fundamental in the learning process. Through the creation of an electronic learning environment, using the internet and e-mail, the student has the opportunity to work individually while tuition is still available when necessary.

## 2. THE NEW WAY OF LEARNING

Effective learning depends on the ability to see connections; to combine subjects from different disciplines and thereby create insight into the bigger picture.

The conventional curriculum is converted into two streams: Science and Humanities. The students learn to comprehend the key concepts.

For example, energy is such a key concept. To understand it in all its aspects it is important to use insights from science, chemistry, physics and biology.

/21 presents those insights in an overall setting and not separated into different subjects. This prevents fragmenting of knowledge.

That is what is necessary. Our thinking is not bound to the barriers of school subjects. Our community, further education and the labour market require adaptable people. What is required are people trained to be able to find effective solutions in a quick and creative way; people who can combine and are able to see connections.

## 3. NEW LANGUAGE TEACHING

/21 follows the principles of intensive language teaching. In a twelve-week period, the students will work intensively in four three-hour periods a week on one modern language. From day one they are motivated to speak in a foreign language, encouraged by an English, French or German native speaker who stimulates, interests and corrects whenever necessary.

Again, the initiative of the student is important. By working on educational projects such as reading, observation and listening projects, the student learns to apply the language effectively. The Internet is useful as an exercise technique when e-mail or chat boxes bring students in contact with students in other countries.

## 4. THE NEW TEACHER

New education requires new teachers. The new teacher is called a tutor, a new name for a new function; a tutor that from the first moment on will be in a position to assist and stimulate if and when necessary, and has the time to do so, since the teaching system is flexible and tutors are complementary to one another.

The tutor will have the opportunity to completely focus on his or her key roles as coach, guide, companion and supporter. The tutor observes the progress and results, intercepts and inspires as necessary and helps the student to achieve his or her full potential.

Teaching assistants take certain tasks and responsibilities from the tutor. This, in addition to the use of an electronic learning environment, provides the tutor with the freedom to fulfill his new role.

Together tutors and teaching assistants form a team guided by a team leader. They are responsible for the education of a group of students for three years, thereby encouraging a close bond between students and staff.

## 5. THE NEW GROUP

Today's youth form groups. Within these groups they gather a wealth of information from one another, they feel free to expose their opinions and emotions. In this situation they support and understand each other by drawing from a huge source of insights and recognition of all aspects of life.

It is the aim of /21 to work the same way. The majority of the time students will work in smaller or larger groups to fulfill specific tasks. In this natural environment they learn quickly and easily. The result of this system of working together is an improved understanding and a more lasting knowledge due to better and more communication, not to mention the 'feel good' factor.

There are no classes in /21, just 'home groups' of about 50 students. Three 'home groups' of three subsequent course years are combined into one 'learning community' under the supervision of a staff team.

The members of the 'home group' will quickly know one another, therefore it is easy to split them into small changing groups to carry out work projects. In order to give course-like tuition, 'home groups' from several 'learning communities' will be joined together from time to time.

## 6. A NEW BUILDING

For this type of education, where the pupils are expected to work in smaller or larger groups, a new type of spacious school building is required.

The home base is the heart of /21. Students and staff of the same 'home group' meet one another in the 'living room' of the school every day. It is the centre of /21, where social contacts are made and experiences are shared. Ample room is available for groups of students to work on their projects.

It has a mediatheek (library for all kinds of media) and a discovery room with a laboratory, a technical corner as well as an art corner. Obviously the building is designed for desk-independent computer usage.

# 7. IMPORTANCE OF ICT

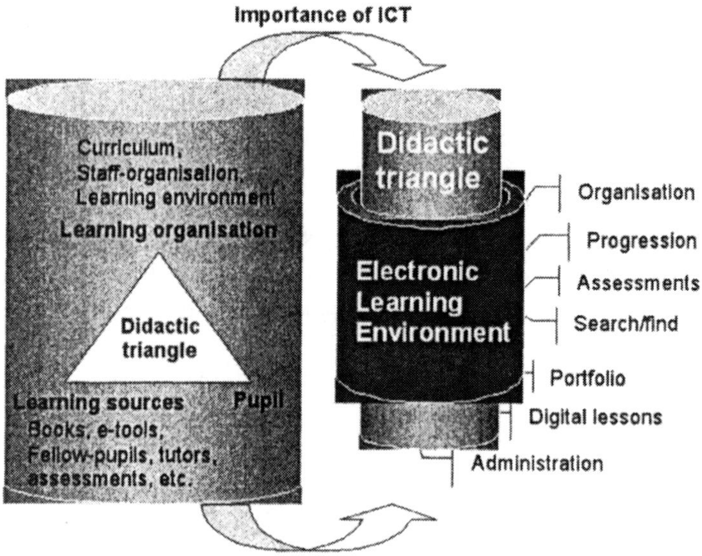


*Figure 1.* The importance of ICT

All this is possible thanks to the power of ICT as a Learning Management System. It provides sources, brings the real world into school, and helps the monitoring of students, sets tutors free from their task to fill students with knowledge and it is a powerful tool to manage the chaos in this learning space. It is an initiative of the Stichting (Foundation) Carmelcollege and KPC Group.

Slash 21 is an extension of the Marianum School which is a member of the Stichting Carmelcollege.

/21 is closely related to the Marianum. The Marianum offers a broad scale of education (vmbo, havo and vwo). The Stichting Carmelcollege is one of the largest schoolboards in the Netherlands for secondary education. It is responsible for 35,000 pupils at 20 schools. Our society and labour market have changed drastically in the last decade. The Stichting Carmelcollege is aware of this and takes as its responsibility the provision of appropriate education. /21 is a logical step for a board that places the pupil in the central role.

The KPC Group is a non profit organization. The KPC groups' major activity is to improve teaching processes. For the government they cooperate in major projects in education innovations. They are also consulted by other schools and school committees to develop ideas in several different areas like school management, personnel and organization.

# Reports of Focus Group Discussions:

# Group E – Teaching Environments: Key Influences and Considerations

**Chair:** Mike Kendall, *Northamptonshire County Council, County Hall, Northampton, NN1 1DN, UK, mkendall@northamptonshire.gov.uk*
**Rapporteur:** Jan Wibe, *Norwegian University of Science & Technology, Trondheim, Norway, jan.wibe@plu.ntnu.no*
**Participants:** Giampaolo Chiappini (Italy), Tony Cruttenden (Australia), Tim Denning (UK), Bronwyn Disseldorp (Australia), Andrew Fluck (Australia), Bernard Holkner (Australia), Andrea Karpati (Hungary), Kristian Kiili (Finland), Johannes Magenheim (Germany)

## 1. INTRODUCTION

Many developments suggest that the teacher of the future should focus upon learning environments that operate with physical and virtual spaces for students. Teaching environments should be flexible and responsive shared spaces, co-constructed within such environments. The focus group considered many arguments about the relationship between learning environments and teaching environments, the influences upon their creation and sustainability, and their outputs. The model overleaf provided a means to represent these relationships and ambiguities, giving a framework for our analysis of teaching environments and the role of the teacher in their creation. Each element in the model provided opportunities to identify new areas of research and development to increase the effectiveness of teaching environments in meeting the needs of learners in a continuously changing ICT rich, e-enabled world, including the power and control relationships within and outside schools in their creation and sustainability.

## 2. DEFINING TEACHING ENVIRONMENTS

The four key influences identified as social actions, learning and teaching resources, usability and learning spaces suggest that teaching and learning environments have a considerable interdependence in enabling learning processes and the development of competencies.

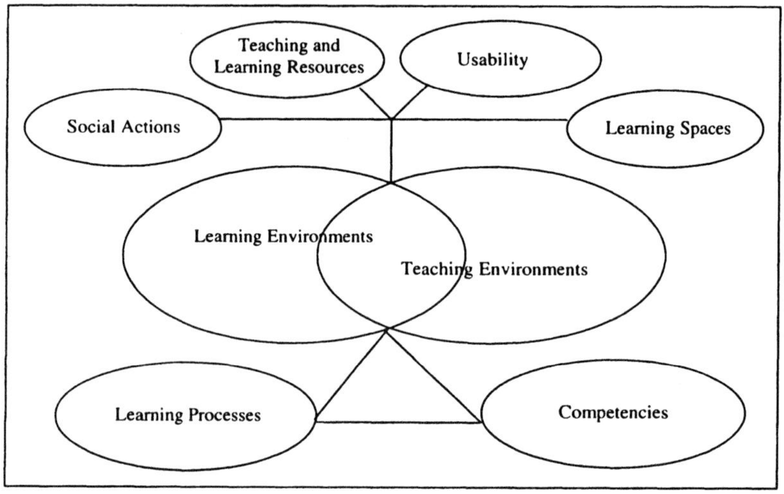


We can describe teaching and learning environments as social systems irrespective of the physical nature and architecture (real or virtual) that define them. Technology supported environments can be recognised as complex social systems which encompass both human and technology actors, rather than technological systems that people are required to negotiate, or social groups to which various technologies are added (Akrich, 1992; Latour 1991). The people include the learner, their contacts, peers, families, the facilitators, technical, helpdesk and other support staff and the developers of hardware and software. This paper recognises the considerable distance that can exist between these actors and the final realisation of the environments for a particular group of learners and teachers. A robust approach to addressing the social and cultural assumptions that are a feature of technologies which frequently find global application needs to be realised for the learner and teacher, acknowledging that developers may ignore cultural matters.

In learning and teaching resources of ICT-enriched environments we may distinguish between a technical and a didactical context. The didactical context provides teachers with a framework to plan a lesson or to draft a learning design. Such designs include a wide range of concepts of face-to-face learning, blended learning and e-learning, to create physical and virtual learning scenarios and cooperation with the community of teachers. ICT enriched environments provide teachers with a wide range of technical resources, such as software tools, educational software, educational agents, groupware facilities, content-management facilities and assessment tools. Learning environments have to provide students with individual content-management and communication features enabling them to organise their individual views on documents, user profiles for resources and personal databases within their often multiple teaching environments.

Another of the influences contributing to the teaching and learning environment is the required characteristics of the learning spaces. This is the physical or virtual space within which teachers and students jointly conduct their development activities. Teaching and learning environments of the future will be spaces where ICT is available in a formal or informal way. Such environments are school spaces with computer labs, classrooms equipped with PCs, open access computer spaces, media rooms; community spaces in youth clubs, telecottages, public access PC areas; home spaces with computer facilities with guidance from family and friends. All these environments contain a strong hidden curriculum that directly influences the choice of methods and teaching aids and, through these decisions, has an indirect impact on teaching content. The OECD study (Venezky & Kárpáti, 2003) of national policies in 23 countries produced 93 anthropological case studies of cutting-edge ICT using schools. It contains descriptions of teaching environments, offering models for the arrangement of computers. Teaching options inherent in these models were widely different. As the provision of ICT in schools between 1998 and 2002 moved from prescriptive provision of computer laboratories to a more cross-curricular approach with computers placed in classrooms, affordances were made available to teachers to start exploring new teaching environments for their disciplines, resulting in significant changes of teaching style. Such changes are accelerated with the provision of wireless and ubiquitous computers, blurring the distinction between real and virtual teaching environments.

Good usability is the basis for meaningful and effective digital learning. Usability tells us how well the users can use the system productively, effectively and pleasantly to reach the defined goals in a certain environment. According to Nielsen (1993) usability is a multidimensional concept that is traditionally associated with five attributes: learnability, memorability, efficiency, errors, and subjective satisfaction. Paying attention to learnability, which should be easy, draws upon previous cognition and is based on the principle of visibility. Memorability is also important when designing learning environments as use can be infrequent and this can in itself create a barrier to learning. In digital learning materials navigation is usually the bottleneck of usability (Sinkkonen et al., 2002) but should allow the structuring of ideas, supporting the finding and location of information and learning objects.

Within the learning process teachers aim to engage students in goal-oriented activity in which the teacher may participate as an assistant or co-participant, giving assistance to the students' performance to achieve pragmatic meaning in developing competencies and as a cultural mediator to epistemic meanings beyond any specific tasks. The characteristics of the ICT tools used in the activity support teachers in: designing activities, providing opportunities for co-participation and instructional conversation with the teacher and with peers and giving assistance to students' performance. ICT tools produce effects that can be interpreted through the metaphorical use of what the interface dynamically and concretely exhibits in the interaction.

The report of professional group 1.4, WCCE 2001 'Indicators of Success', provides a helpful discussion of the broad range of competencies needed by citizens of the third millennium. As lifelong learners living and working in a networked society where 'ICT changes knowledge itself' (Cornu, 2003) they will need access to flexible and adaptive learning environments. Such environments will support an active engagement with information of all kinds and develop the capacity to use reasoning, enquiry, evaluation and creative thinking skills (DfES, 2002). The capacity to work autonomously or as an effective part of a wider team, perhaps separated by time and space, will also become increasingly important as patterns of work and employment change and the benefits of collaborative problem solving associated with authentic and open-ended challenges become more established. Closely associated with this is the need to "give learners the time and opportunity to talk about thinking processes, to make their own thought processes more explicit, to reflect on their strategies and thus gain more self-control" (McGuiness, 1999). This will promote the development of key metacognitive skills that will support lifelong learners in the decisions that they will need to make so that their learning activities are well matched to their preferred learning styles or 'dispositions' (Facione, 1990 in Pouts Lajus et al., 2003).

## 3. RECOMMENDATIONS

This paper raises many development issues and research questions that need to be addressed if the teacher of the future is to be provided with the opportunity to create teaching environments that meet learning needs, including their own. Teachers are part of a growing team of education professionals supporting, often leading, the learning of students. In determining research questions, consideration should be given to issues of power and control; the relationship between technical and pedagogical leadership; organisational metaphors; leadership in establishing a vision and the management of implementation; assessment and validation of student work; and consequences of changes in teaching environments. At the beginning of our four meetings we agreed the focus should be upon learning environments. As you see in this paper our conclusion is that the interrelationship of teaching environments and learning environments is the key issue for the teacher of the future.

## REFERENCES


Akrich, M. (1992). The de-scription of technical objects. In W. E. Bijker & J. Law (Eds), *Shaping Technology/Building Society* (pp. 205-224). Cambridge, MA: MITPress.

Cornu, B. (2003). *The Teaching Profession: A Networked Profession in New Networked Environments* Keynote Presentation at the IFIP Working Conference on ICT and the Teacher of the Future 26th January, Melbourne, Australia

DfES (2002). *Transforming the Way We Learn: A Vision for the Future of ICT in Schools.* London: DfES.

Latour, B. (1996). Social theory and the study of computerized work sites. In W. J. Orlikowski, G. Walsham, M. R. Jones & J. DeGros (Eds), *Information Technology and Changes in Organizational Work* (pp. 295-307). London: Chapman & Hall.

McGuiness, C. (1999). *From Thinking Skills to Thinking Classrooms.* Research Brief No. 115, Department for Education and Employment, UK.

Nielsen, J. (1993). *Usability Engineering*. London: Academic Press.

Pouts Lajus, S., Wegerijf, R. & Kárpáti, A. (Eds) (in press). EMILE – Observation and analysis of uses of ICT in European primary and secondary schools: An intercultural approach. *Studies in Educational Research in Europe – European Educational Research Association (EARLI).* Amsterdam: Kluwer.

Sinkkonen, I., Kuoppala, H., Parkkinen, J. & Vastamäki, R. (2002). *Käytettävyyden Psykologia*. Helsinki, Finland: IT Press.

Venezky, R. & Kárpáti, A. (Eds) (in press). Case studies on ICT and educational change – Issues from the OECD project: ICT and the quality of learning. A special Issue of *ECI (Education, Communication and Information)*.

# Reports of Focus Group Discussions:

# Group F – Knowledge Building Communities: Creating New Learning and Teaching Environments

**Chair:** Jari Multisilta, *Tampere University of Technology, jari.multisilta@pori.tut.fi*
**Rapporteur:** Bernard Cornu, *La Villa Media, France, bernard.cornu@la-metro.org*
**Participants:** Henk van Dieten (The Netherlands), John Murnane (Australia), Paul Newhouse (Australia), Nicholas Reynolds (Australia), Patricia Reynolds (UK), Ferran Ruiz Tarrago (Spain), Nicole Veelo (Norway), John Vincent (Australia), Nicola Yelland (Australia)

## 1. INTRODUCTION

This paper takes learning environments as its focus, with an emphasis on interactions and engagement with ideas in order to create knowledge building communities. The psycho-social learning environment (Fraser, 1991) is viewed as a facilitator for learning and teaching (see figure).

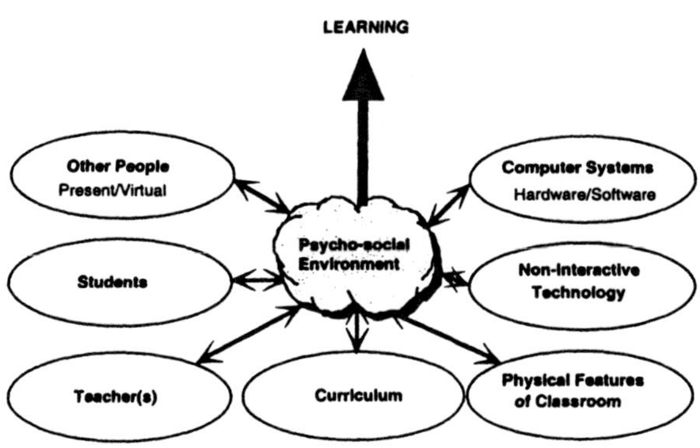

This is considered to be different from a teacher's 'work environment' which includes being in classrooms, offices, at home etc. However, it is contended that these do connect with the overall environment. The focus is on learning and interactions rather than on instruction and the teacher.

Teaching is an integral part of learning environments. Therefore it is important to consider the roles of teachers in learning environments. The interactions between all the components of the learning environment are important when considering the work of teachers. Knowledge building communities involve learning and teaching environments and the available tools, including ICT-based tools, and the way in which they are used.

Pre-computing teaching and learning tools were separate and linear for the worker and learner in schools. It may be said that when the microcomputer was first put into schools in the 1980s the activities conducted on them were very much isolated from the regular or routine activities in the classroom. They were sometimes a reward for students who completed their set tasks or students programmed them with languages such as Logo and Pascal which, it was claimed, trained the mind to think in more coherent ways which were not necessarily connected to authentic activities. Then they incorporated electronic word processing which had the potential to stimulate the writing process. In this way the technology was regarded as a tool that many thought would help learners in the new age to come.

At the current time we seem to be at the crossroads between the "Road to nowhere" and the "Pioneering road to the west" in terms of the use of ICT in schools. The way to the new territories is emerging in which we have the potential to reconceptualise new learning with new pedagogy and technologies. In this zone ICT is used as an artefact of innovation which supports pedagogical practices that promote learning in new and dynamic ways. Learners appropriate technologies when necessary and choose to embark on authentic tasks that may or may not involve new technologies and media. New technologies are not mapped onto old curricula, but pedagogues are involved in discussions that engage them in thinking about new curricula for the knowledge era.

In this context, teachers are viewed as pedagogues instead of a purveyors of knowledge, organisers of content, deliverers of materials or transmitters of fact, while learners actively construct their learning in social contexts. This enables them to generate their own understanding of processes and knowledge.

## 2. ENVIRONMENTS FOR KNOWLEDGE BUILDING COMMUNITIES

In 2000 the U.S.A. Committee on Developments in the Science of Learning addressed the issue of what should be considered in developing learning environments in their report *How People Learn: Brain, Mind, Experience, and School.* They defined "four interrelated attributes of learning environments that need cultivation" (p.23).

1. Schools and classrooms must be **learner-centred**. This includes taking into account different cognitive and learning styles. Learning is goal-oriented with learners having individual goals.
2. To provide a **knowledge-centred** classroom environment, attention must be given to what is taught (information, subject matter), why it is taught (understanding), and what competence or mastery looks like. Schools need to aim to foster the creation of 'deep' knowledge rather than the typical range of 'superficial' knowledge.
3. In the **assessment-centred** classroom environment, formative assessments help both teachers and students monitor progress. This may include self and peer evaluation and feedback.
4. Learning is influenced in fundamental ways by the context in which it takes place. A **community-centred** approach requires the development of norms for the classroom and school, as well as connections to the outside world that support core learning values. This emphasizes the local and global communities.

This structure provides an image of the ideal and thereby throws some challenges at education systems. Some of these challenges may be met with ICT support.

The Committee on Developments in the Science of Learning (2000) suggested five ways to use ICT to establish and sustain effective learning environments: Real world problems, Scaffolding, Feedback, Reflection and guidance, Local and global communities and Extending teacher learning. David Jonassen's "Designing a Constructivist Learning Environment" web-site has a section on Tools (http://tiger.coe.missouri.edu/~jonassen/courses/CLE/) where five ICT tool categories for designing constructivist learning environments are outlined. These tools provide the teacher with the means to design learning frameworks to implement the use of computers to support high quality learning environments (Harper, 2003).

## 3. THE ROLE OF ICT IN KNOWLEDGE BUILDING COMMUNITIES

ICT provides a new set of dimensions for learning. The use of ICT in learning environments has the potential to extend and facilitate new and dynamic ways of teaching. Via the use of ICT students can do things in different ways and experience ideas and concepts that they may not have encountered without new technologies.

The use of ICT can stimulate cooperative and collaborative learning conditions in the classroom, for example by giving the teacher tools to collect data about how cooperation is taking place, as well as tools in order to share knowledge and manage different access to different tasks. It also enables the teacher to construct an open classroom, which gives access to authentic contexts and resources without physically going out. It helps promote autonomous engaged learners, through managing the pupils' learning process more individually. Learners are not totally dependant on the physical presence of the teacher.

ICT provides tools that help us to materialise ideas and our thoughts and manipulate them. Our thoughts take material form as text, graphics, pictures, sound, numbers, moving images ... the new dimension is the integrated creativity that is allowed by the common digital format. Since all these different formats can now be created, processed, manipulated and edited with the same technology and the same techniques, all sorts of other things that were previously out of reach become possible.

New technologies allow us to reach out to the world: we can bring the world into the room where we are and communicate and disseminate our ideas to the world when we wish. Another new dimension is the way to access data or information because of the system based on indexes and data retrieval technology.

ICT provides for the development of social and collaborative experiences and knowledge in a way that was not possible before. The use of ICT supports and facilitates a social/collaborative/group experience through the computer remembering all your ideas and discoveries as well as the journey you travelled to arrive at them, through the easy and powerful communication technology that now exists.

## 4. THE HUMAN DIMENSION IS ESSENTIAL

An effective learning environment as part of a knowledge building community is also a social environment. Is it possible or advisable to replace the good teacher as a human dimension from that society?

Traditional roles such as the master/apprentice relationship are still valid learning/teaching methods. A good teacher possesses the ability to adapt to different social and learning situations, can act as a mediator and an agent, has the ability to learn and an understanding of knowledge and information.

New technology can present a social context through chat rooms and BBS, it can also provide information, but does the ICT possess knowledge? Regardless of the advances in ICT, the basis for good teaching remains the love of teaching and of the sharing and building of knowledge. The challenge is to create environments in which effective teaching and learning are supported by and through the new technologies.

# 5. CONCLUSIONS

Regardless of the advances in ICT, the basis for effective teaching remains the love of teaching and of the sharing and building of knowledge. We think that teaching and learning environments should be conceptualised as knowledge building communities in which ICT is an integral component that promotes new dimensions for learning and understanding.

# REFERENCES

Committee on Developments in the Science of Learning (Ed.) (2000). *How People Learn: Brain, Mind, Experience, and School.* Washington, D.C.: National Academy Press.

Fraser, B. J. & Walberg, H. J. (1991). *Educational Environments.* Oxford: Pergamon Press.

# Index of Contributors


Bocconi, S. 71
Bottino, R. 41
Carlsen, R. 49
Chambers, D. 137
Chiappini, G. 217
Chung, A. 165
Cornu, B. 3, 301
Cox, M. 145, 203
Davis, N. 53
Domenjoz, J-C. 183
Downes, T. 109, 129
Godinet, H. 229
Haaksma, T. 209
Harper, B. 15
Hartnell-Young, E. 159
Johnson, N. 53
Jones, A. 65
Kárpáti, A. 235
Keiho, H. 257
Kemis, M. 53
Kendall, M. 295
Kennewell, S. 203, 247
Ketamo, H. 257
Ki, W-W. 165
Kiili, K. 251
Lachat, C. 183
Lam, H-C. 165
Law, N. 171
Martin, A. 71
Midoro, V. 71
Morel, R. 125, 183
Multisilta, J. 257, 301
Newhouse, P. 267
Nicholson, P. 125
Pedemonte, B. 217
Pozzi, F. 71
Robotti, E. 217
Romeo, G. 191
Rossi, C. 183
Ruiz Tarragó, F. R. 279
Sarti, L. 71
Schubert, S. 85, 129
Valente, J. 97
van Dieten, H. 291
Watson, D. 29
Webb, I. 109
Weber, W. 115, 209
Wibe, J. 295

CPSIA information can be obtained at www.ICGtesting.com
Printed in the USA
LVOW071422020513

332031LV00009B/207/P

9 781402 076046